IMAGES
of America

ANNVILLE TOWNSHIP

I0807088

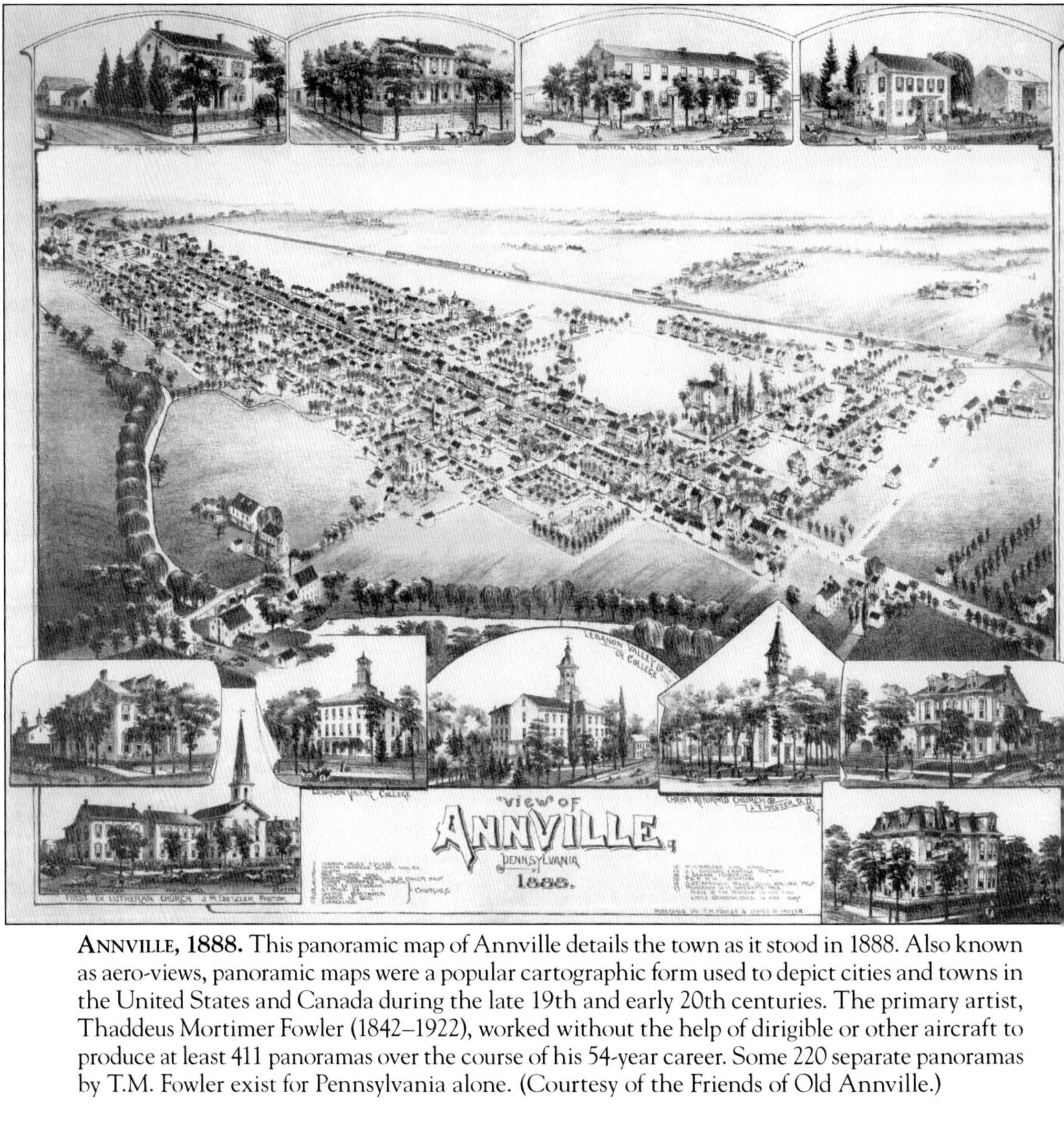

ANNVILLE, 1888. This panoramic map of Annville details the town as it stood in 1888. Also known as aero-views, panoramic maps were a popular cartographic form used to depict cities and towns in the United States and Canada during the late 19th and early 20th centuries. The primary artist, Thaddeus Mortimer Fowler (1842–1922), worked without the help of dirigible or other aircraft to produce at least 411 panoramas over the course of his 54-year career. Some 220 separate panoramas by T.M. Fowler exist for Pennsylvania alone. (Courtesy of the Friends of Old Annville.)

ON THE COVER: BATDORF BUILDING, AROUND 1880. Local residents pose for a picture in front of the Batdorf Building in Annville around 1880, which was before the addition of the third story to the building. (See page 55.) (Courtesy of Betty Streicher.)

IMAGES
of America

ANNVILLE TOWNSHIP

Paul M. Fullmer and
the Friends of Old Annville

ARCADIA
PUBLISHING

ISBN 978-0-7385-7460-8

Published by Arcadia Publishing
Charleston, South Carolina

Printed in the United States of America

Library of Congress Control Number: 2010937259

For all general information, please contact Arcadia Publishing:
Telephone 843-853-2070
Fax 843-853-0044
E-mail sales@arcadiapublishing.com
For customer service and orders:
Toll-Free 1-888-313-2665

Visit us on the Internet at www.arcadiapublishing.com

To my mother, Ruth Maison Fullmer, a member of Lebanon Valley College's class of 1961, without whose loving influence I would never have known Annville.

CONTENTS

ACKNOWLEDGMENTS

The Friends of Old Annville was formed in 1979 by a group of young Annville residents with a willingness to throw themselves in front of a wrecking ball. We wish to thank the founders for their passion and pride in Annville's history, which inspires the present volume. Dr. Owen Moe, past and current president as well as faculty member at Lebanon Valley College, stands as principal among them. Unless otherwise noted, all images appearing in this book have been provided through the archives of the Friends of Old Annville.

Most notable among the many individuals who generously supplied images for this volume are Dick and Betty Streicher, without whose massive collection of slides and photographs this book would not be possible. Doris Flory's careful research on the history of almost every historic property in Annville has been as informative as it is awe-inspiring. Also informative has been the work of those who gathered data regarding structures on West Queen Street and Main Street for submission to the Pennsylvania Historic and Museum Commission; all of these structures are now included on the National Register of Historic Places. We thank Fredric Richter and Kenn Kreiser who, together with the Streichers, developed a previously published pictorial history that has inspired this book. Blanche Schaeffer shared many pictures, insights, and an appreciation for Pennsylvania history that is unique, perhaps, to native Californians.

We are thankful for the helpfulness of Maureen Anderson, Tom Hanrahan, Bob Riley, and Donna Miller at Lebanon Valley College who responded to inquiries with a promptness that characterizes the college's service to the local community. Paul Baker and staff of the *Lebanon Daily News* provided many helpful photographs. We also wish to specifically thank Phil and John Feather, Hughey May, Scott Saylor, Paul Kettering, Peter and Jane Aftosmes, Robert and Suanne Long, Howard Starry, Bob and Carol Werni, Anne Shroyer Shemeta, Art Shearer, Mike Bowman, Valerie Weiner, Jill and Dave Palanzo, Michael and Laura Charelian, Marty and Patti Brandt, Lori Unger Nalley, Ammon Balaster, Edward and John Bernardo, Linnea Miller, Kevin Pry, Tanya Richter, Rachel Noll, Alice Diehl, Michelle Poorman, Vicki Gingrich, Dennis Flake, and Nancy Darkes for their contributions.

Juliana Fullmer accompanied her daddy on many visits and errands associated with the research for this book.

Finally, Paul Fullmer would like to thank his wife, Becky, who balanced our late nights with her own unending enthusiasm for current activities in Annville and Lebanon County.

INTRODUCTION

The tradition of historic walking tours through Annville can be traced back to June 16, 1899, when Dr. E. Benjamin Bierman read his paper, "A Visit to Annville Sixty Years Ago," before the Lebanon County Historical Society. The study's detail of a stroll through Annville in 1839 describes people and businesses on many of the same streets surveyed in this volume: Main and "Whiteoak," Queen and Mill, Chestnut and Cherry.

However, the current practice of annual walking tours seems to have been inspired by a paper entitled "Annville Landmarks," which was read by Anna E. Kreider to Annville's Home Study Circle at 444 East Main Street on November 30, 1962. Walking tour booklets, ranging from the previously mentioned date to the present, can be perused via the electronic archives of the Friends of Old Annville. Particularly enjoyable is a review of the information relayed on the November 3, 1991, Outhouse Tour, sponsored by the Friends. The story prompted headlines such as "Annville's Alleys Flush with Old-time Facilities" in both national and international media.

Like the present tour, most historic walking tours of Annville start on the 200 block of South White Oak Street. After receiving permission, walkers leave their cars in the parking lots of Annville Elementary School or Christ Church and then gather on adjacent lawns to prepare for departure. A trip through either the west end or the east end of town will result in a 90-minute adventure. Attempting to amble through both ends, however, may leave even the most seasoned walkers exhausted and overwhelmed by a wealth of history. (See the Walking Tour Map on page 126.)

The street addresses provided in the captions of this book allow the reader to either walk the entire distance of a tour, down a specific block, or simply to a single address. Situated as they are at particular locations, the pictures inspire the reader to engage the dynamics of history by comparing the past with the present. For those who are unable to visit the town, the pictures may stand on their own as powerful testimonies to entire communities of ages past and the contributions they have made to the present.

Walking along the streets of Annville, one is struck by the nearness of the homes to the streets. Two men who had acquired property from William Penn, Andrew Miller and Abraham Ulrich, along with investor Abram Raiguel, developed a grid work of streets through a series of negotiations between 1763 and 1764. The average lot was 66 feet wide, a familiar figure in historical real estate because it is the length of Gunter's chain (a standard surveying device invented in 1620) and 198 feet long, or 12 perches (a perch being an English linear measure equal to 16.5 feet). Building specifications were established such that eight feet were allotted for sidewalks. Homes were built with no front yards allowing for the optimum size back yard to be used for gardens. Alleys running behind the lots provided access to barns and carriage sheds.

Although the town was called Millerstown by its earliest settlers, upon the completion of its layout, the town received the name Annville, presumably after Miller's wife Anna, or both Miller's and Ulrich's wives, Anna and Julianna. A second version of the naming of the town suggests that Queen Ann of England is its namesake. Andrew Miller, a descendent of the Palatines given land

and freedom by Queen Ann, may have desired to show his appreciation to her majesty by calling the town Ann Will. Evidence of this loyalty to English leadership may be noted in the use of the names Queen and King in streets that were central to the town at the time.

Selecting a site surrounded by a stream was typical for the town builders and homemakers of early America. The stream was a source of water for home and farm, as well as a means of transportation. Most of all, streams translated to waterpower for the mills. In the mid-18th century, mills operated by Andrew Miller on Queen Street, the primary street at the time, and Abram Raiguel on South White Oak Street were the livelihood of the community. A trip to the mill was an important occasion. The miller was a respected man whose opinions were sought in addition to the use of his grinding stone. In his capacity as host to the countryside, the miller built himself a stately house. Several fine examples of houses built by millers Raiguel and Herr remain in Annville. (See pages 23–29.)

In 1789, Capt. Alexander Graydon wrote a letter to geographer Jedediah Morse in which he tabulated 35 houses in Annville, constructed principally of log. A stroll along the streets in the southwest quadrant of the town reveals that a number of Annville's log houses are still standing. Materials such as aluminum siding, tar paper shingles, and weatherboarding conceal the log construction.

Beginning around 1790, several hotels were constructed on Main Street to service travelers along the local portion of the Allegheny Path, a footpath established by Native Americans that extended from Philadelphia to Harris Ferry (later Harrisburg) and westward. It is rumored that George Washington traveled along this path in the late 18th century, and may have even stopped at a tavern in Annville. (See page 102.)

In 1817, the Berks-Dauphin Turnpike was built as a toll road through the town. A toll house was established at the 600 block of East Main Street at that time. By 1839, Annville already had a number of fine residences that were examples of excellent craftsmanship in the area. Between 400 and 500 people lived here. In 1840, I.D. Rupp listed 120 houses (only three of which were brick), five stores, and five taverns. There were also four churches, three schools, and one academy at that time.

The mid-19th century saw the development of large limestone quarries west of the town. The coming of the railroad in 1860 led to the building of factories in town for the manufacture of shoes, hosiery, flags, handkerchiefs, and shirts. The new industrialists who developed these factories would build their mansions on the eastern side of this place, adding to the historic beauty of Annville, the details of which we invite you now to explore, from mill to mansion.

One

FIT FOR A KING

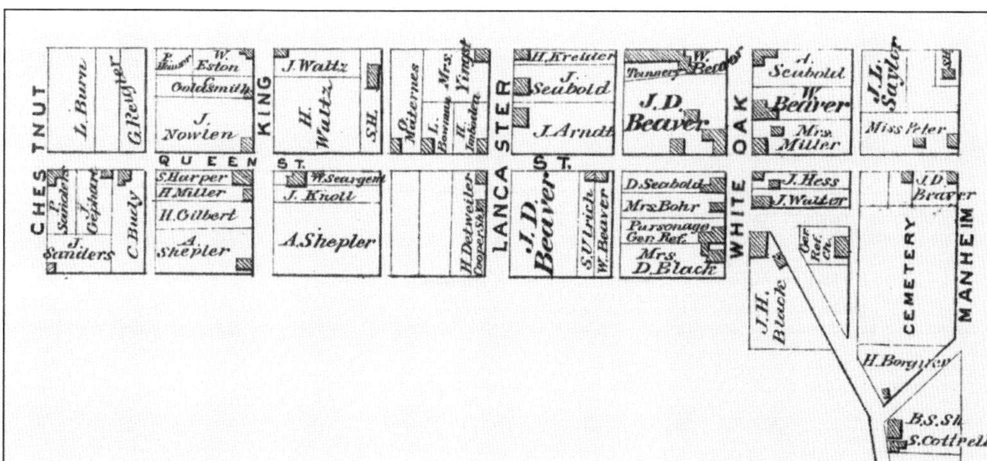

THE 1875 ATLAS. This portion of the *County Atlas of Lebanon, Pennsylvania* details the building footings and surnames of residents from the 200 block of South White Oak Street through the 200 block of West Queen Street as they existed in 1875.

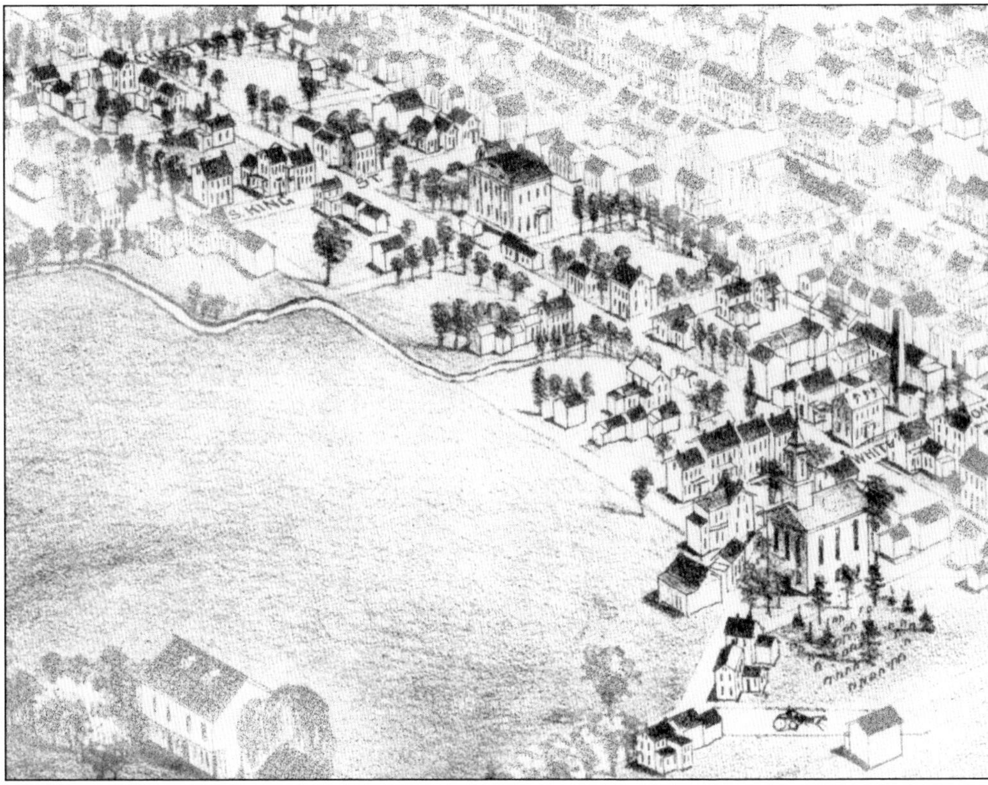

An 1888 View. T.M. Fowler's panoramic view of Annville portrays the buildings of the 200 block of South White Oak Street through the 200 block of West Queen Street as they appeared from the southeast in 1888.

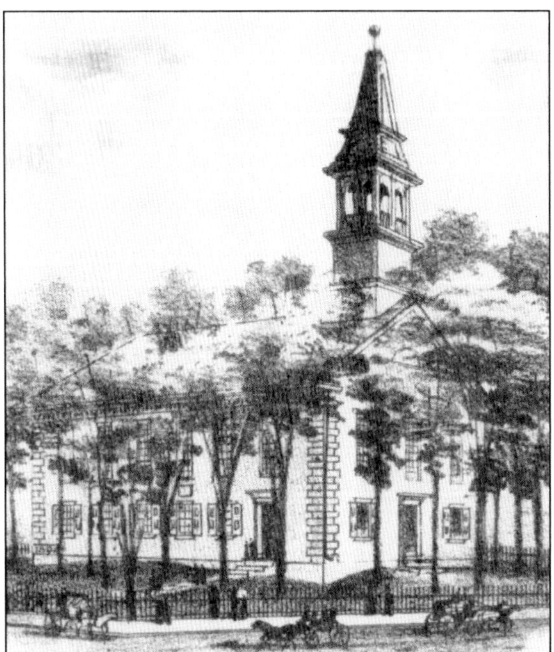

No. 200 South White Oak Street. On this site in 1804, the Lutheran and Reformed congregations that had worshipped in Annville since the 1730s built Jerusalem Church, as pictured in the 1888 view of Annville. A three-story limestone structure, the church housed a sanctuary with a grand balcony encircling three walls and the first pipe organ in Annville. In 1872, the Lutherans sold their share of the building to the Reformed congregation, and the church became known as Christ Reformed Church. When church expansion was deemed necessary in 1903, the present building replaced the original church. Shortly after the national Reformed Church became the United Church of Christ in 1957, the church was renamed with a palindrome: Christ Church United Church of Christ.

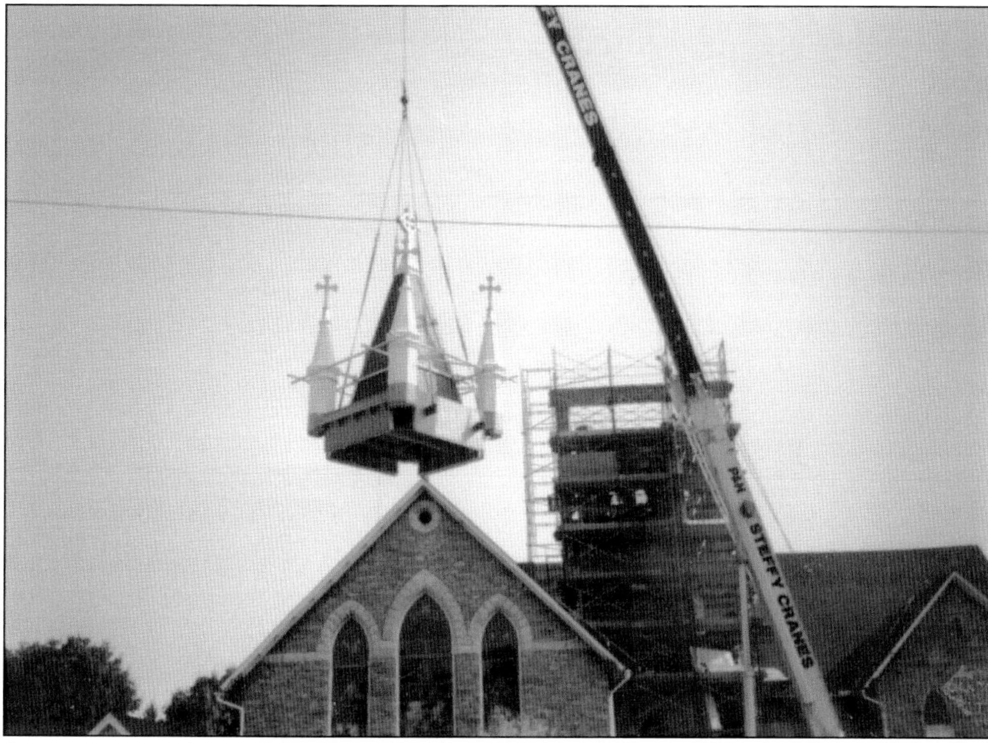

Replacing the Steeple. In time, the effects of weather and gravity required that the 1903 square bell tower and steeple be removed entirely or replaced at significant cost. Many members of the local community gathered in a show of support for the congregation's restoration of the structure in 1991.

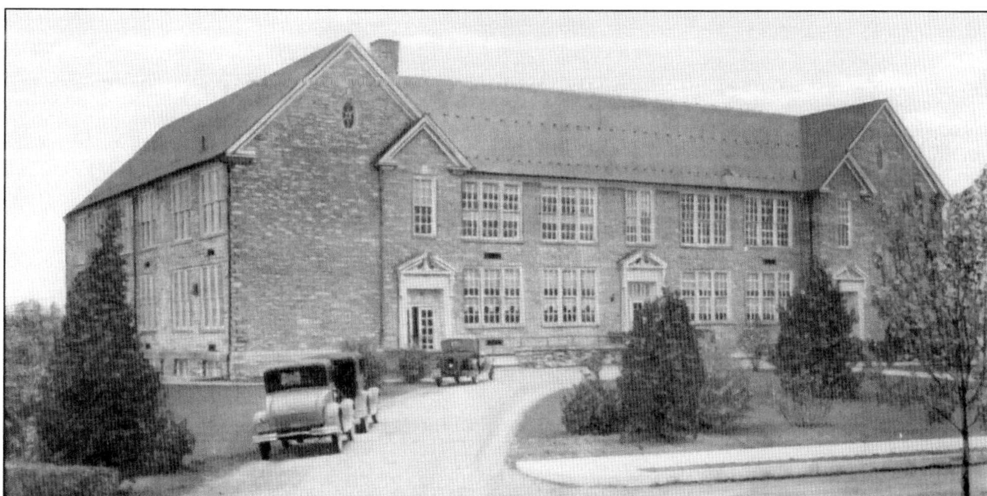

No. 205 South White Oak Street. The stately school edifice west of the church was built in 1926 as a new high school for the area, replacing the building at 145 West Queen. (See page 14.) The stone for its construction was hand-cut from the quarries of Annville. When a larger high school building was completed in 1959 farther south on White Oak Street, the elementary school moved into this building. (Courtesy of Dick and Betty Streicher.)

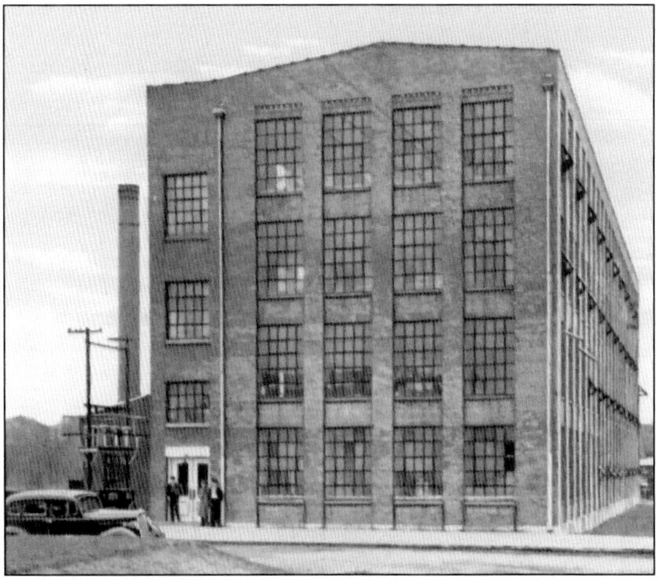

No. 201 South Lancaster Street. Glancing to the west, one notes the presence of this large, historic brick building. Apartments named the Anvil Mill Quarters now occupy the site of the Annville branch of the Carlisle Shoe Company. In the early 1900s, there were two large shoe factories in Annville, one here and one on North Railroad Street. (See page 116.) Prior to the building's conversion to apartments, t-shirts were manufactured at this facility from 1940 to 2002. (Courtesy of Dick and Betty Streicher.)

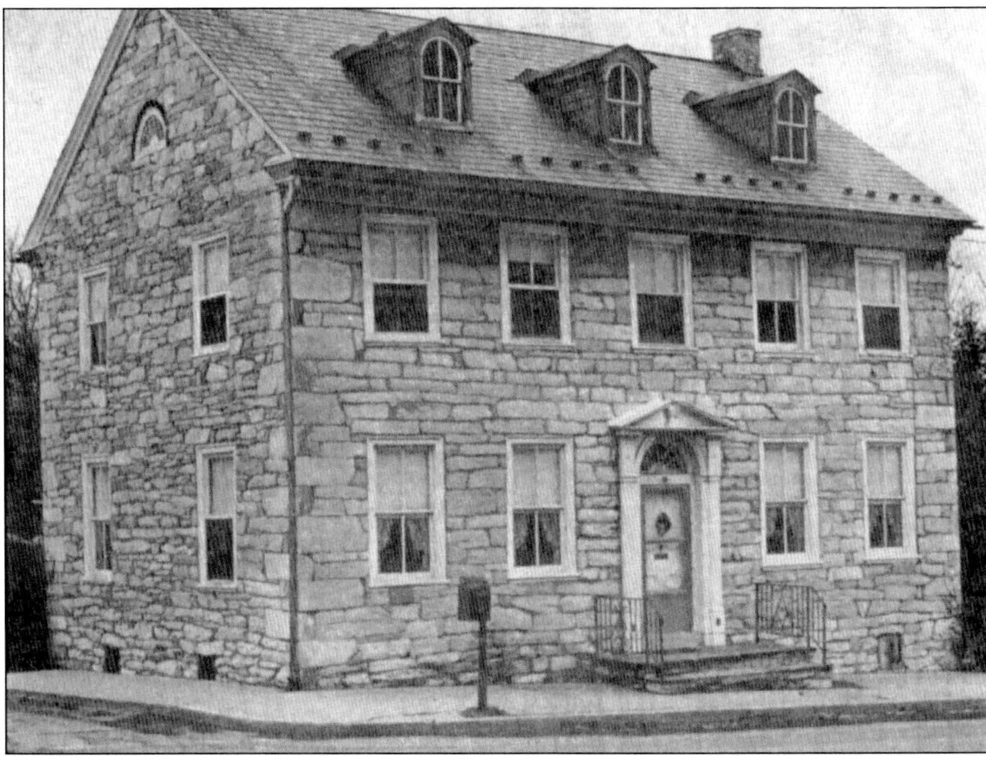

No. 49 South White Oak Street. John D. Beaver Sr. (1776–1858) constructed this limestone house in the Georgian style in 1814. Note the pegged-and-mortised window frames. The reeded pilasters at the main doorway are decorated with a fine pick-work pattern, which recurs throughout the front of the building. One of the house's long-term residents, John D. Beaver Jr. (1812–1880) donated the land and significant funds for the building of a Lutheran church. (See page 91.) For the West End Walking Tour, head west on Queen Street. For the East End Walking Tour, head north on White Oak Street and turn to page 71, which features 16 South White Oak Street.

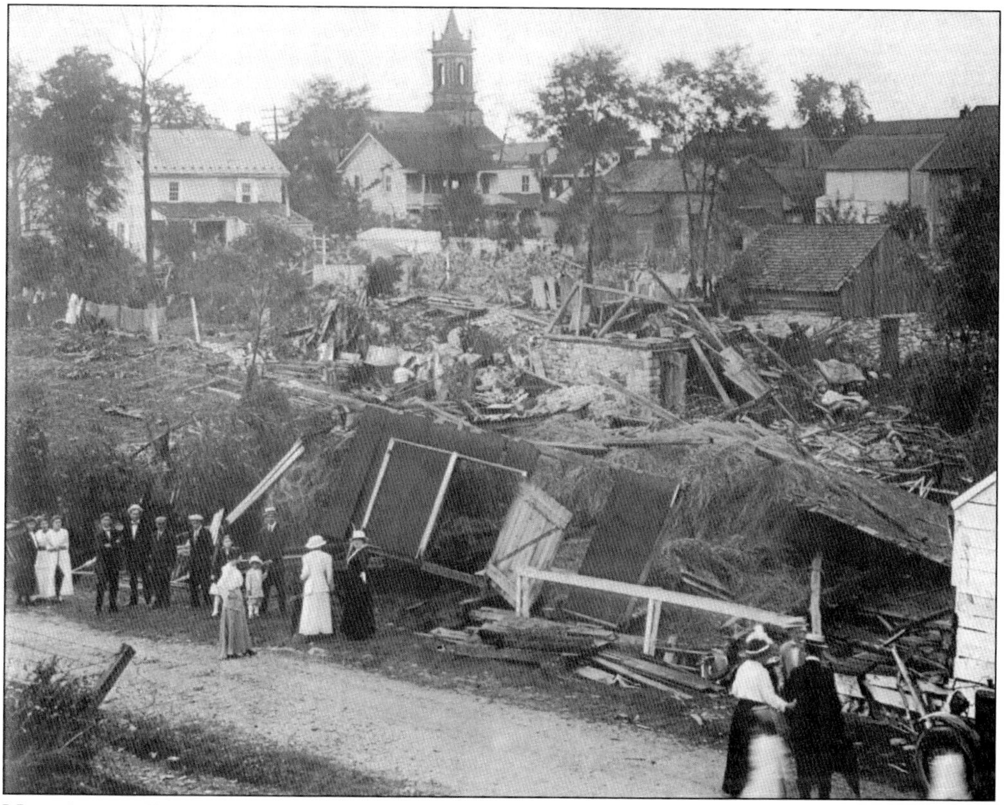

Nos. 30–49 West Queen Street. On August 23, 1915, a cyclone blew from the first block of West Queen, down the first block of East Queen Street (see page 125), over to the first block of East Main (see page 82), down to the 300 block of East Main (see pages 100–101), and eventually to the 400 block of East Maple (see pages 106–107). This picture shows the havoc that resulted. The foundations of some of the damaged buildings still remain on the property. (Courtesy of Dick and Betty Streicher.)

No. 101 South Lancaster Street. Although the 1915 cyclone peeled the facade off of the building, its current state testifies to the fact that community members supported the Bowman family such that the residence might be restored.

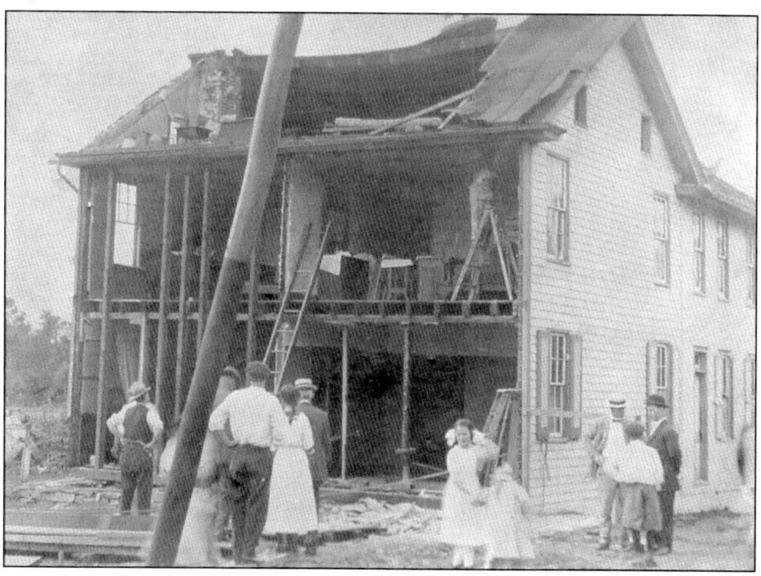

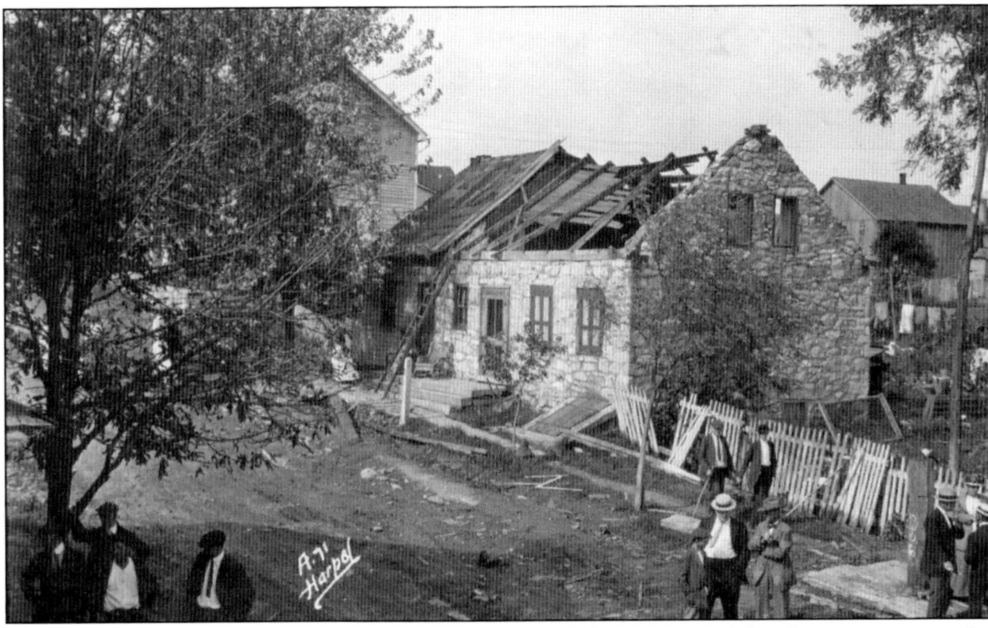

No. 46 South Lancaster Street. The Joseph Arndt home, named for the stonemason who lived here in the late 19th century, lost much of its roof in the 1915 cyclone. Note the hitching post and vaulted cellar door. The huge limestone slabs that serve as a sidewalk were installed by Arndt; they cover one of the early town wells.

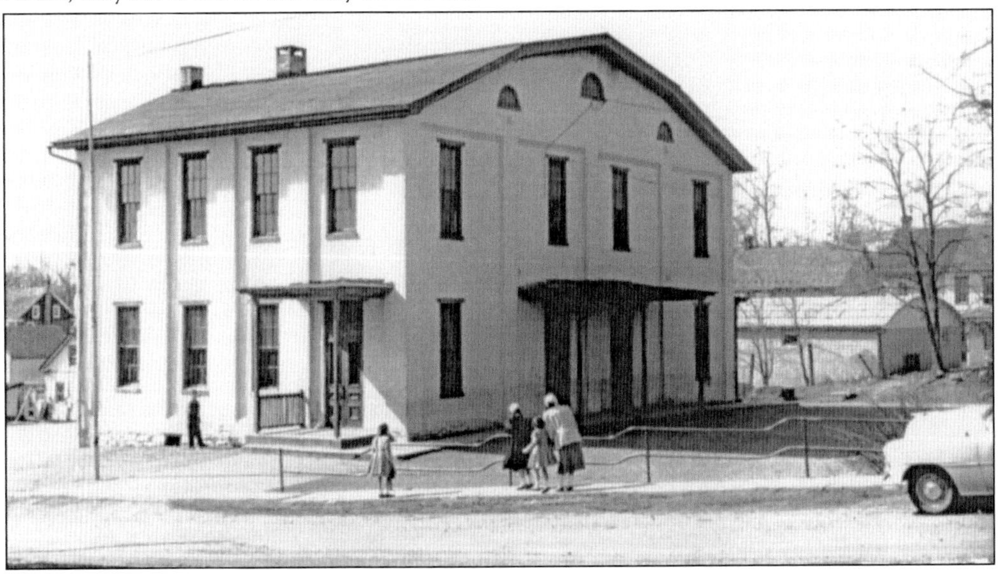

No. 145 West Queen Street. Washington School was built on this site in 1873 for high school–aged students in Annville Township, as well as in North and South Annville. After a new high school facility was completed in 1926 (see page 11), the building functioned as an elementary school. In the 1970s, the school was razed and replaced by Viozzi's Food Market. Illustrative of the many kindnesses of grocer Earnest Viozzi (1929–1995) was the relationship that he maintained with the fire company in Annville; groceries were always available to families who suffered from house fires. In 1996, Lebanon Valley Child Care and Learning Center moved to this location from Lebanon Valley College. (Courtesy of Nancy Darkes.)

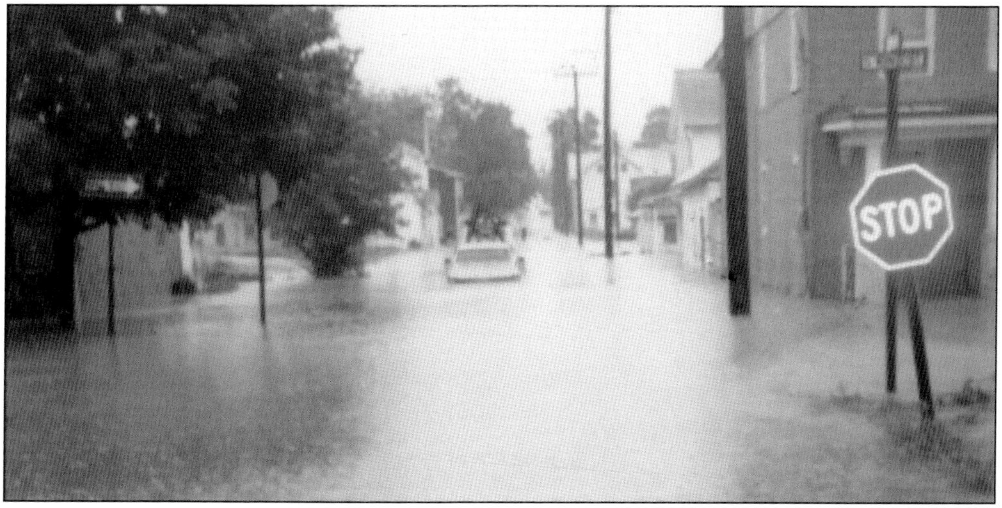

KING AND QUEEN STREETS. When the streets of Annville were formally laid out in 1763–1764, America had not yet earned its independence. Perhaps as a show of loyalty to George III, the most prominent streets of the time were named King and Queen. However, the intersection did not end up as the center of business and livelihood in Annville. It is likely that the owners of the several taverns situated along the old Allegheny Path, one block north of Queen Street (now Main Street), convinced the engineers who designed the Berks-Dauphin Turnpike in 1816–1817 to direct the thoroughfare there rather than along Queen Street. Certainly, they may also have argued, such low lands would not serve a turnpike well. The area was susceptible to floods, such as those later brought by Hurricane Agnes on June 22, 1972, as seen in this picture.

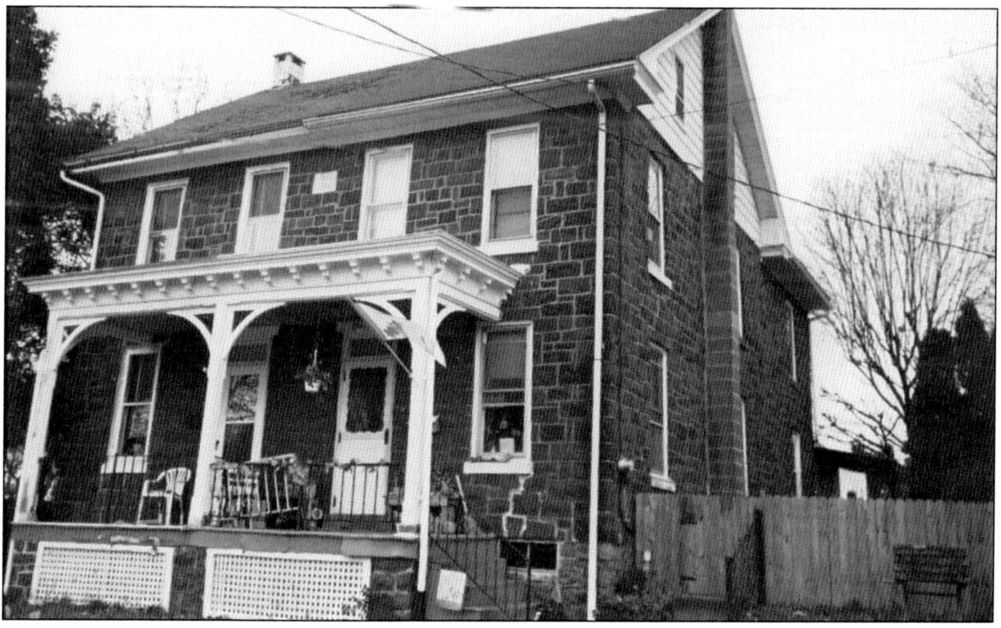

NOS. 113–115 SOUTH KING STREET. Located a few houses south of King and Queen Streets on the west side of the street is one of a few sandstone structures left in Annville. It was built in 1905 with the surviving stones of the Administration Building at Lebanon Valley College from the 1904 Christmas Eve fire. (See page 115.) From 1960 to 1980, Earl and Mary Wolfe raised seven children at 113 South King. (Courtesy of Robert and Suanne Long.)

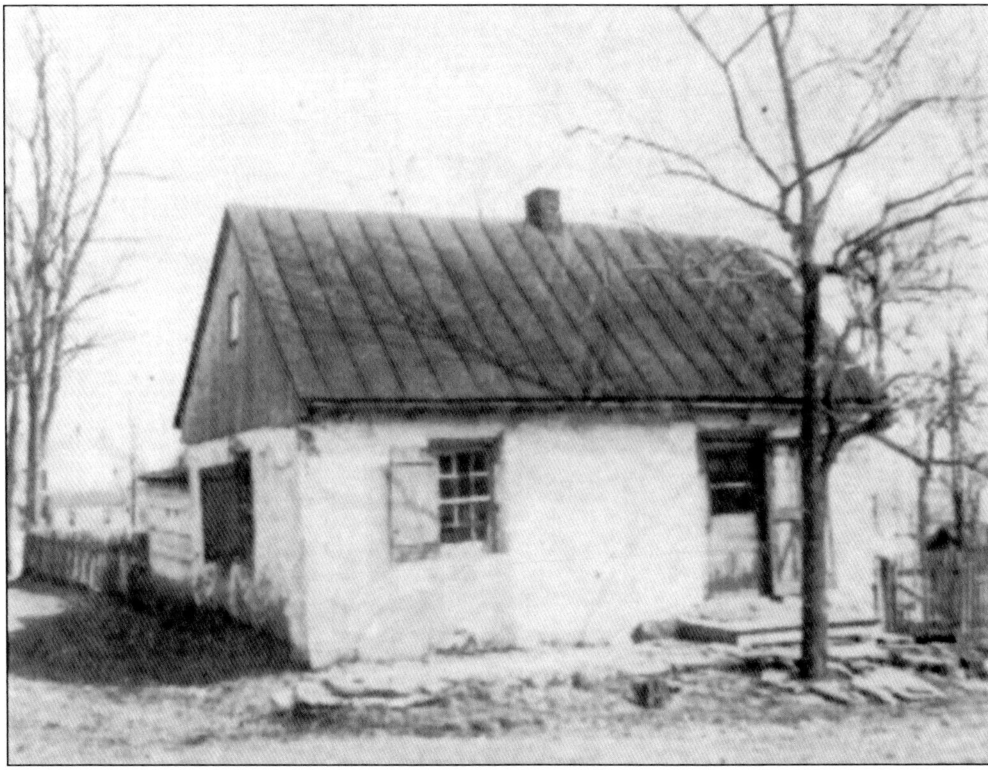

No. 28 South King Street. A short jaunt north on King Street leads one to the Mary Gass house, named for widow Mary Gass (1843–1923), who lived in the home for several decades at the turn of the 19th century. The building is thought to be one of the oldest in Annville, constructed in the mid– or late 18th century. It is shown here in its original form as a one-room structure with a loft, a large central fireplace, and a pitched roof typical of the era. Not long after this picture was taken in 1904, the building was remodeled, and the roofline changed.

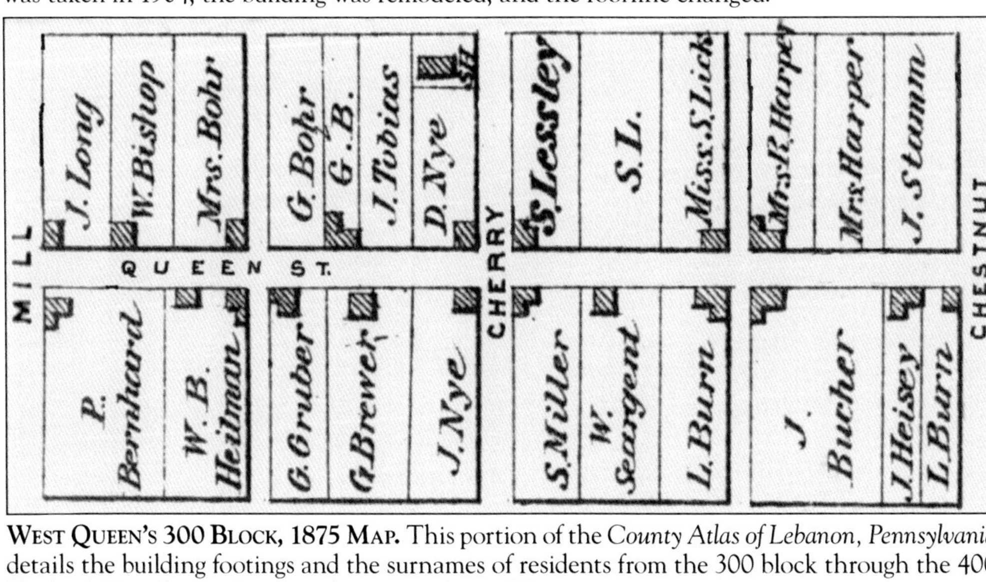

West Queen's 300 Block, 1875 Map. This portion of the *County Atlas of Lebanon, Pennsylvania* details the building footings and the surnames of residents from the 300 block through the 400 block of West Queen Street as they existed in 1875.

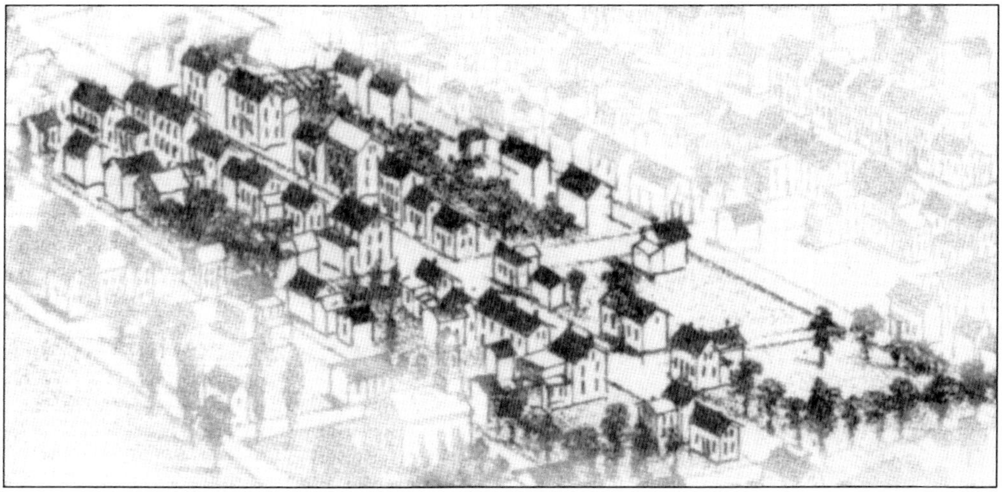

West Queen's 300 Block, 1888 View. T.M. Fowler's panoramic view of Annville portrays the buildings of the 300 block through the 400 block of West Queen Street as they appeared from the southeast in 1888.

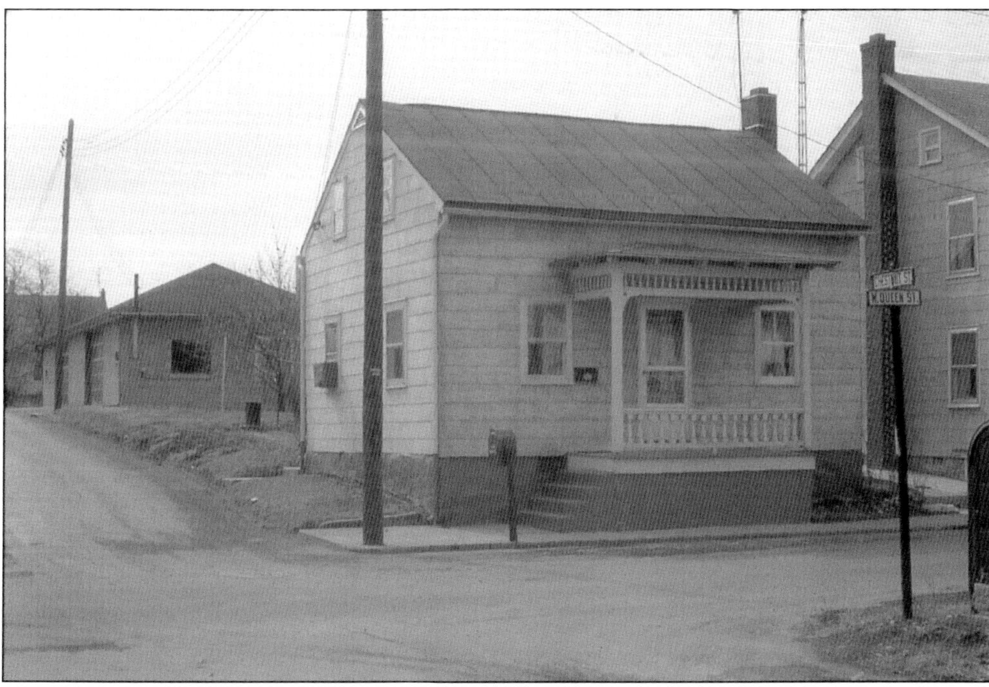

No. 304 West Queen Street. The small size and 1.5-story height of this log-construction home, built in the 1820s, is illustrative of the log homes that dominated Annville before the 1850s. No. 332–334 West Queen Street is an unusually large log construction. The log home at 415 West Queen Street once housed an Italian grocery store.

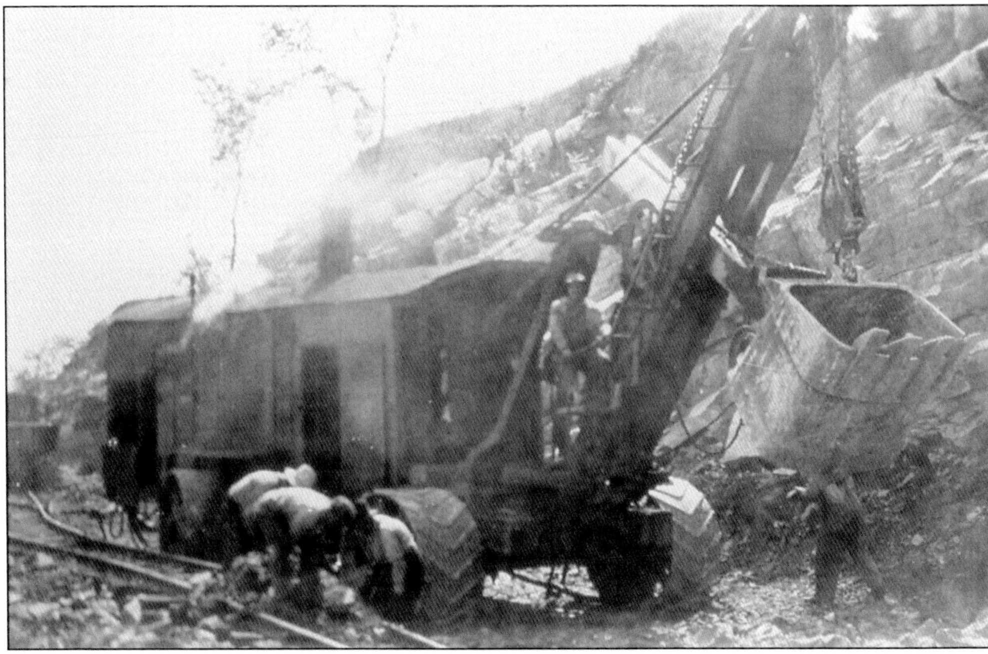

Workers of Millard Quarry. From 1880 to 1920, America welcomed an influx of European immigrants to its shores. In Annville, a significant Italian community developed on the west end of town, consisting largely of people who worked, and sometimes died, in local stone quarries such as the Millard Quarry on the far west end of Annville (beyond the boundaries of this tour).

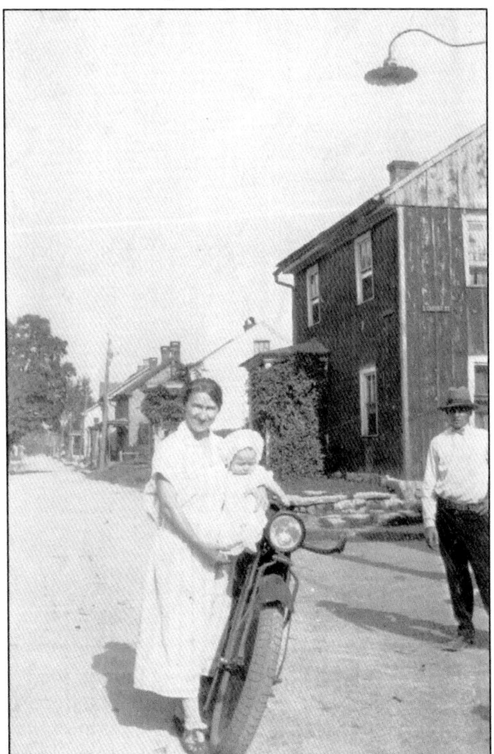

Queen and Cherry Streets. A vibrant community of Italian Americans was centered on the intersection of Queen and Cherry Streets and extended to the west end of Queen Street at Nellie Bernardo's house. (See page 24.) (Courtesy of John Bernardo.)

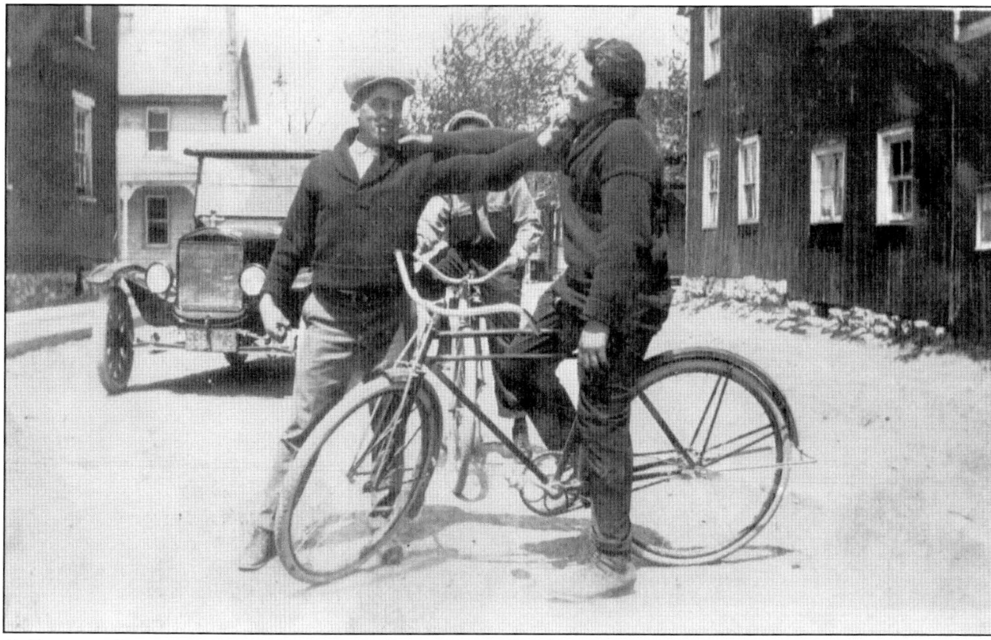

A Lively Community. West Annville native Charlie Mariani recalls the following about the good old days of the 1920s and 1930s: "Those streets were alive with people enjoying one another; there were not too many automobiles to keep us on the sidewalks, many of which were still dirt paths." This picture looks north to the intersection of Queen and Cherry Streets. (Courtesy of John Bernardo.)

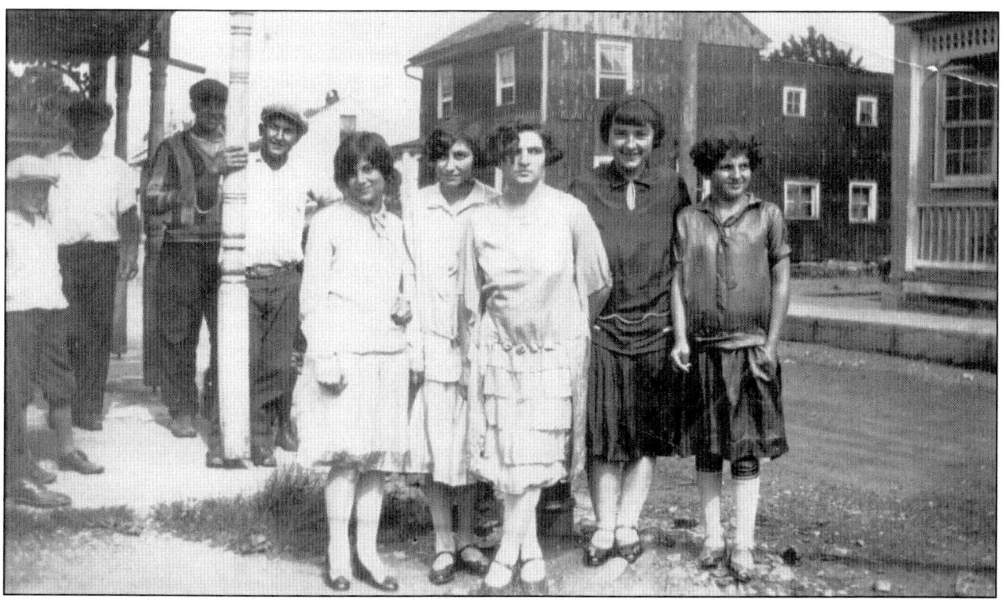

Frequent Celebrations. "Religious holidays," continues Mariani, "usually began with going to church, coming home, changing clothes . . . and then enjoying camaraderie, food, and games like Bocce, town ball, caddy, hiddy go, et cetera." This picture looks east toward Queen and Cherry Streets. (Courtesy of John Bernardo.)

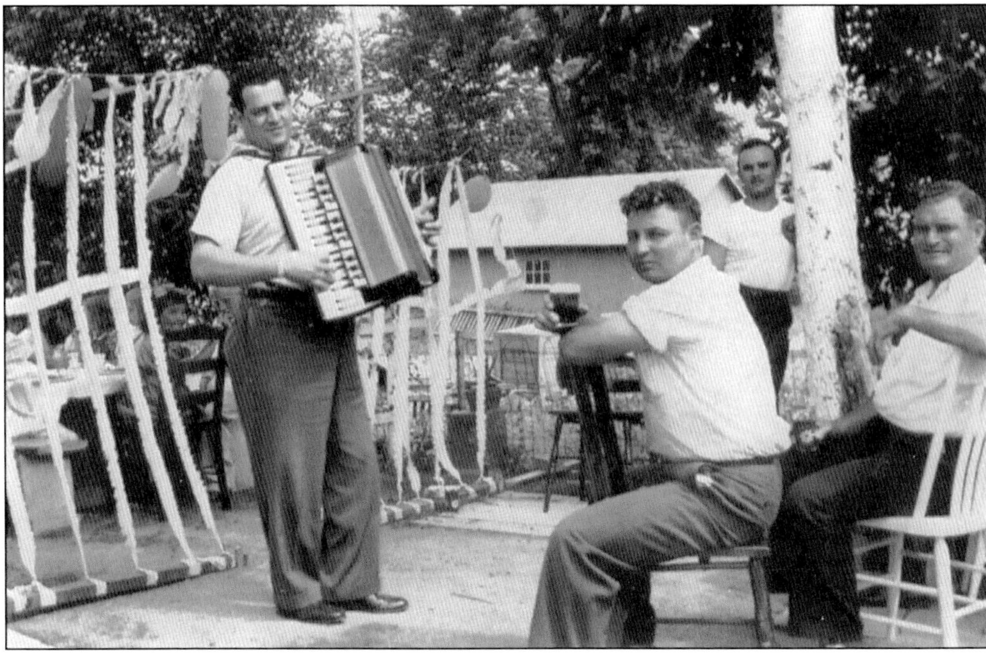

Streets Filled with Music. "The end of the day was left for resting with singing accompanied by the neighborhood musicians who would play guitar, banjo, mandolin," Mariani notes. "My hero was Tony Mariani with his accordion [pictured here around the 1930s]. I would stay to listen to him play for us rather than go to the movies." (Courtesy of Ammon Balaster.)

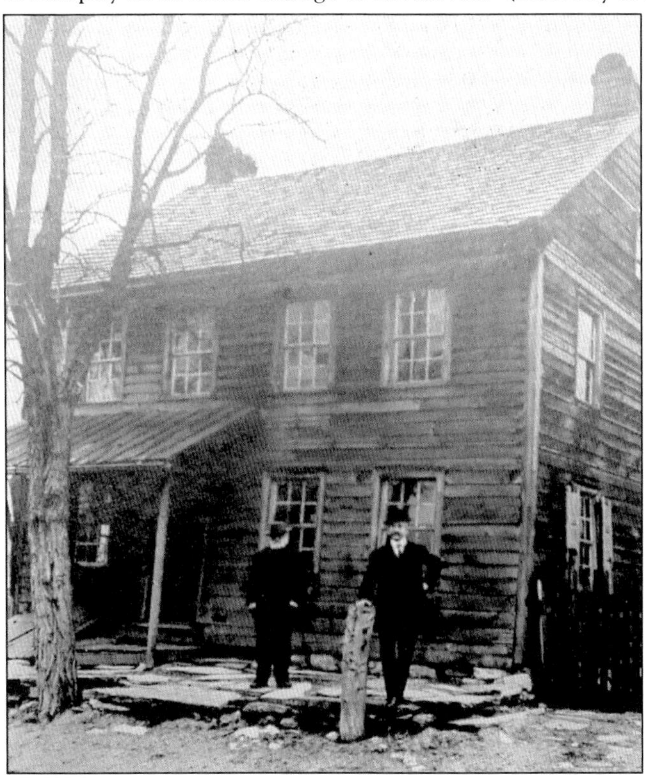

No. 440 West Queen Street. Peter Bernhard (1832–1887) built this home in the late 1870s. Wood siding protected most of the log- and frame-construction homes in Annville through the first half of the 20th century. After seeing how paint bonded to aluminum fuselages on World War II planes, Jerome Kaufman invented aluminum siding in 1947. The durability, lower maintenance costs, and improved insulation afforded by aluminum, and later vinyl siding, would transform this section of West Queen Street as it did much of America.

Two

UP FROM THE BANKS OF THE QUITTAPAHILLA

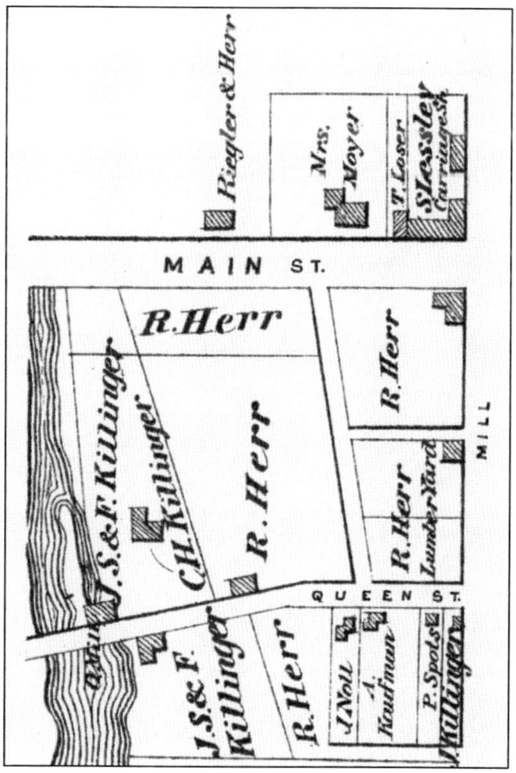

WEST QUEEN'S 500 BLOCK, 1875 MAP. This portion of the *County Atlas of Lebanon, Pennsylvania* details the building footings and residents' surnames from the 500 block of West Queen Street to the 500 block of West Main Street as they existed in 1875.

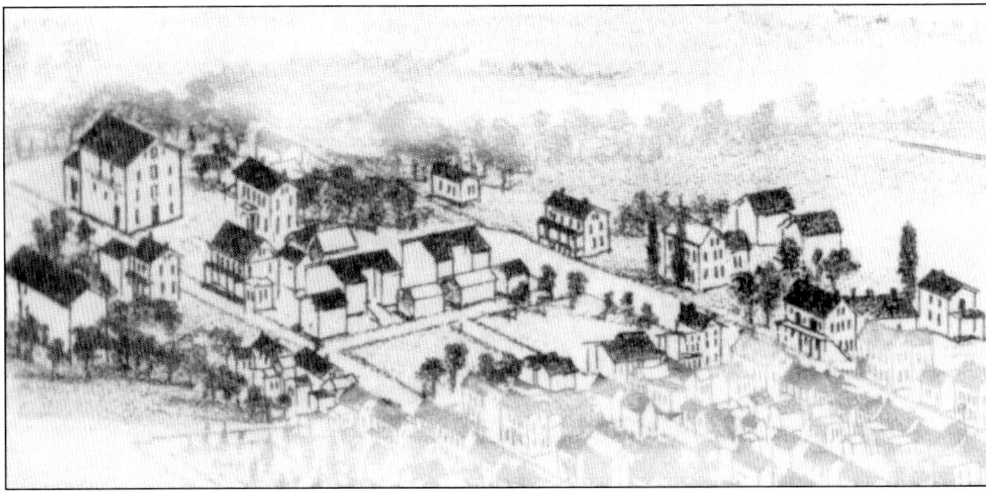

West Queen's 500 Block, 1888 View. T.M. Fowler's panoramic view of Annville portrays the buildings of the 500 block of West Queen Street and the 500 block of West Main Street as they appeared from the southeast in 1888.

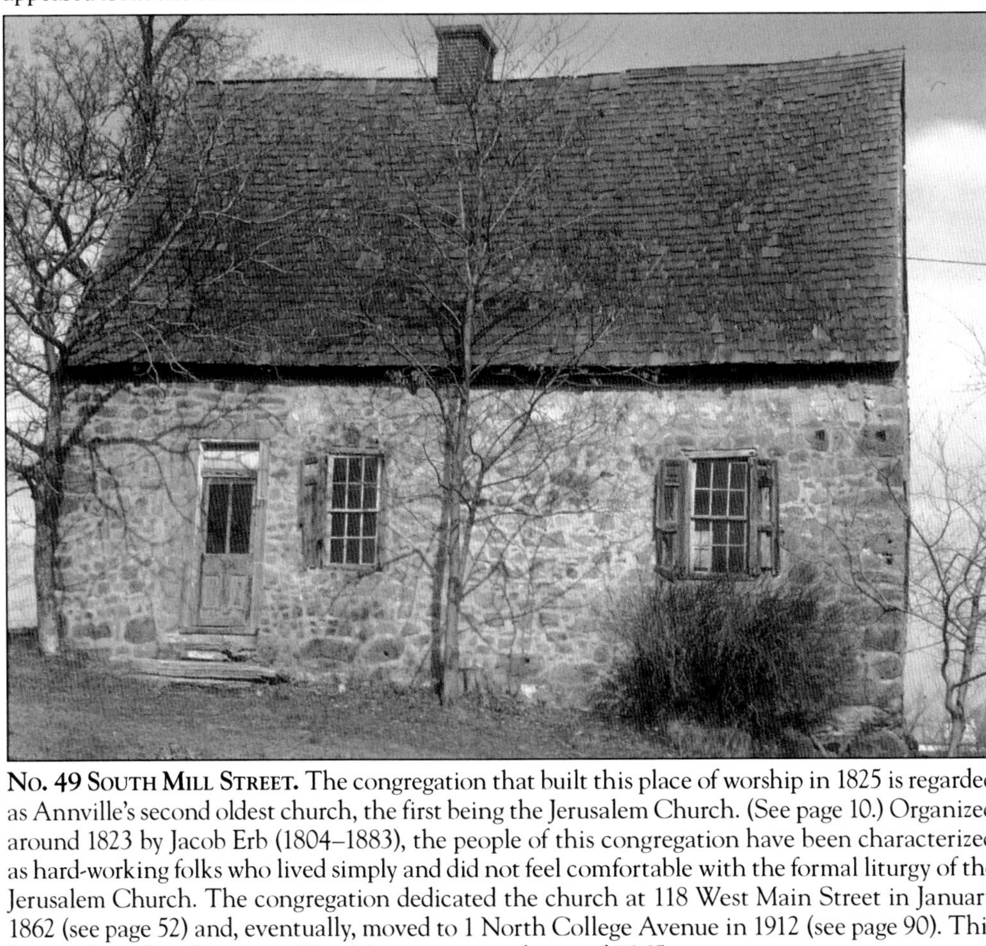

No. 49 South Mill Street. The congregation that built this place of worship in 1825 is regarded as Annville's second oldest church, the first being the Jerusalem Church. (See page 10.) Organized around 1823 by Jacob Erb (1804–1883), the people of this congregation have been characterized as hard-working folks who lived simply and did not feel comfortable with the formal liturgy of the Jerusalem Church. The congregation dedicated the church at 118 West Main Street in January 1862 (see page 52) and, eventually, moved to 1 North College Avenue in 1912 (see page 90). This house of worship, known as Herr House, was razed around 1965.

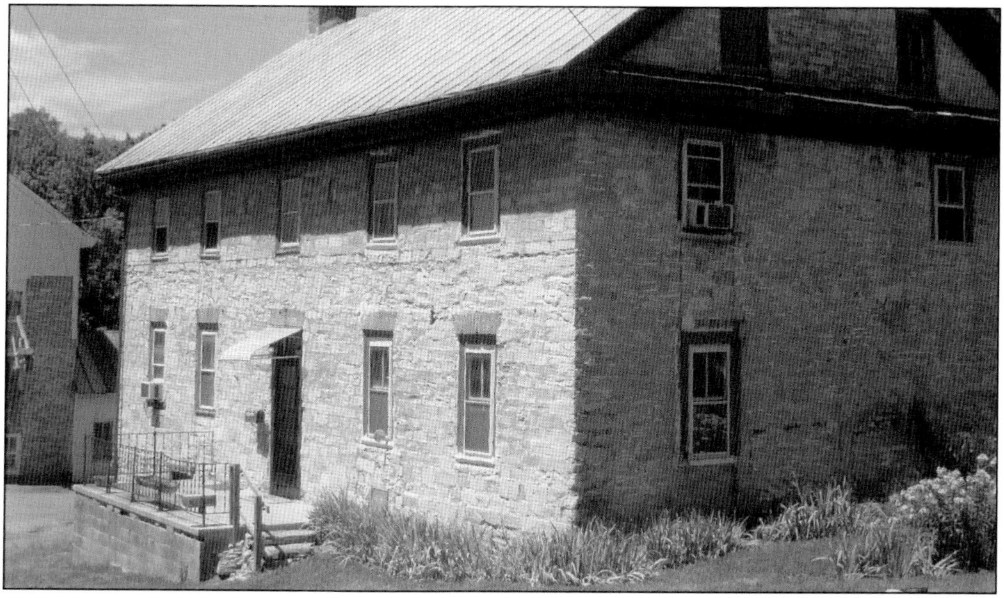

No. 533 West Queen Street. Records from a local window tax collected in 1798 indicate that Abraham Herr (1762–1812), who owned and operated the mill on this property at that time, also owned this large home, built around 1795 in the Georgian style. Note the fine Greek key designs that frame the roof, as well as the pent eaves between the first and second floors on the gable ends of the structure. Unfortunately, no record or recollection exists of the date stones missing from the front of the building.

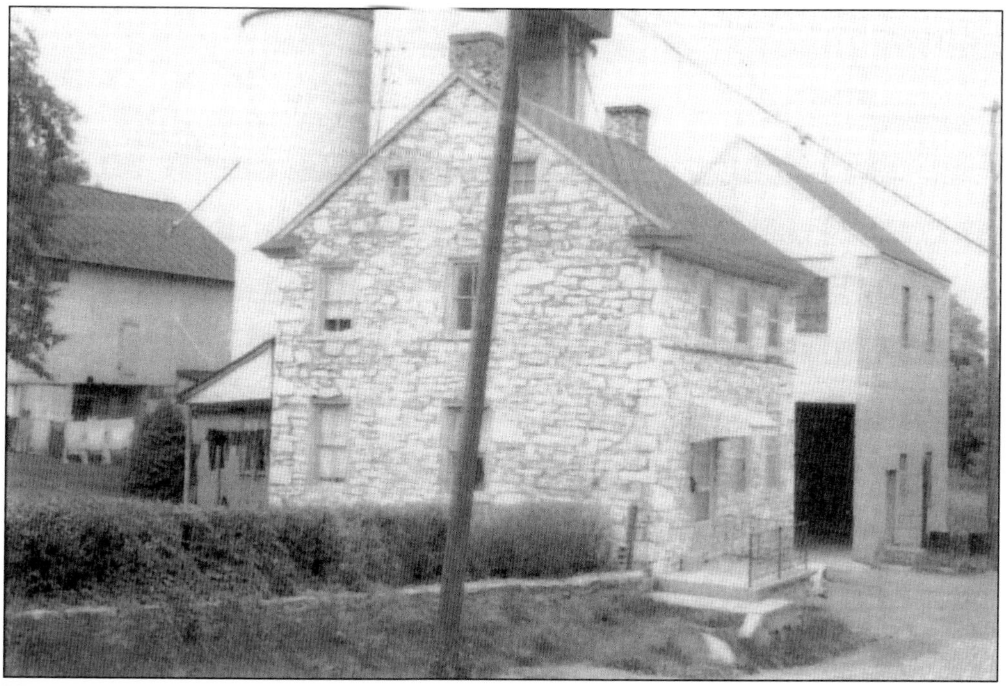

No. 536 West Queen Street. Abraham Herr's son Henry (1790–1827) and his wife, Sarah (1798–1870), built this home in 1822 for themselves and their six children. The building is no longer standing. (Courtesy of Lori Unger Nally.)

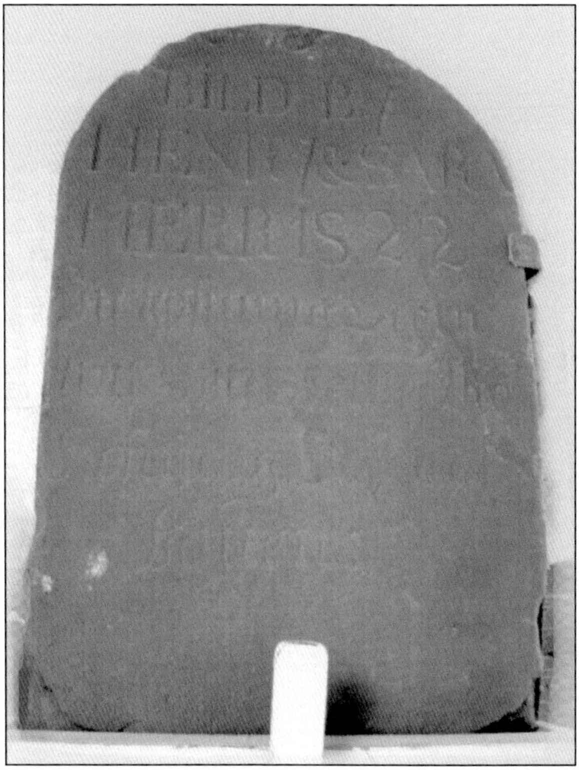

THE 1822 DATE STONE. Following its basic indication that Henry and Sarah Herr built the house, the inscription on the date stone for the building reads: "*In hofnung legen wir den stein. Auf hofnung las uns bauen,*" which translates to "In hope we lay the stone. On hope let us build."

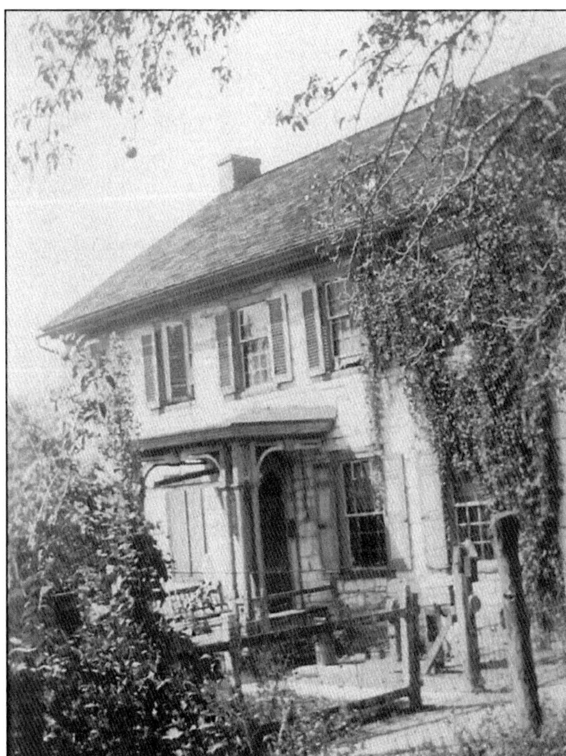

NO. 539 WEST QUEEN STREET. Features of the interior stairwell of this building, which are similar to features of the stairwell at 533 West Queen Street, suggest that this home was also built by Abraham Herr, possibly for his brother Samuel (1766–1806). The house is pictured here in the 1930s, when the Bernardos, a family of Italian immigrants, lived here. At that time, Nellie Bernardo maintained a vegetable garden that extended from the back of the property to Route 422 to the north. (Courtesy of Edward Bernardo.)

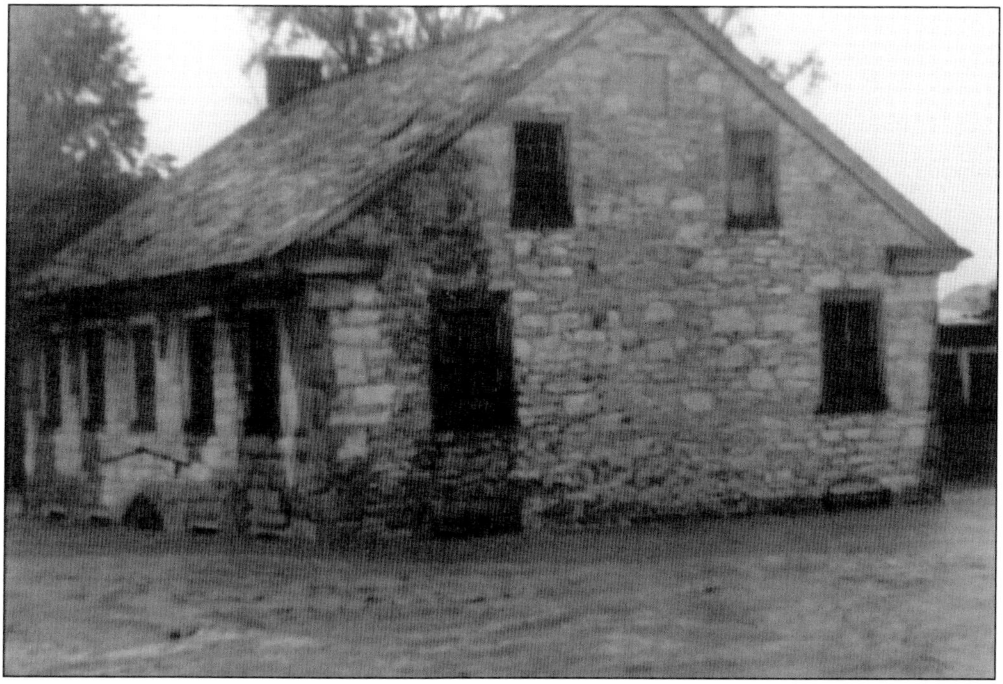

Hurricane Agnes. Located as close to the Quittapahilla Creek as it is, this house suffered significant damage when Hurricane Agnes hit the region on June 22, 1972. The home was not occupied at the time.

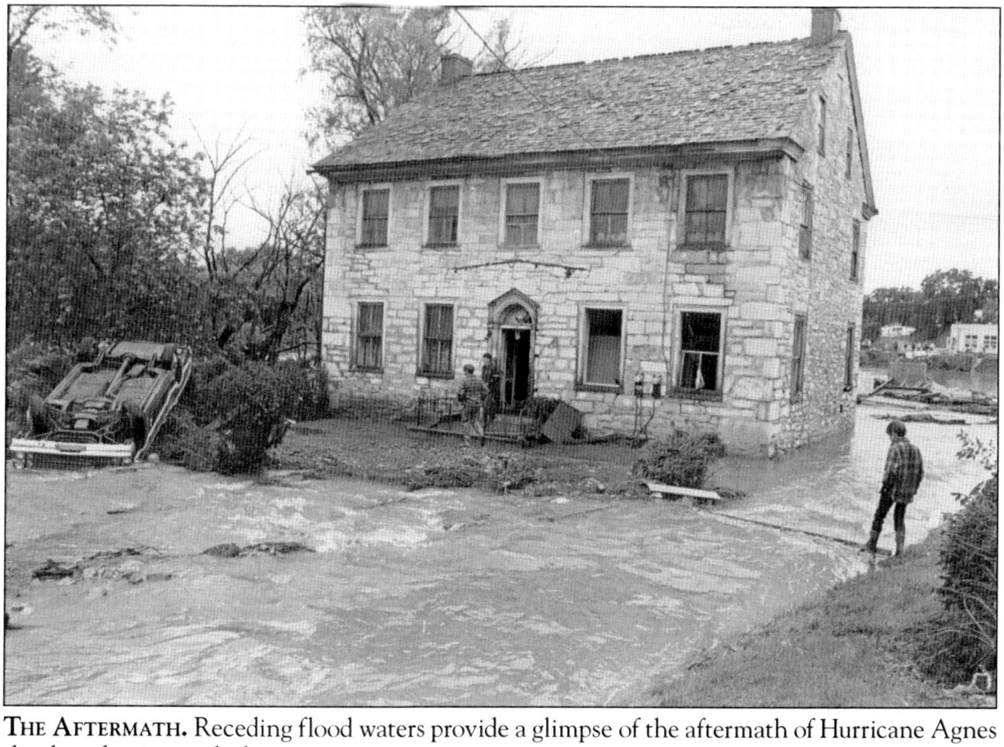

The Aftermath. Receding flood waters provide a glimpse of the aftermath of Hurricane Agnes the day after it struck the area.

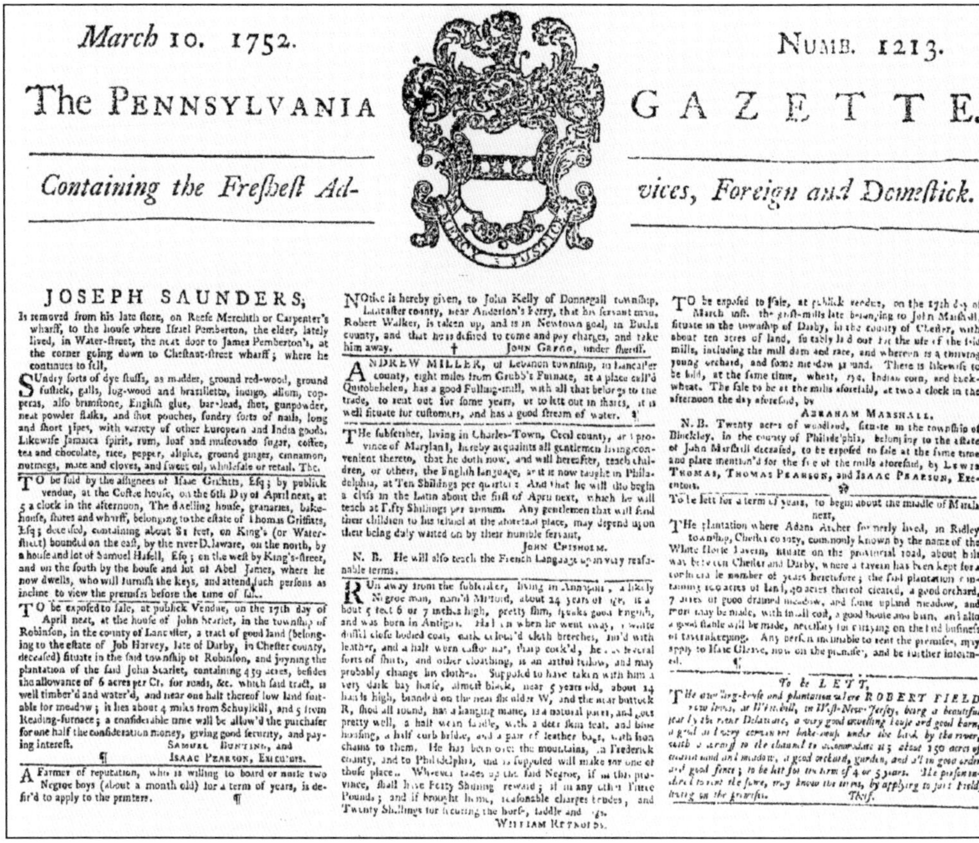

March 10. 1752. NUMB. 1213.

The PENNSYLVANIA GAZETTE.

Containing the Freshest Advices, Foreign and Domestick.

JOSEPH SAUNDERS,

Is removed from his late store, on Reese Meredith or Carpenter's wharff, to the house where Israel Pemberton, the elder, lately lived, in Water-street, the next door to James Pemberton's, at the corner going down to Chestnut-street wharff; where he continues to sell,

SUndry sorts of dye stuffs, as madder, ground red-wood, ground fustick, galls, log-wood and brasilletto, indigo, allom, copperas, also brimstone, English glue, bar-lead, shot, gunpowder, neat powder flasks, and shot pouches, sundry sorts of nails, long and short pipes, with variety of other European and India goods. Likewise Jamaica spirit, rum, loaf and muscovado sugar, coffee, tea and chocolate, rice, pepper, allspice, ground ginger, cinnamon, nutmegs, mace and cloves, and sweet oil, wholesale or retail. The.

TO be sold by the assignees of Isaac Griffitts, Esq; by publick vendue, at the Coffee house, on the 6th Day of April next, at 5 a clock in the afternoon, The dwelling house, granaries, bakehouse, stores and wharff, belonging to the estate of Thomas Griffitts, Esq; deceased, containing about 81 feet, on King's (or Water-street) bounded on the east, by the river Delaware, on the north, by a house and lot of Samuel Hasell, Esq; on the west by King's-street, and on the south by the house and lot of Abel James, where he now dwells, who will furnish the keys, and attend such persons as incline to view the premises before the time of sale.

TO be exposed to sale, at publick Vendue, on the 17th day of April next, at the house of John Scarlet, in the township of Robinson, in the county of Lancaster, a tract of good land (belonging to the estate of Job Harvey, late of Darby, in Chester county, deceased) situate in the said township of Robinson, and joyning the plantation of the said John Scarlet, containing 459 acres, besides the allowance of 6 acres per Ct. for roads, &c. which said tract, is well timber'd and water'd, and near one half thereof low land suitable for meadow; it lies about 4 miles from Schuylkill, and 5 from Reading-furnace; a considerable time will be allow'd the purchaser for one half the consideration money, giving good security, and paying interest.

SAMUEL BUNTING, and
ISAAC PEARSON, Executors.

A Farmer of reputation, who is willing to board or nurse two Negroe boys (about a month old) for a term of years, is desir'd to apply to the printers.

NOtice is hereby given, to John Kelly of Donnegall township, Lancaster county, near Anderson's Ferry, that his servant man, Robert Walker, is taken up, and is in Newtown goal, in Bucks county, and that he is desired to come and pay charges, and take him away.

JOHN GARGO, under sheriff.

ANDREW MILLER, of Lebanon township, in Lancaster county, eight miles from Grubb's Furnace, at a place call'd Quitobehelen, has a good Fulling-mill, with all that belongs to the trade, to rent out for some years, or to lett out in shares, it is well situate for customers, and has a good stream of water.

THe subscriber, living in Charles-Town, Cecil county, in the province of Maryland, hereby acquaints all gentlemen living convenient thereto, that he doth now, and will hereafter, teach children, or others, the English language, as it is now taught in Philadelphia, at Ten Shillings per quarter: And that he will also begin a class in the Latin about the first of April next, which he will teach at Fifty Shillings per annum. Any gentlemen that will send their children to his school at the aforesaid place, may depend upon their being daily waited on by their humble servant,

JOHN CHISHOLM.

N. B. He will also teach the French Language upon very reasonable terms.

RUn away from the subscriber, living in Annapolis, a likely Negroe man, nam'd Milford, about 24 years of age, is about 5 feet 6 or 7 inches high, pretty slim, speaks good English, and was born in Antigua. Had on when he went away, a white duffil close bodied coat, dark colour'd cloth breeches, lin'd with leather, and a half worn castor hat, sharp cock'd, he has several sorts of shirts, and other cloathing, is an artful fellow, and may probably change his cloths. Suppos'd to have taken with him a very dark bay horse, almost black, near 5 years old, about 14 hands high, branded on the near shoulder W, and the near buttock R, shod all round, has a hanging mane, is a natural pacer, and goes pretty well, a half worn saddle, with a deer skin seat, and blue housing, a half curb bridle, and a pair of leather bags, with iron chains to them. He has been over the mountains, in Frederick county, and to Philadelphia, and is supposed will make for one of those places. Whoever takes up the said Negroe, if in this province, shall have Forty Shillings reward; if in any other Three Pounds; and if brought home, reasonable charges besides, and Twenty Shillings for securing the horse, saddle and bags.

WILLIAM REYNOLDS.

TO be exposed to sale, at publick vendue, on the 17th day of March inst. the grist-mills late belonging to John Marshall, situate in the township of Darby, in the county of Chester, with about ten acres of land, suitably laid out for the use of the said mills, including the mill dam and race, and whereon is a thriving young orchard, and some meadow ground. There is likewise to be sold, at the same time, wheat, rye, Indian corn, and buckwheat. The sale to be at the mills aforesaid, at two a clock in the afternoon the day aforesaid, by

ABRAHAM MARSHALL.

N. B. Twenty acres of woodland, situate in the township of Blockley, in the county of Philadelphia, belonging to the estate of John Marshall deceased, to be exposed to sale at the same time and place mention'd for the sale of the mills aforesaid, by LEWIS THOMAS, THOMAS PEARSON, and ISAAC PEARSON, Executors.

To be lett for a term of years, to begin about the middle of March next,

THe plantation where Adam Archer formerly lived, in Ridley township, Chester county, commonly known by the name of the White Horse Tavern, situate on the provincial road, about half way between Chester and Darby, where a tavern has been kept for a considerable number of years heretofore; the said plantation containing 100 acres of land, 40 acres thereof cleared, a good orchard, 7 acres of good drained meadow, and some upland meadow, and more may be made, with small cost, a good house and barn, and also a good stable will be made, necessary for carrying on the said business of tavernkeeping. Any person inclinable to rent the premises, may apply to Isaac Glease, now on the premises, and be further inform'd.

To be LETT,

THe dwelling-house and plantation where ROBERT FIELD *now lives, at Whitehill, in West-New-Jersey, being a beautiful seat by the river Delaware, a very good dwelling house and good barn, a good and very convenient bake-house under the bank by the river, with a [illegible] to the channel to accommodate it; about 150 acres of* [illegible] *and meadow, a good orchard, garden, and all in good order and good fence; to be lett for the term of 4 or 5 years. The person inclined to rent the same, may know the terms, by applying to* [illegible] *Field, living on the premises.*

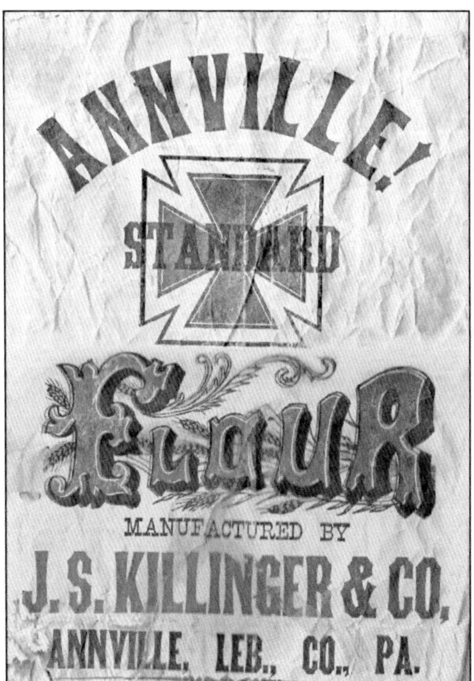

AN 18TH-CENTURY MILL. The structure that housed the grindstone of the mill, originally built in the mid-18th century, began as a 2.5-story building and was expanded to four stories later in that same century. This advertisement to lease the mill ran in the March 10, 1752, edition of the *Pennsylvania Gazette*. The owner at that time, and probably its builder, was Andrew Miller, Annville's founder. The advertisement, which appears second from the top of the middle column, reads as follows: "Andrew Miller, of Lebanon township, in Lancaster County, eight miles from Grubb's Furnace, at a place call'd Quitobehelen, has a good Fulling-mill, with all that belongs to the trade, to rent out for some years, or to lett [sic] out in shares, it is well situate [sic] for customers, and has a good stream of water."

KILLINGER FLOUR BAG. Jacob S. Killinger owned and operated the mill from 1865 to 1878, during which time this bag was filled with flour and sold to a member of the local community. (Courtesy of John Feather.)

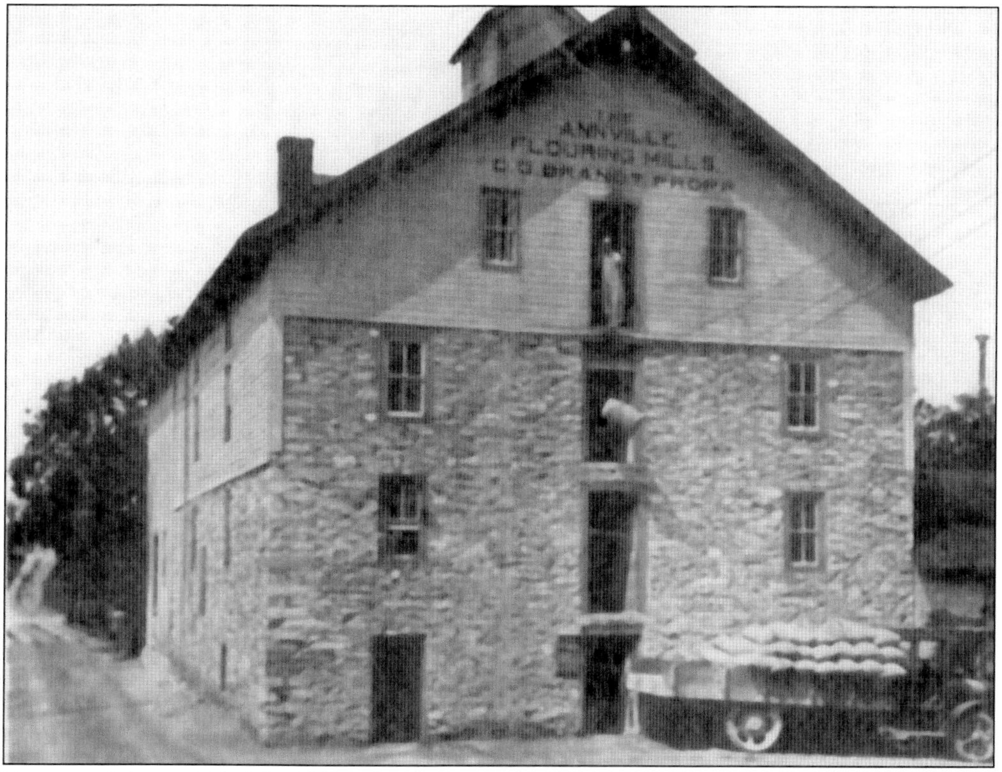

Front of Mill, 1909. The Killinger family sold the mill to David G. Brandt and family on April 3, 1906. Shortly after that time, the principal source of power for the mill was shifted from an undershot waterwheel, turning horizontal grinding stones, to a single-cylinder diesel engine. The Brandts would manage the property and business until 1980. (Courtesy of Lori Unger Nalley.)

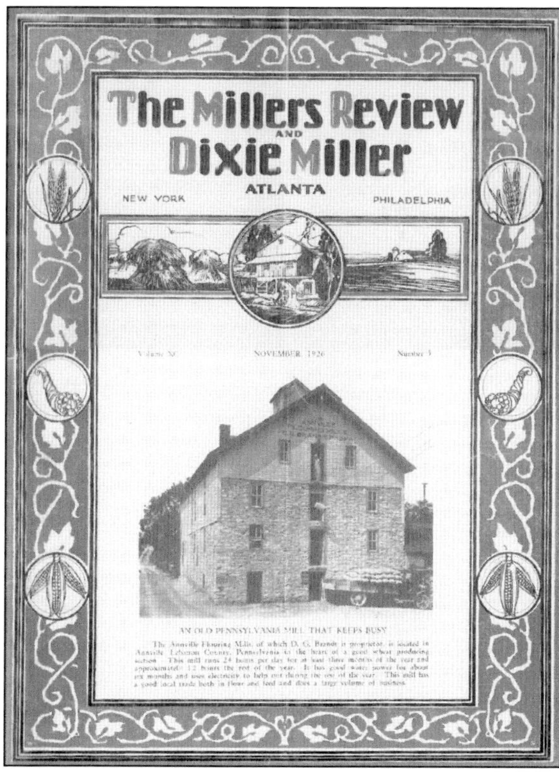

Magazine Cover, 1926. In November 1926, the *Millers Review and Dixie Miller* magazine featured the Annville mill on its cover. "This mill runs 24 hours per day for at least three months of the year," the caption states, "and approximately 12 hours the rest of the year." (Courtesy of LeRoy Brandt.)

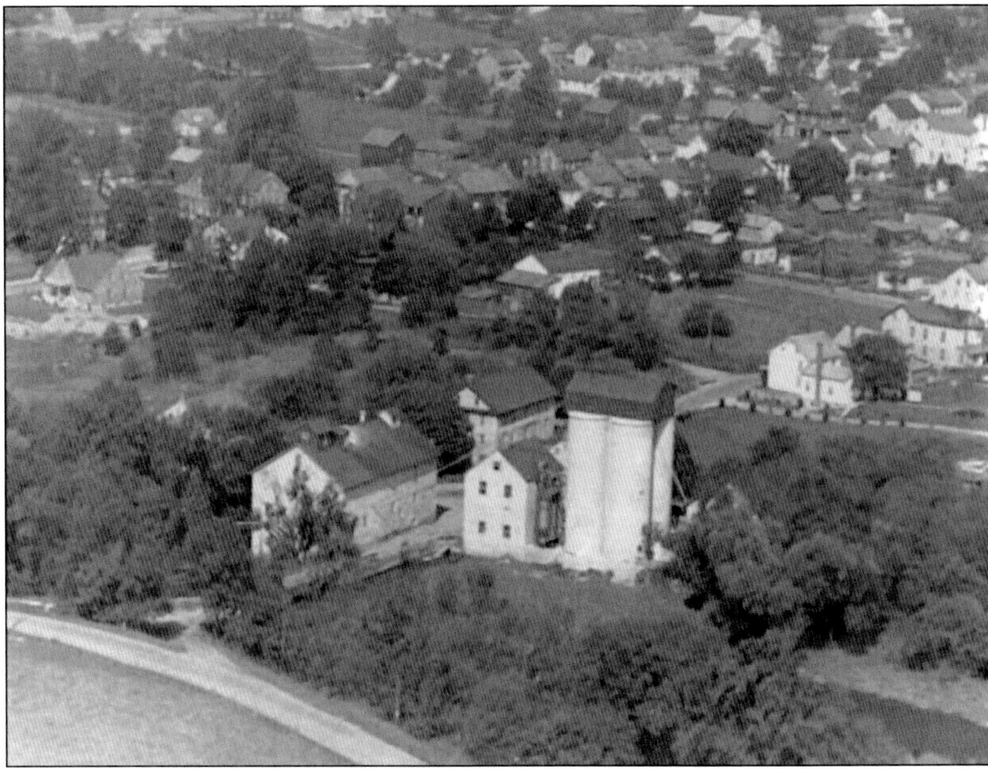

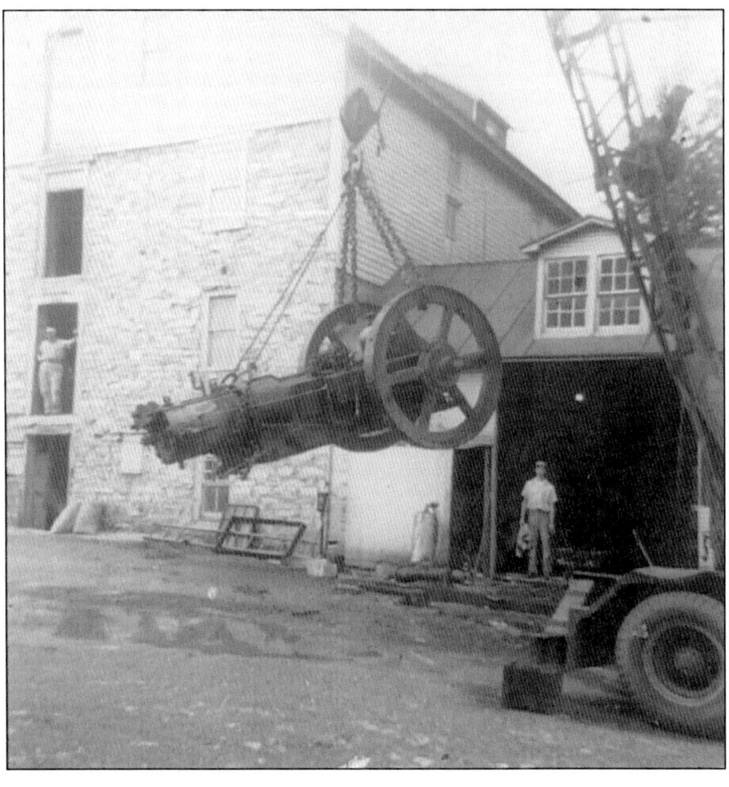

A 1950s Aerial View. This aerial view of the mill features concrete grain silos and a scale house that was built in 1951. (Courtesy of Lori Unger Nalley.)

A New System. Around the time of the building of the scale house, the diesel engine that powered the mill was replaced by an electric motor. Members of the local community were glad to see the diesel engine go; its frequent backfires were loud enough to wake even the deepest sleeper. (Courtesy of Marty and Patti Brandt.)

AGNES AT THE MILL. Taken shortly after Hurricane Agnes struck the region on June 22, 1972, this picture provides some indication as to how high the floodwaters reached at that time.

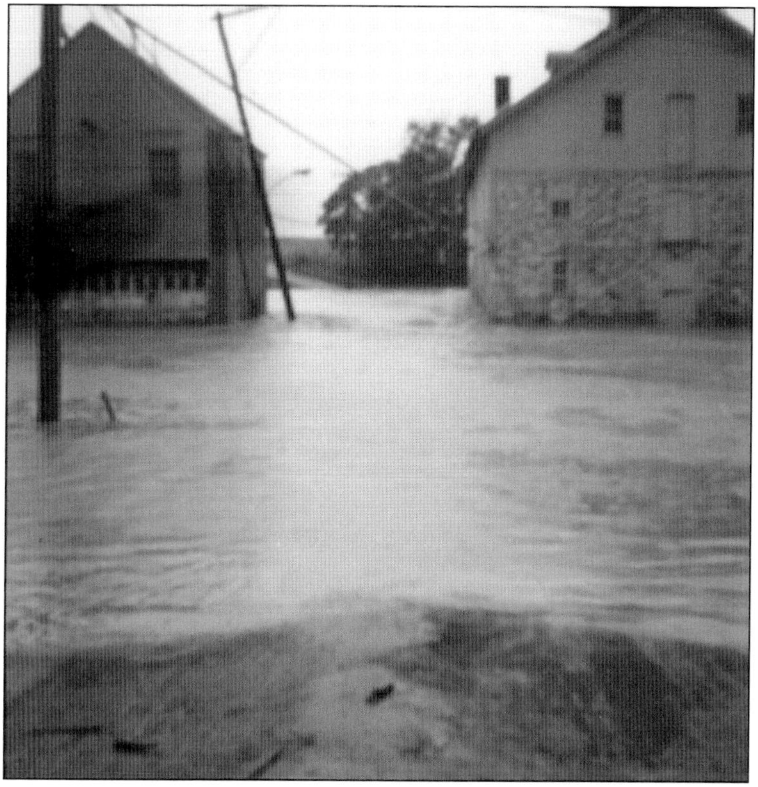

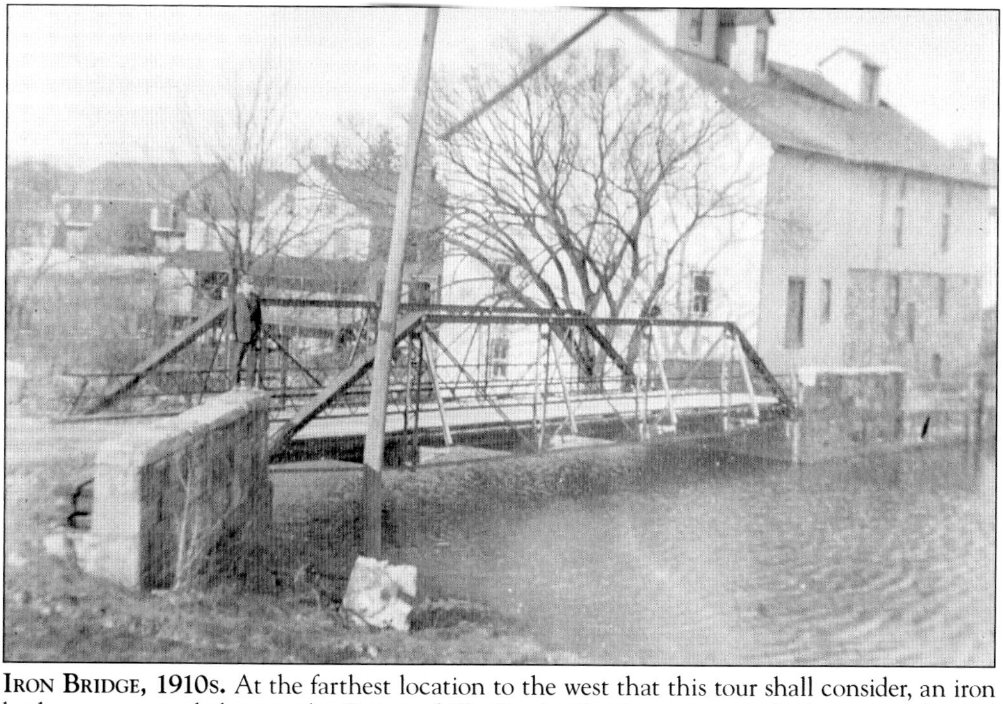

IRON BRIDGE, 1910S. At the farthest location to the west that this tour shall consider, an iron bridge once extended across the Quittapahilla Creek, allowing passage to both automobiles and pedestrians. (Courtesy of Dick and Betty Streicher.)

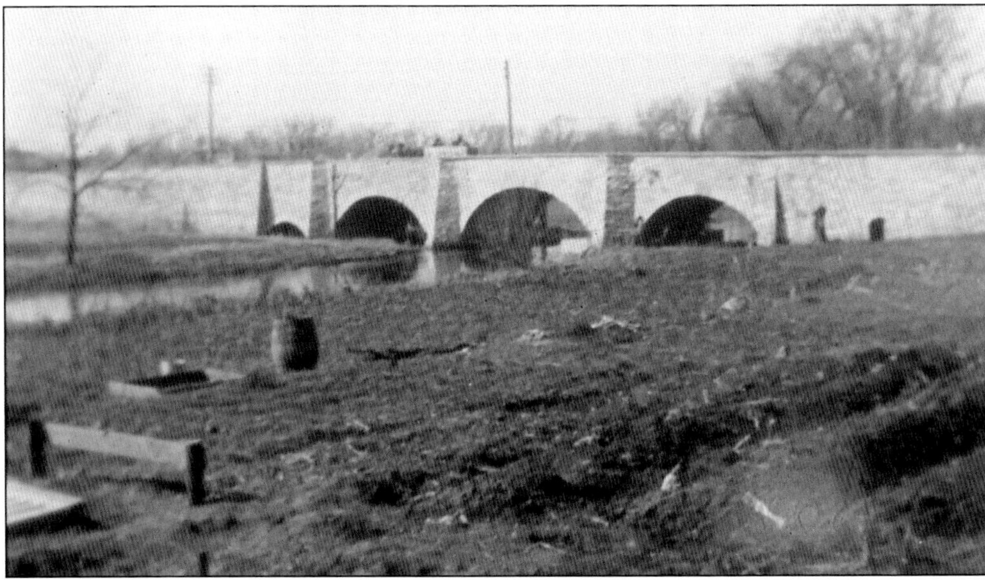

VIEW OF ROUTE 422. This 1900s view from the back of 539 West Queen Street reveals the bridge that once took the Dauphin-Berks Turnpike (later Route 422) over the Quittapahilla when the turnpike was constructed in 1817. (Courtesy of Dick and Betty Streicher.)

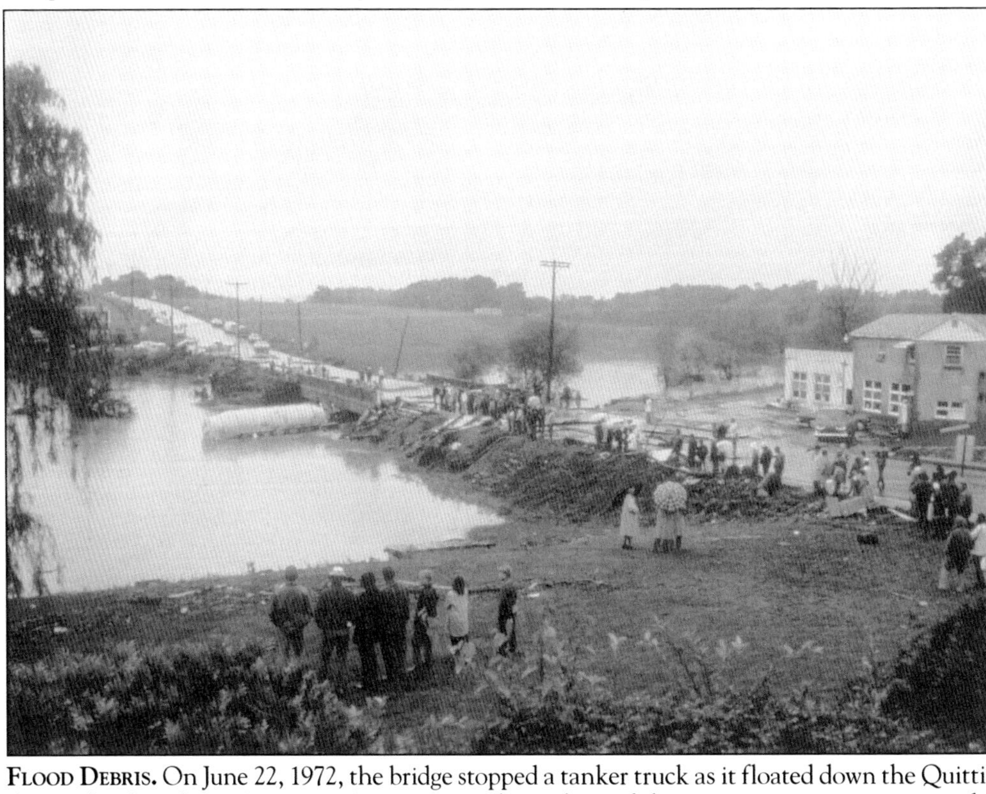

FLOOD DEBRIS. On June 22, 1972, the bridge stopped a tanker truck as it floated down the Quittie during flooding from Hurricane Agnes. Several members of the community came to view the spectacle the next day. In time, the tanker was able to be pulled from the current with the help of a tow truck and cinch.

Three

Nos. 500–300 West Main Street

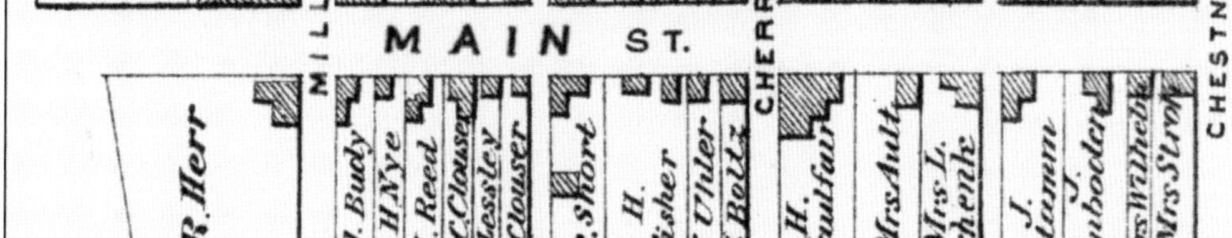

West Main's 500 Block, 1875 Map. This portion of the *County Atlas of Lebanon, Pennsylvania* details the building footings and residents' surnames from the 500 block through the 300 block of West Main Street as they existed in 1875.

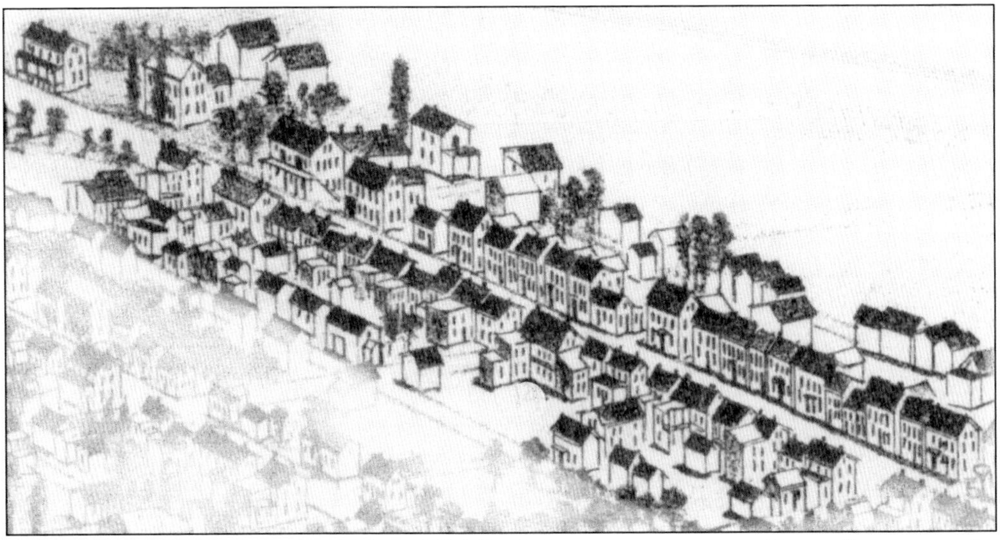

West Main's 500 Block, 1888 View. T.M. Fowler's panoramic view of Annville portrays the buildings of the 500 block through the 300 block of West Main Street as they appeared from the southeast in 1888.

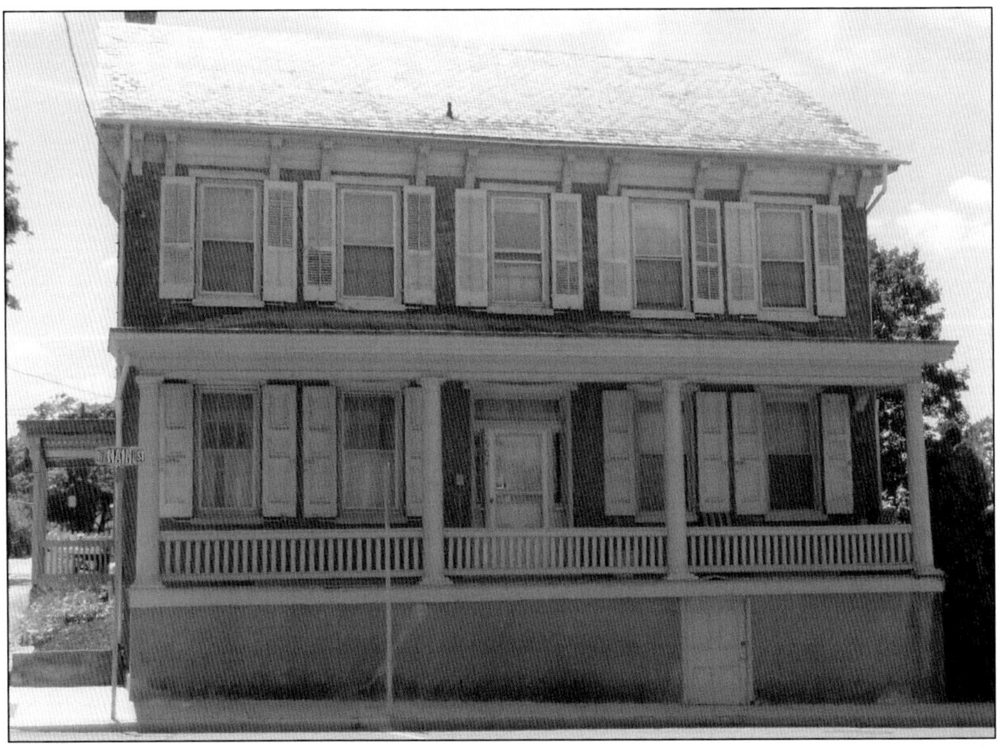

No. 504 West Main Street. Rudolph Herr (1827–1914), a grandson of Abraham Herr, built this home in 1860 to house his family, including his wife, Sarah, and five children. A rod placed through this brick house during its construction runs between the floors to keep the middle of the exterior walls from buckling out. The end of the rod takes the form of a star on the Mill Street side and the letter "S" on the west side.

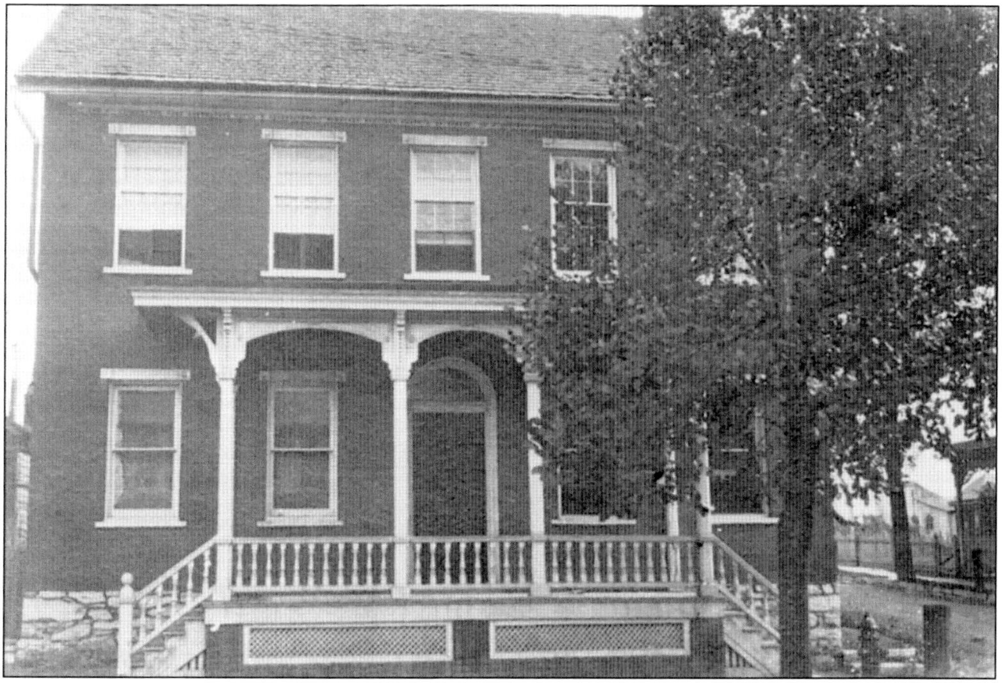

No. 450 West Main Street. On the southeast corner of Main and Mill Streets stands one of the three earliest brick homes in Annville, pictured here in the 1930s with an early porch. The stone section to the rear housed one of the first subscription schools in the area. In February 1845, Annville Township scheduled a vote as to whether or not it would adopt a public school system. The idea was opposed by German residents of the rural areas who were sufficiently wealthy to pay for private schooling and hesitant to have their children learn English. The rural areas would have outvoted the town had a snowstorm not hit Annville on the night preceding the vote, making the roads impassable. (Courtesy of Ron and Doris Flory.)

No. 437 West Main Street. This log house was originally constructed sometime before the Revolutionary War. The steep rear roofline resembles that of Saltbox houses popular in the northeastern United States at that time, named for their resemblance to wooden-lidded boxes in which salt was once kept. Sometime in the 19th century, a single, centralized chimney was replaced by two chimneys on either end.

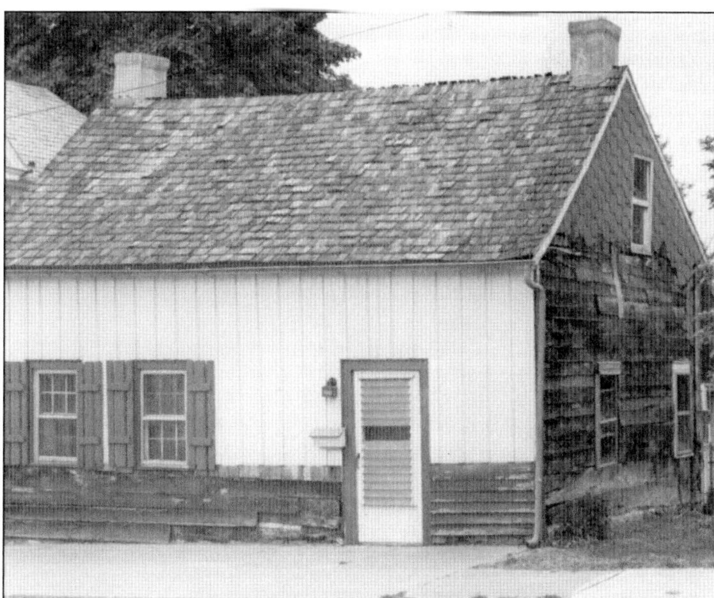

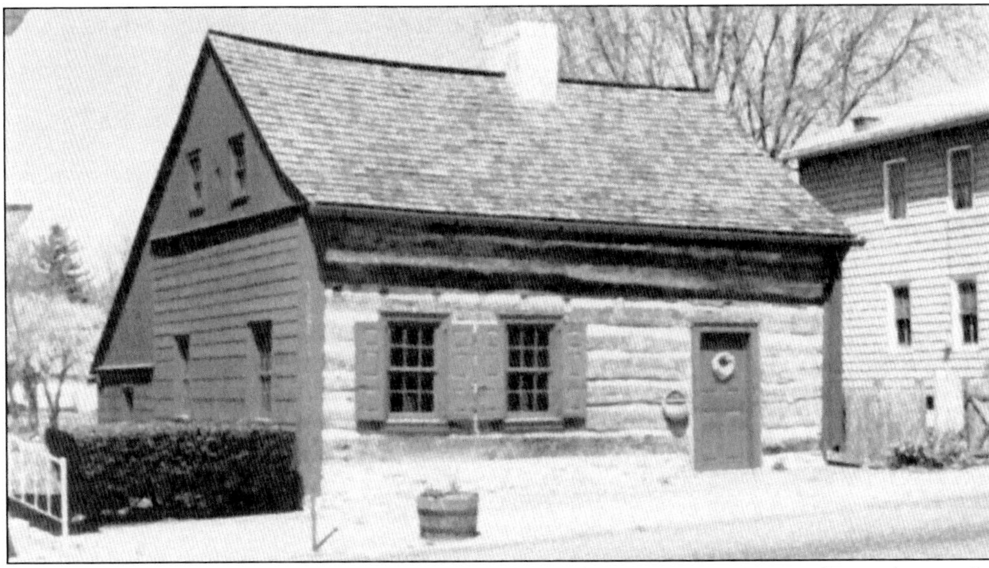

No. 437 Restored. From 1979 to 1999, Annville resident Mary Lou Harris directed a careful restoration of the home, assisted by the expertise of William R. Ross, restoration constructor; mason Thomas Sattazahn; and interior finisher Jonathan Horst. The process returned the single chimney to its original footings along with a central fireplace and a pre-Revolution, five-plate cast-iron stove. Archaeological work conducted by Harris on the site has turned up colonial buttons, brass shoe buckles, and clay marbles, among many other items. The traditional blessing in Pennsylvania Dutch inscribed over the front door translates to: "May the blessing of God crown this house." (Courtesy of Blanche Schaeffer.)

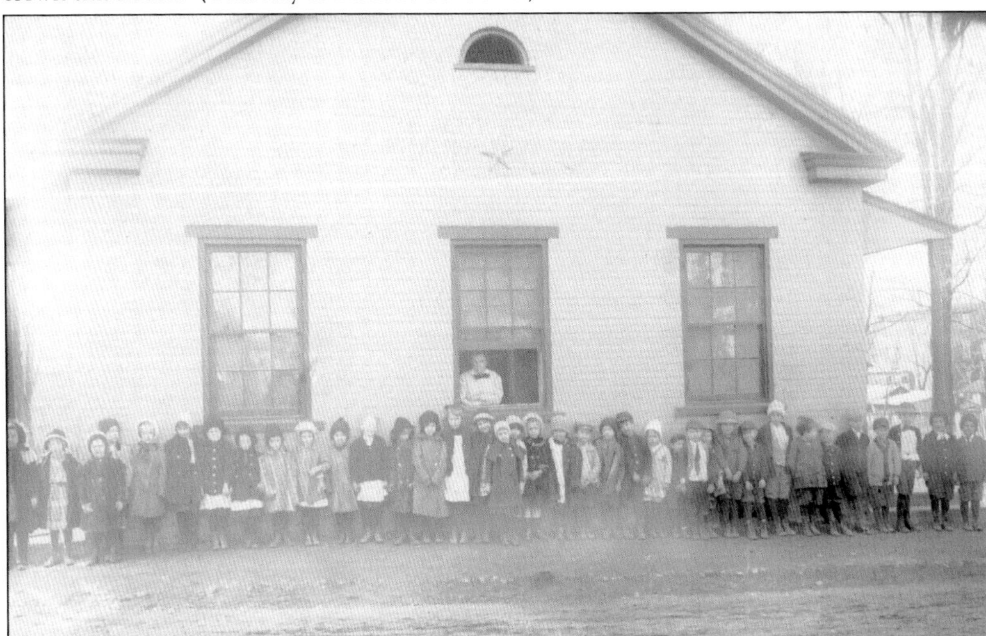

No. 29 South Cherry Street. Walking a few hundred yards south from West Main Street on Cherry Street brings one to a private residence that once served as a public elementary school and, before that, a subscription school founded by Daniel Stroh Jr. (1802–1864).

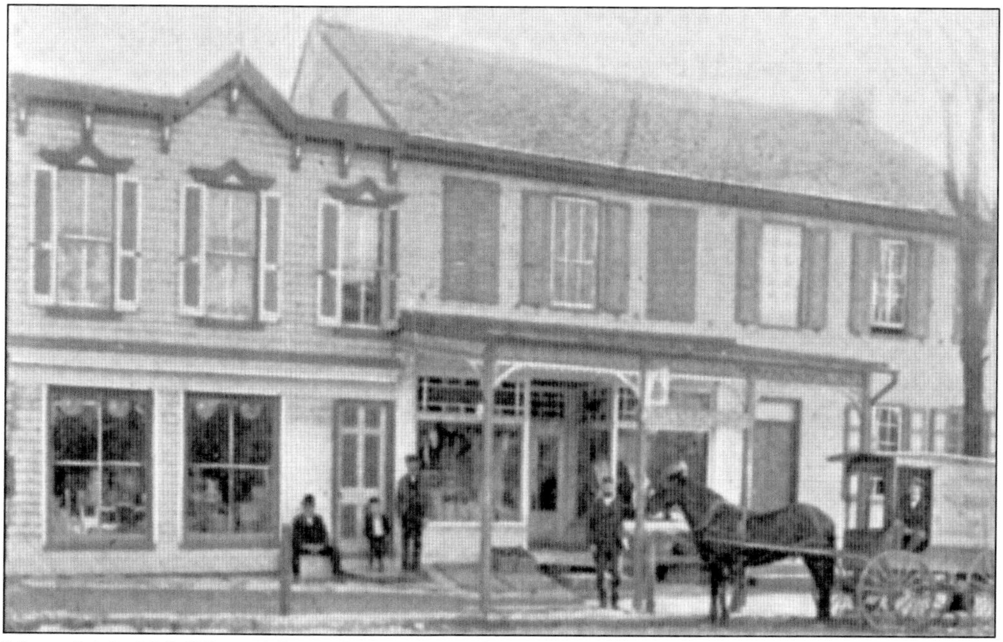

NOS. 346–350 WEST MAIN STREET. In the 1900s, this long building housed Shoop's Department Store. The structure dates to the first half of the 19th century. (Courtesy of Lebanon Valley College.)

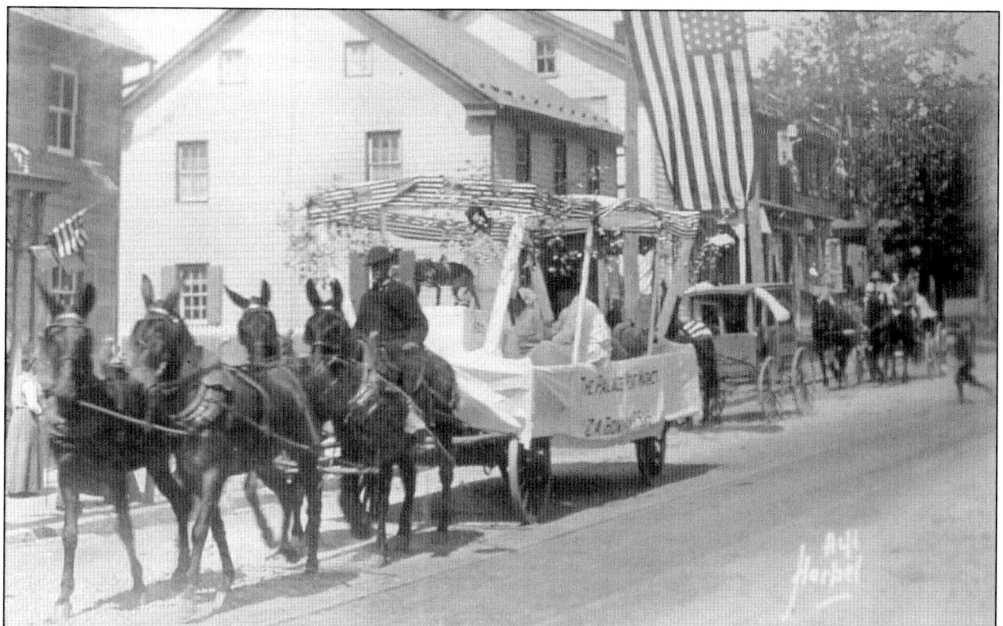

NO. 343 WEST MAIN STREET. The parade that passed by this residence in the early 1900s featured several teams of horses. The team pictured here pulls a float advertising Z.A. Bowman's Palace Meat Market. The building to the far left is no longer standing.

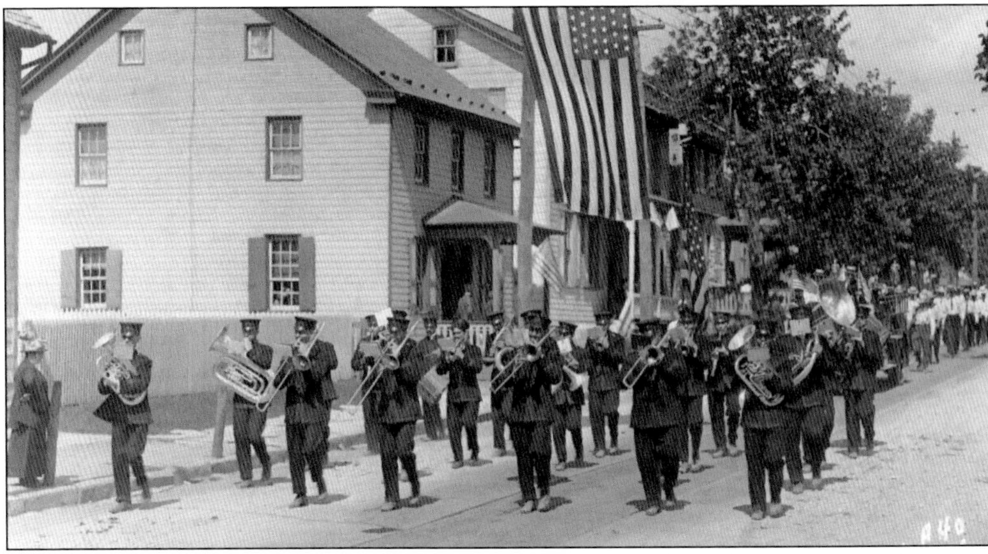

THE WASHINGTON BAND. On August 2, 1856, nine men from Annville gathered in the tavern known as Washington House (see page 43) to form a band that would become known as the Washington Band. Before the days of radio, television, or electronics, this band provided musical entertainment at many of Annville's affairs, such as this parade. By the turn of the 20th century, the band was sufficiently large to rehearse at the Hippodrome Theatre. (See page 84.) A permanent home and rehearsal hall was established in the 1920s when the band purchased an implement shop from Saylor's Carriage Works at 35 North Lancaster Street. The Washington Band has stayed active there ever since. (Courtesy of Dick and Betty Streicher.)

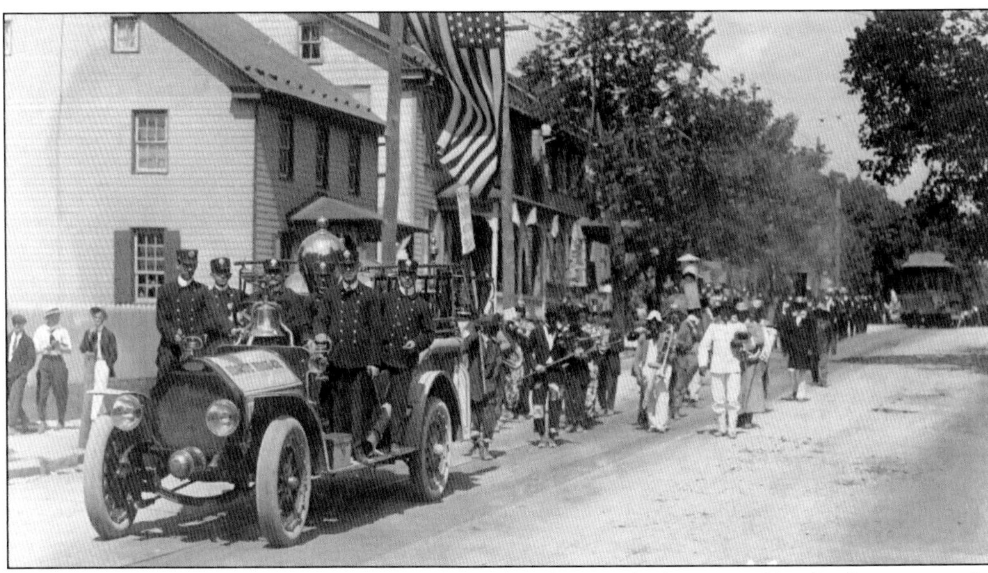

FIRE COMPANY. As is common in local parades today, the parade that passed by this location in the early 1900s provided the fire company an opportunity to display its latest equipment. (Courtesy of Dick and Betty Streicher.)

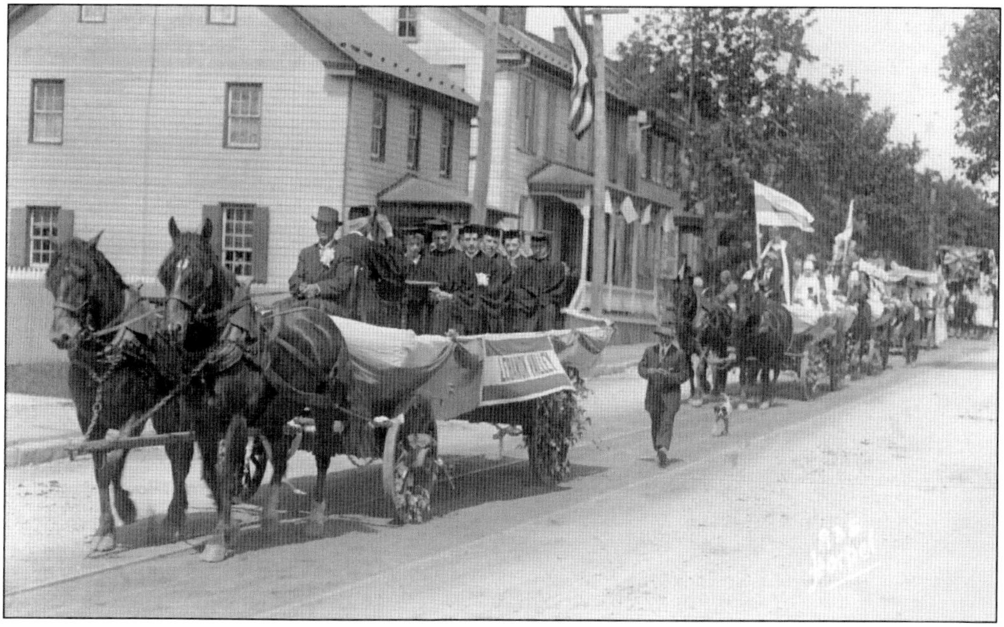

LEBANON VALLEY COLLEGE'S FLOAT. Several local businesses, as well as Lebanon Valley College (LVC), whose float is pictured here, were represented in the parade. (Courtesy of Dick and Betty Streicher.)

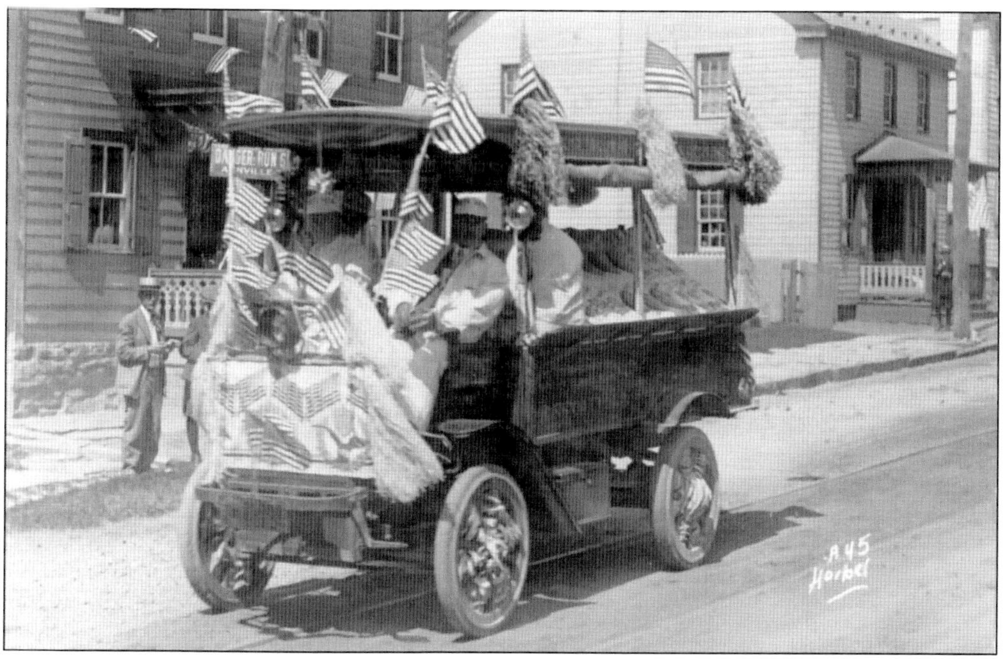

FOOD. Although the end of World War I was the occasion for similar large parades around the United States, the limited number and style of vehicles featured in this parade suggest a date about 10 years earlier. Note that the message of the early traffic sign is directed primarily to horse-drawn carriages, "Danger: Run Slow." (Courtesy of Dick and Betty Streicher.)

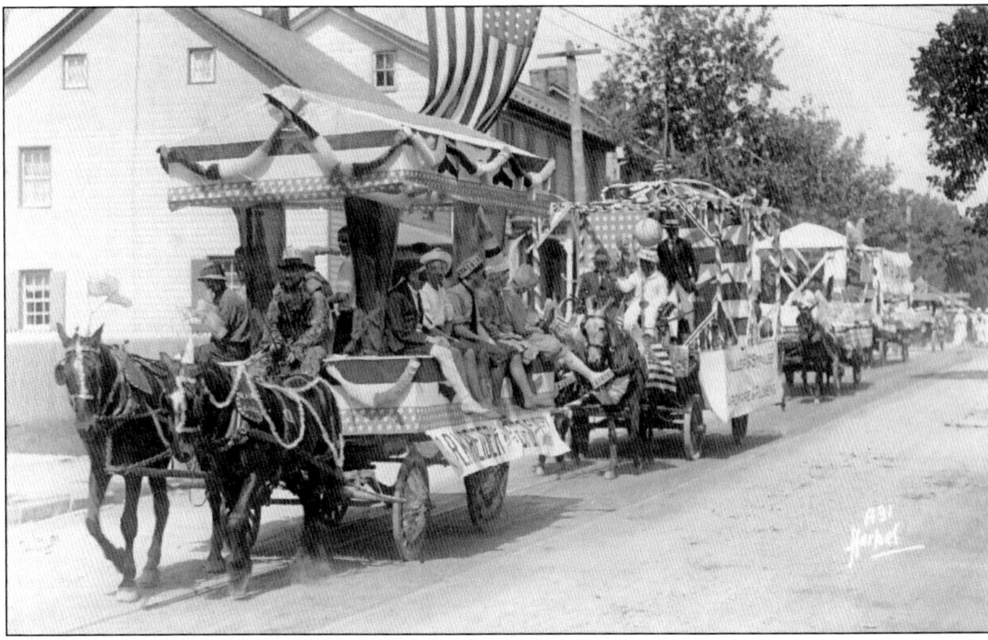

FUN. Male employees of A.R. Kreider's Hosiery enjoy the opportunity to flaunt their well-garbed legs from a float in the parade. (See pages 121–122.) (Courtesy of Dick and Betty Streicher.)

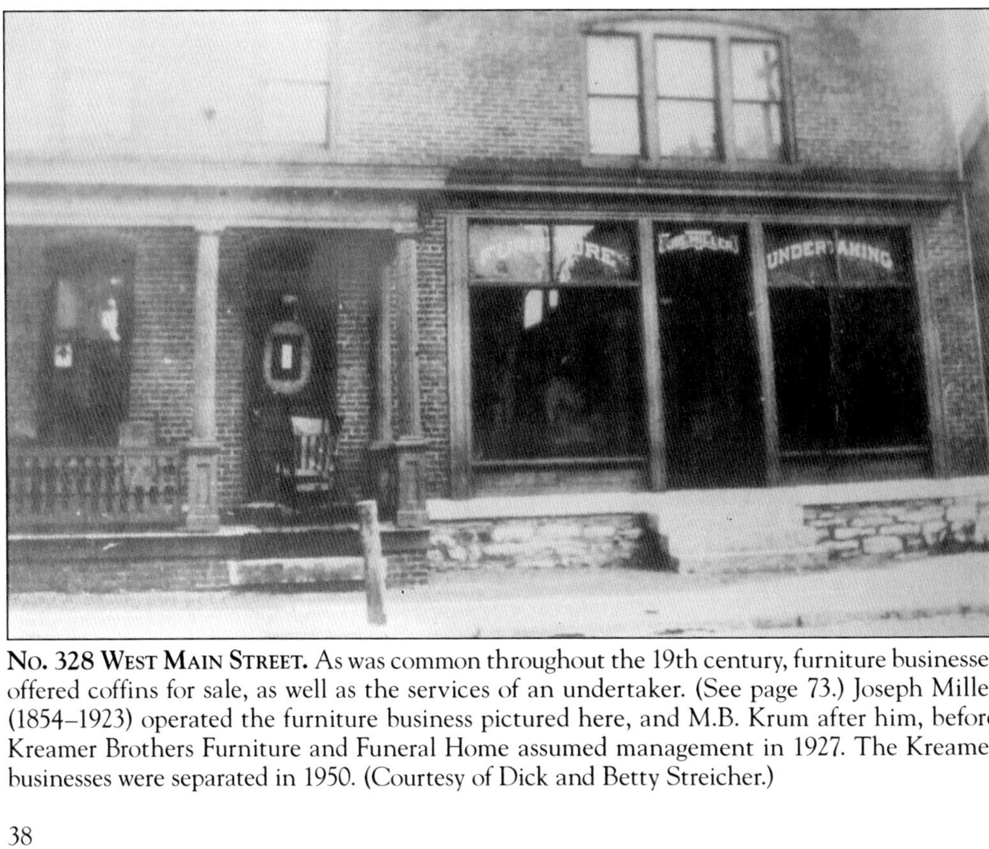

NO. 328 WEST MAIN STREET. As was common throughout the 19th century, furniture businesses offered coffins for sale, as well as the services of an undertaker. (See page 73.) Joseph Miller (1854–1923) operated the furniture business pictured here, and M.B. Krum after him, before Kreamer Brothers Furniture and Funeral Home assumed management in 1927. The Kreamer businesses were separated in 1950. (Courtesy of Dick and Betty Streicher.)

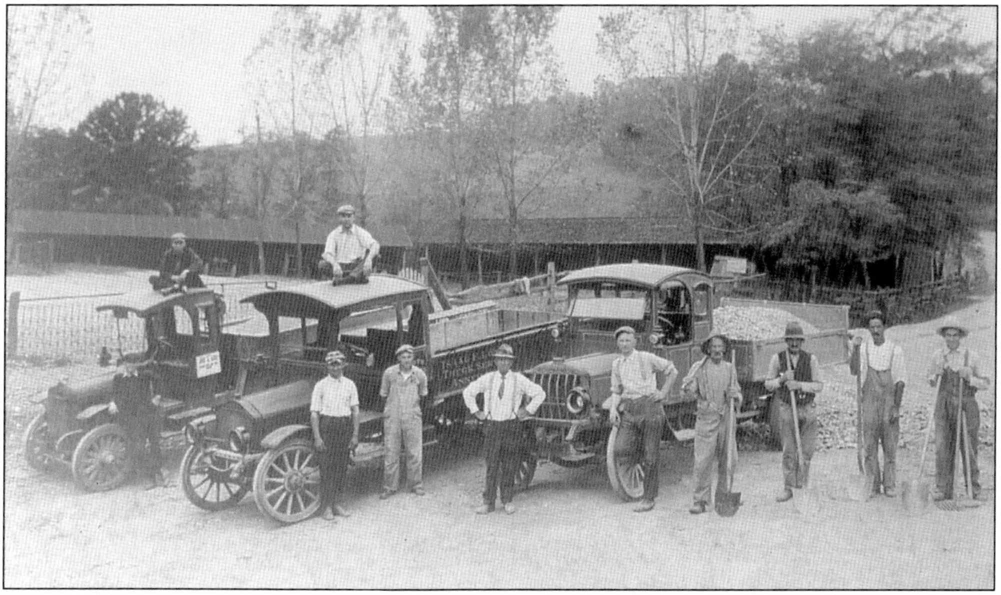

Street Maintenance. Before the advent of pavement, maintaining a busy road such as Main Street involved a process that began with the gathering of small stones. Annville's quarries provided for this need. (Courtesy of Dick and Betty Streicher.)

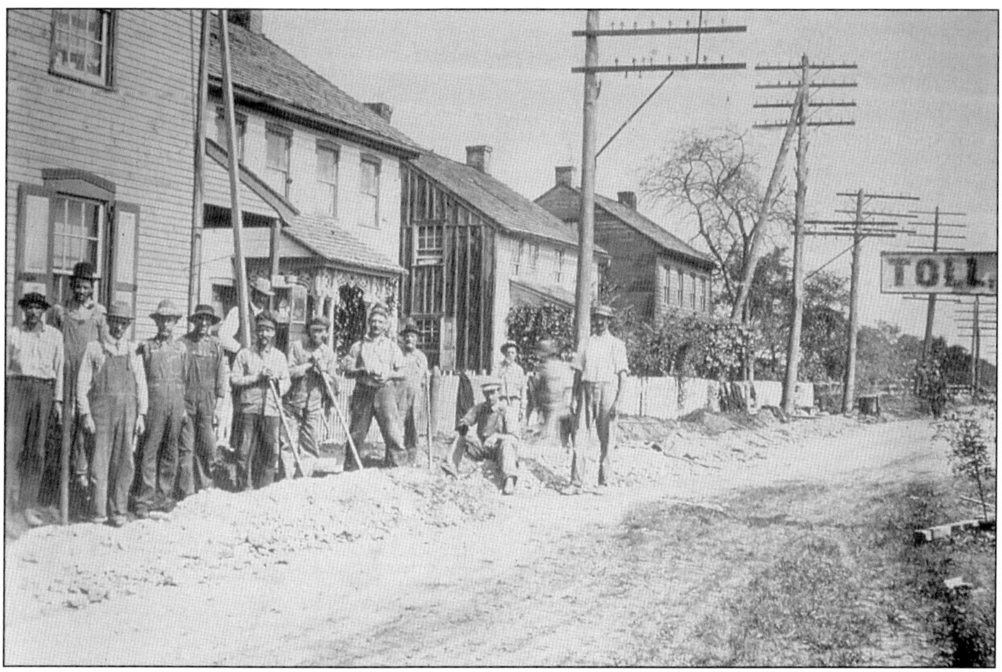

Clearing. As a second step in the street maintenance process, roads would need to be cleared and smoothed, particularly following a year of harsh weather. (Courtesy of Blanche Schaeffer.)

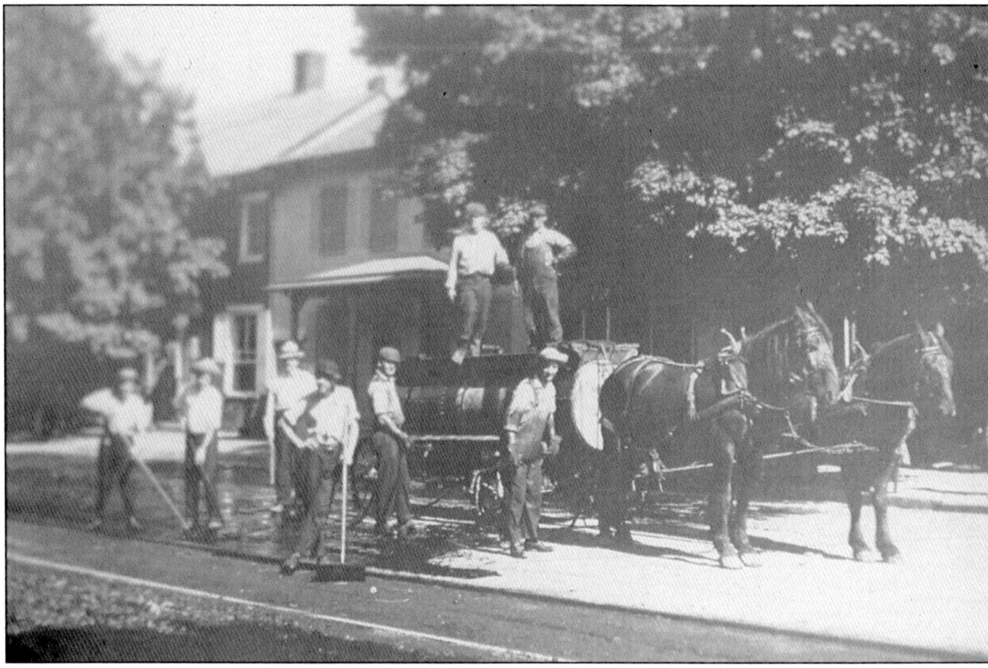

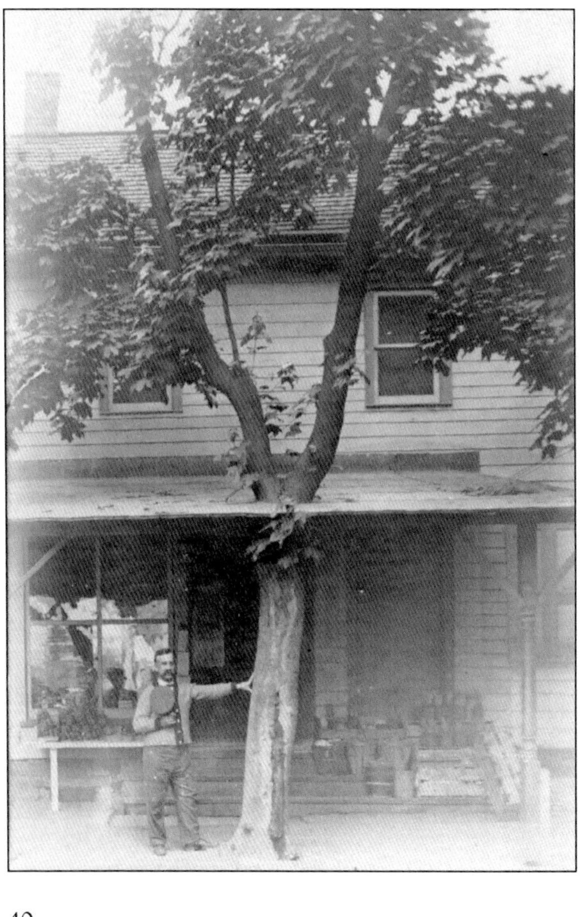

TARRING. Finally, the application of tar kept dust and pot holes at a minimum. (Courtesy of Dick and Betty Streicher.)

NOS. 301–303 WEST MAIN STREET. Harold Boltz (1866–1940) stands in front of the grocery store that he operated out of this building in the early 1900s. Evidence of the large store window still remains in the front wall of this building. (Courtesy of Blanche Schaeffer.)

Four

Nos. 200–100 West Main Street

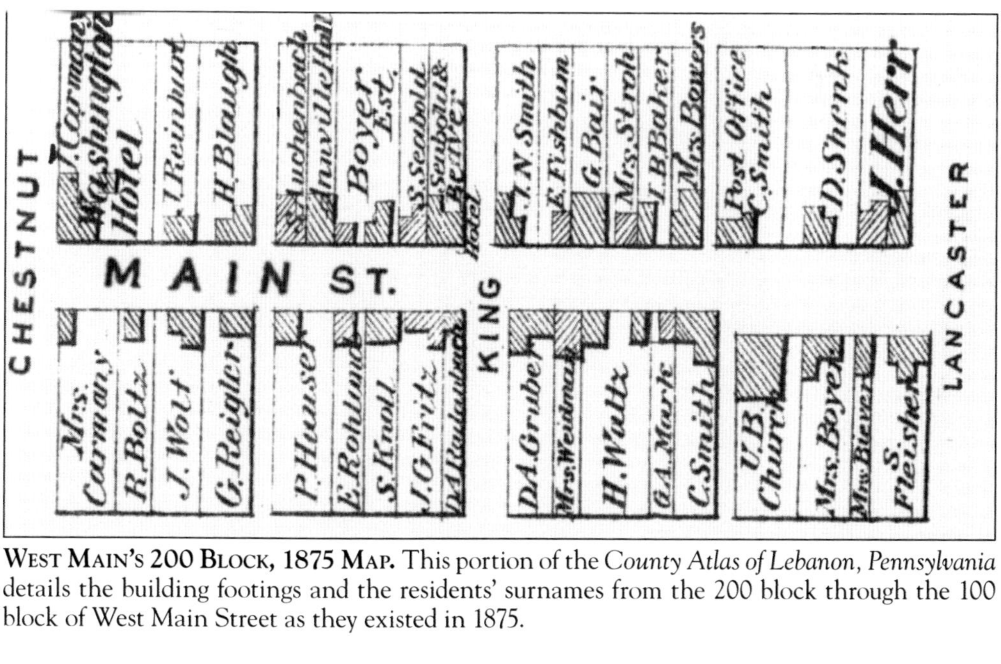

West Main's 200 Block, 1875 Map. This portion of the *County Atlas of Lebanon, Pennsylvania* details the building footings and the residents' surnames from the 200 block through the 100 block of West Main Street as they existed in 1875.

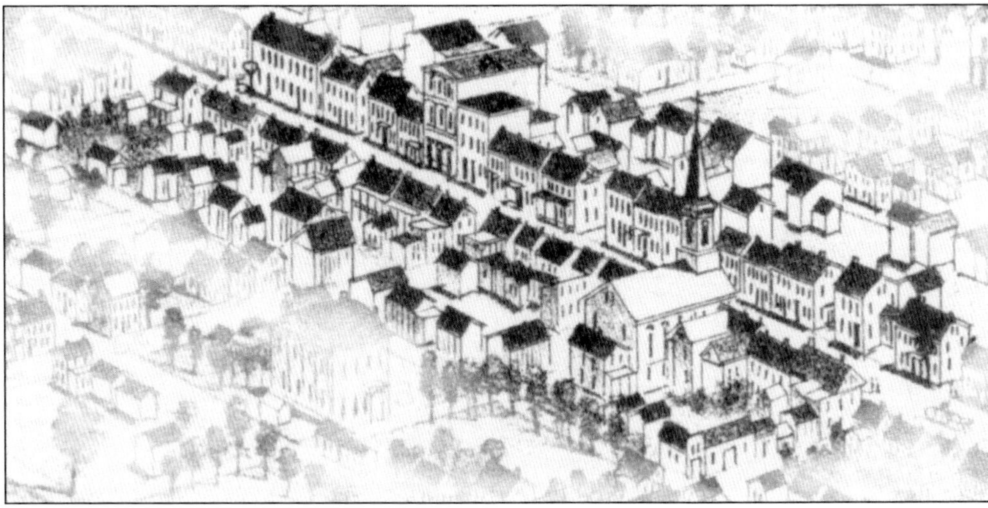

West Main's 200 Block, 1888 View. T.M. Fowler's panoramic view of Annville portrays the buildings of the 200 block through the 100 block of West Main Street as they appeared from the southeast in 1888.

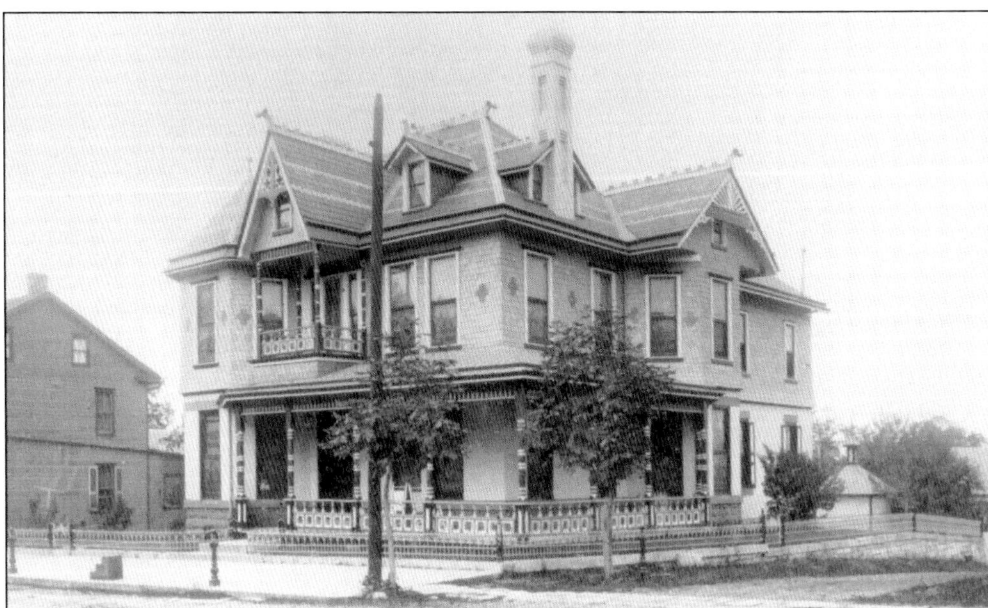

No. 246 West Main Street. This fine home, built in the 1880s for Annville physician I.K. Urich and pictured here in 1895, was once a quintessential Queen Anne residence. A comparison of this picture with the current structure requires some study; the ornate woodwork and detailed painting is costly to preserve. (See page 94.)

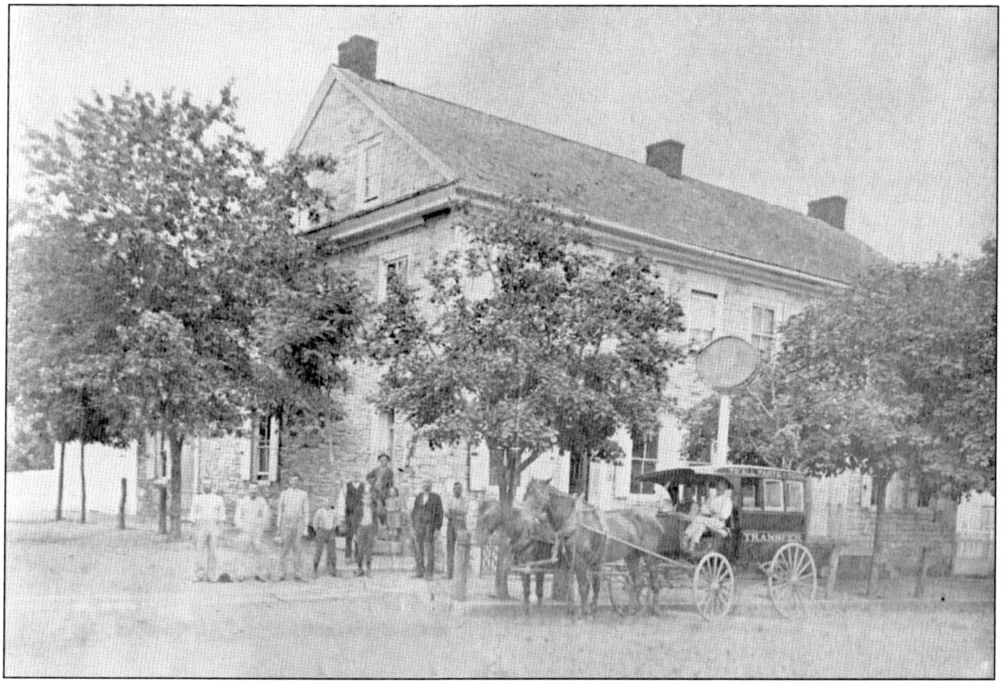

No. 245 West Main Street. Washington House, built around 1795, actively served travelers on the Berks-Dauphin Turnpike throughout the 19th century. William Dietzler Miller (1838–1911), pictured here around 1884 wearing a dark suit with coat, operated Washington House as a tavern from 1884 to 1904. (Courtesy of David, Richard, Michael, and Linnea Miller.)

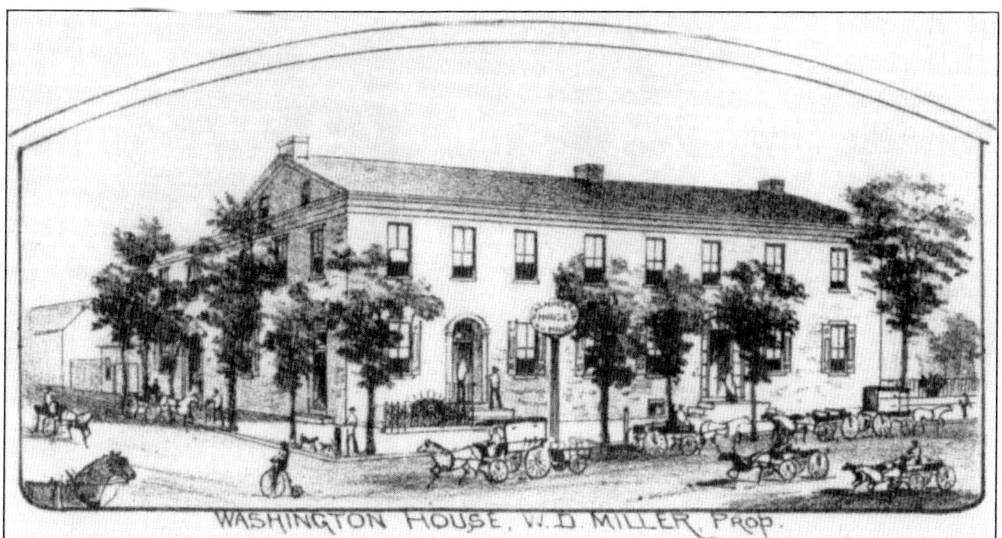

An 1888 Sketch. This sketch captures the full length of the Washington house. Although most of the building's original limestone exterior has been covered, some of the stone is visible on the east side of the building. Note the boxed cornice and large stone lintels.

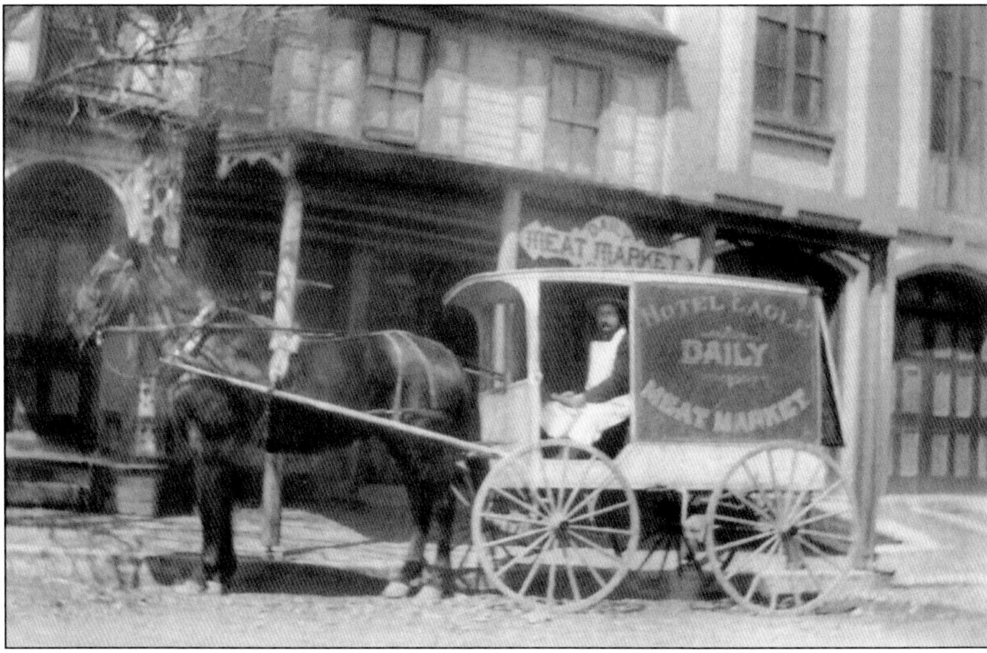

Nos. 223–225 West Main Street. In 1903, Samuel H. Lutz and Daniel P. Spangler moved their Daily Meat Market business from the Eagle Hotel at 2 East Main Street to this shop. In 1904, the two men built an additional store at 3 East Main Street, a venture that lasted until 1933. (See page 76.) (Courtesy of Michael Bowman.)

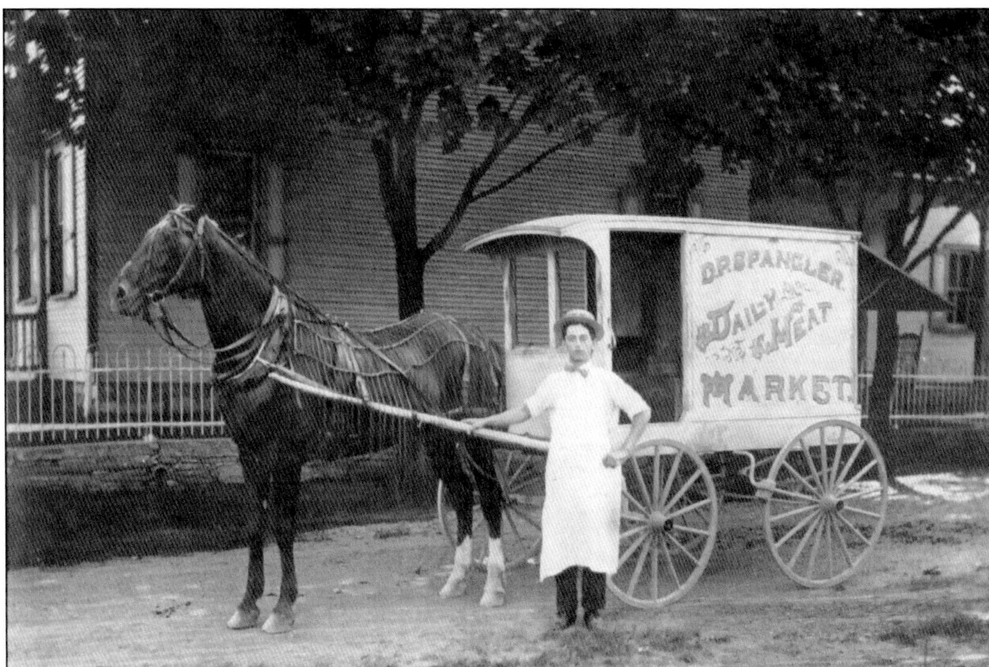

Spangler's. D.P. Spangler's Daily Meat Market operated at 223–225 West Main Street until 1941. The space has housed an antique store since the 1960s. The current name of the store pays homage to the heritage of the place—Butcher Block Antiques. (Courtesy of Dick and Betty Streicher.)

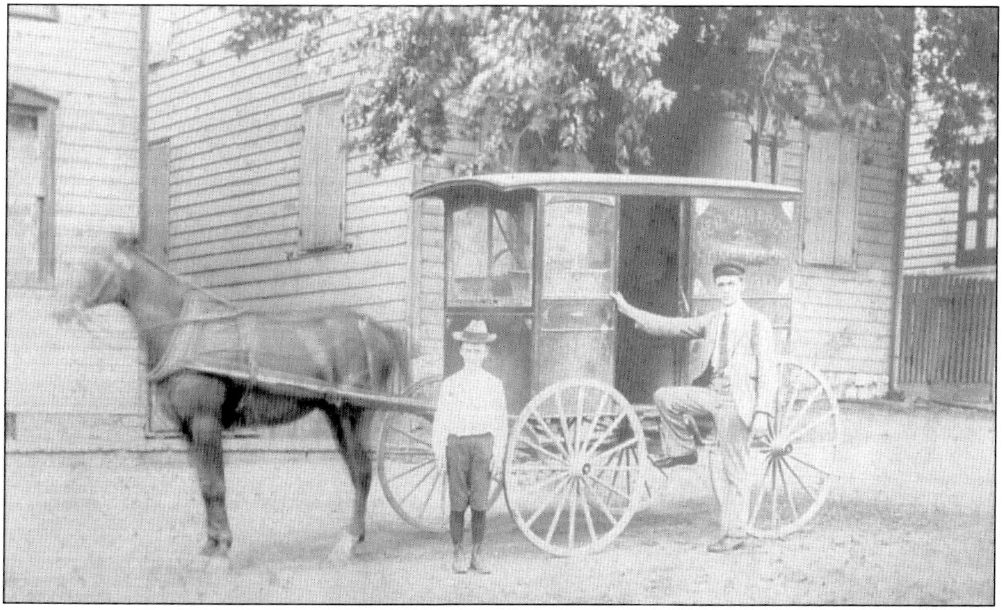

CART VENDORS. Vending by cart was a prominent mode of doing business in the 1880s and 1890s. The Heilman Brothers Bakery operated without a storefront and was based from a small home located off of Main Street. The cart pictured here provided a means of living for this family. (Courtesy of Dick and Betty Streicher.)

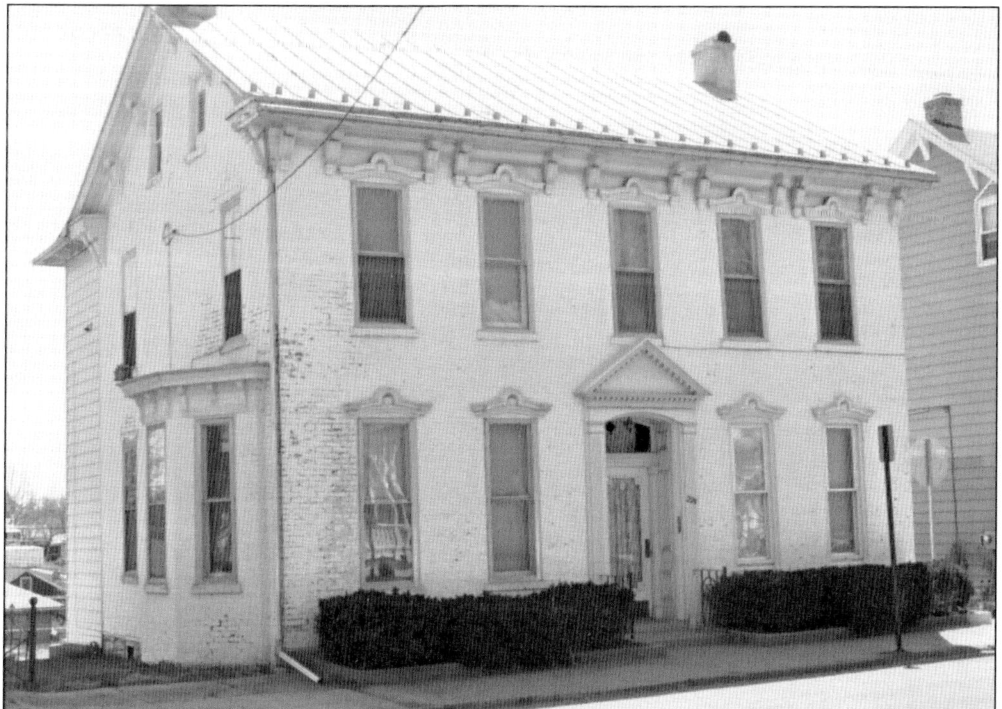

NO. 224 WEST MAIN STREET. Built around 1860, this structure features a classical pediment over the doorway inset with an etched ruby transom. The house, remembered most often as the family home of Judge L. Ehrman Meyer (1904–1993), was repainted in four historic colors in 2006.

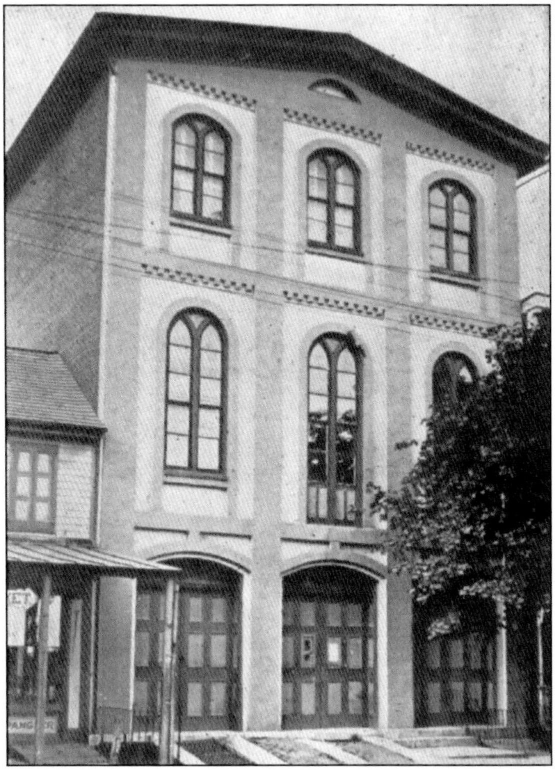

Nos. 219–221 West Main Street. According to Warner's 1909 *Annville: Township and Town*, this town hall was built in 1857. The date stone indicates that the building was dedicated in 1869 for the local Independent Order of Odd Fellows (IOOF). At that time, the first floor of this building was leased to the township by IOOF to house Annville's Rescue Fire Company and the town jail. The second floor, now a private apartment, originally served as a public auditorium for community entertainment, high school graduation exercises, and the like. The third floor was a meeting place of IOOF members and other community lodges. (For more on lodges, see page 56.) (Courtesy of Dick and Betty Streicher.)

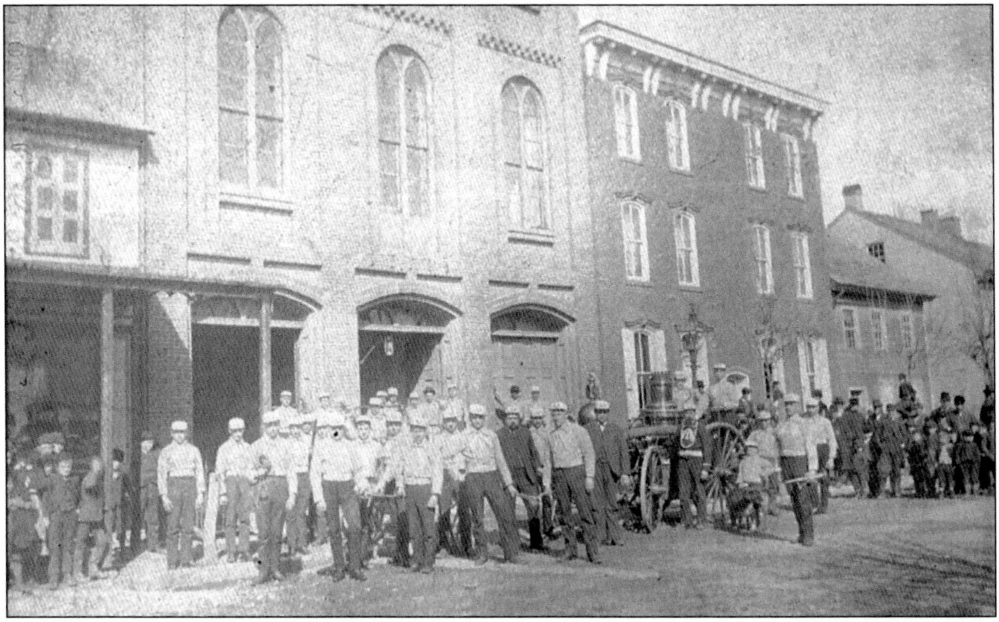

Nos. 217, 215, 213, and 219–221 West Main Street. Annville's Rescue Fire Company, organized in 1881, is seen gathered outside of the old fire hall for this picture, taken around 1883. The steam fire engine, which was pulled and pumped by hand, could be connected by hose to 16 water pumps, both iron and wooden, that extended down Main from Mill to Railroad. (Courtesy of Dick and Betty Streicher.)

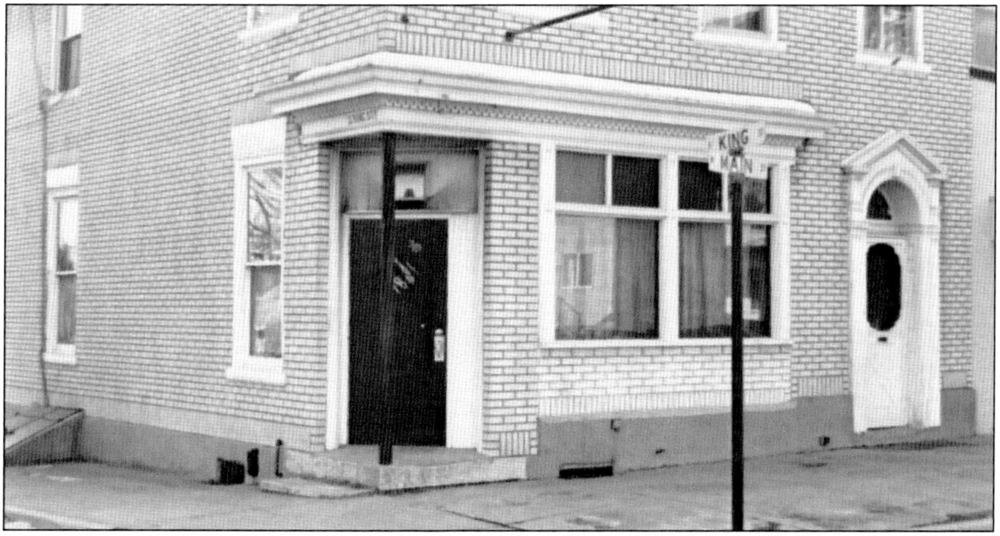

No. 202 West Main Street. In 1907, William Dietzler Miller purchased this former site of D.A. Radenbach's music school so that his granddaughter Lottie and her husband, Arthur S. "Ussie" Miller, might establish a restaurant here. The couple operated the restaurant until 1946, when their son Richard Miller assumed management and changed it to Rich's Bar. His son Michael Miller took over in 1976. The Corvette Bar and Grill was established here in 1990. Although faux white brick has covered the very early brickwork, the classical ornamentation of the building is apparent in its external woodwork and doorways, which feature dentil and beaded molding.

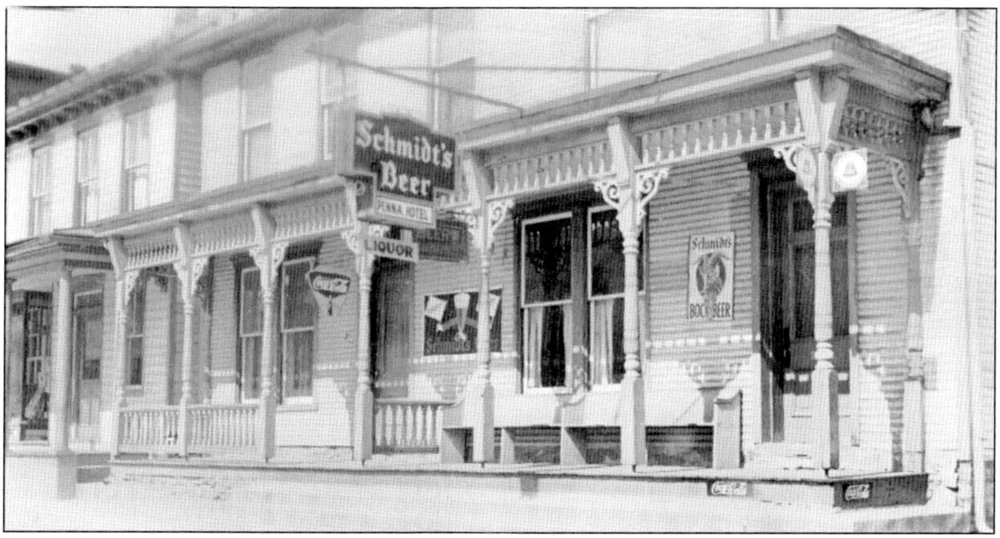

Nos. 201–203 West Main Street. Originally known as the Golden Swan Hotel, this building has served as a public house since its construction as early as 1800. By 1875, the business was known as the Pennsylvania Hotel. The west front door of the building, designated the "Ladies Entrance," led to a formal dining room; behind the east door was a bar that provided a place of rest for men. From 1889 to 1934, Daniel R. Speck Sr. and his son, Daniel R. Speck Jr., managed the business. In 1934, Louis and Angelica Rotunda purchased the hotel and assumed its management. In 1959, another Johnson family, that of John E. and Nancy J. Johnson, reinvented the establishment as Johnson's Bar, "where friends meet friends." Their son, Steve Johnson, and his family assumed management of the bar in the late 1980s. (Courtesy of the Rotunda Family.)

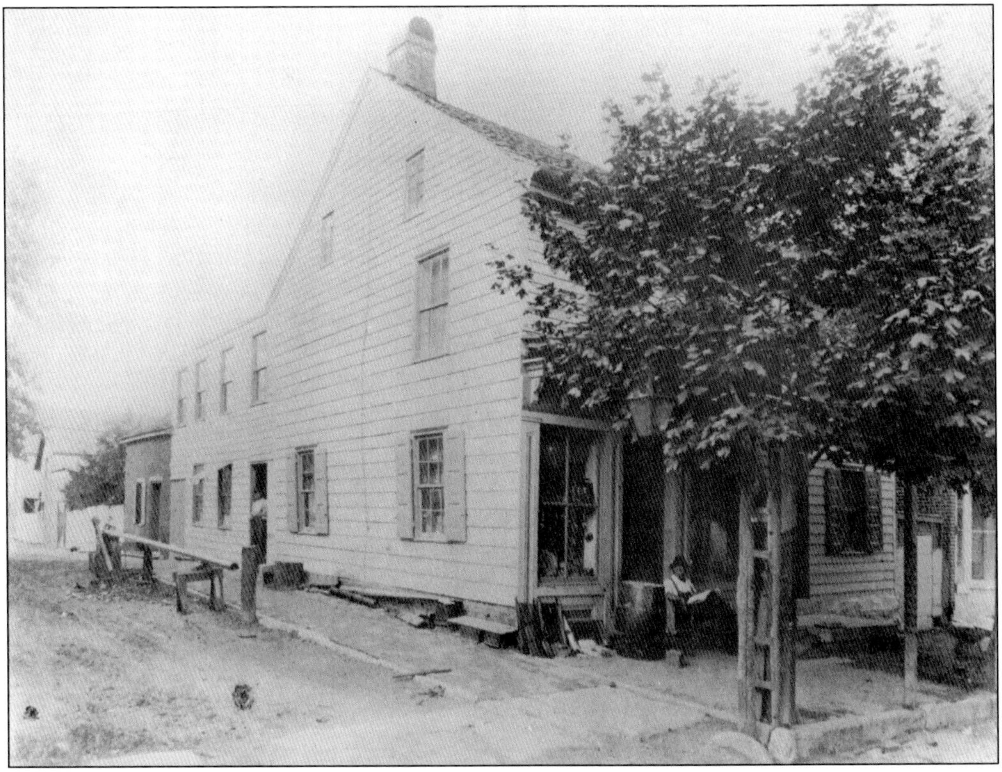

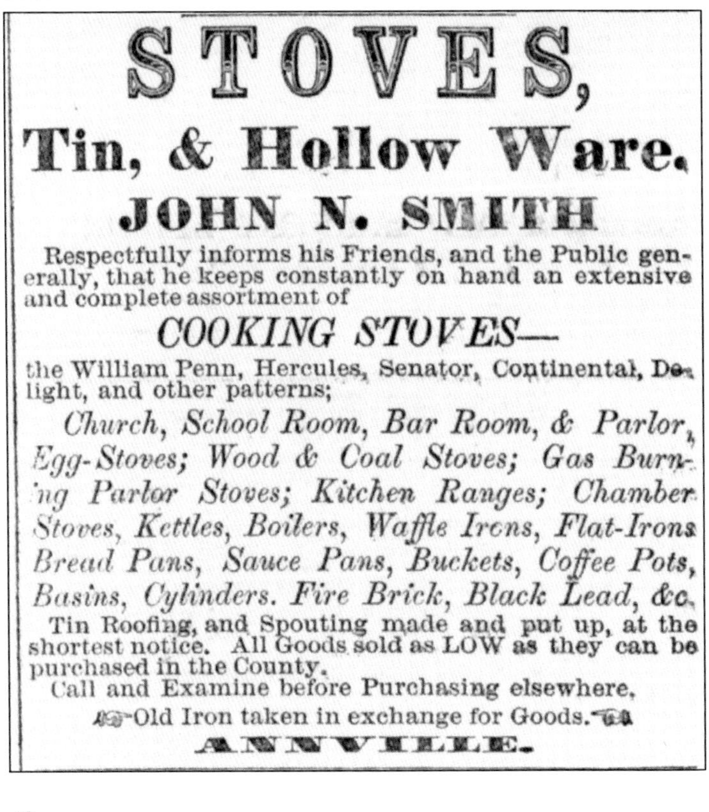

No. 149 West Main Street. Perhaps the longest lasting family business venture in Annville is Smith's Metal and Hardware Store, established on this corner by Joseph Smith (1795–1862) in the 1820s.

Vintage Advertisement. Some of the early work of the business can be discerned from this detailed ad printed in the May 1864 edition of the *Student's Monthly*, a publication of the Lebanon Valley Institute (the immediate precursor of Lebanon Valley College).

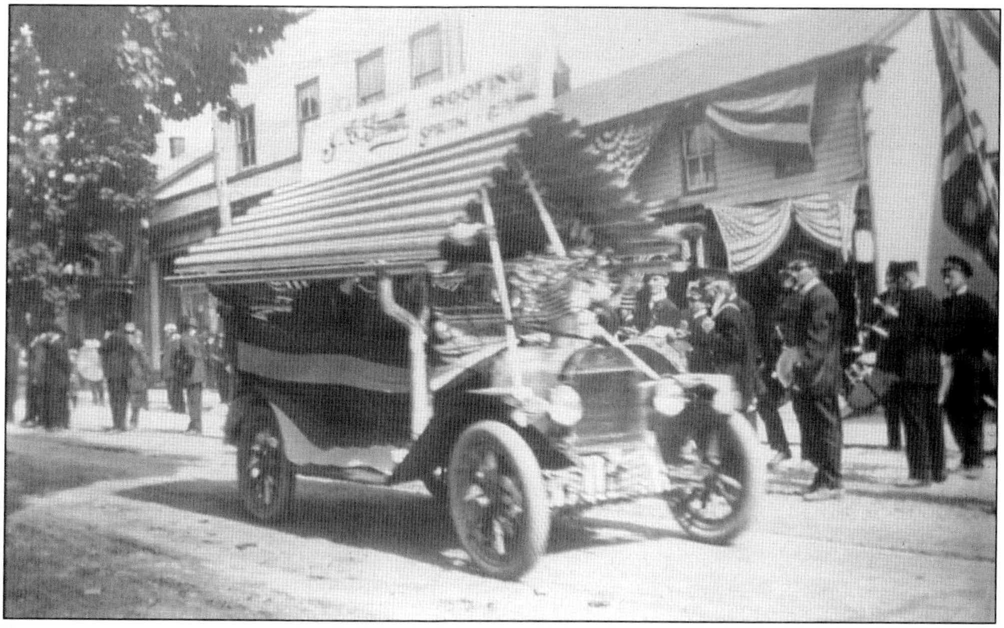

Parade Entry. A creative parade entry from Smith's Metal and Hardware Store passes by 30 East Main Street in the early 1900s. (Courtesy of Dick and Betty Streicher.)

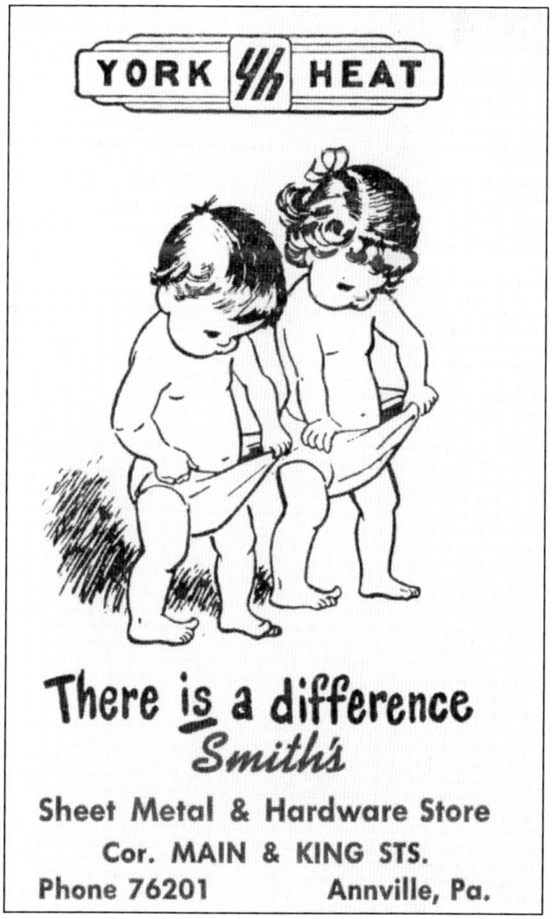

Creative Advertisement. The longevity of Smith's Metal may be attributed in part to its creativity in advertising. The business operates in Annville to this day, though at a location other than the northeast corner of Main and King Streets.

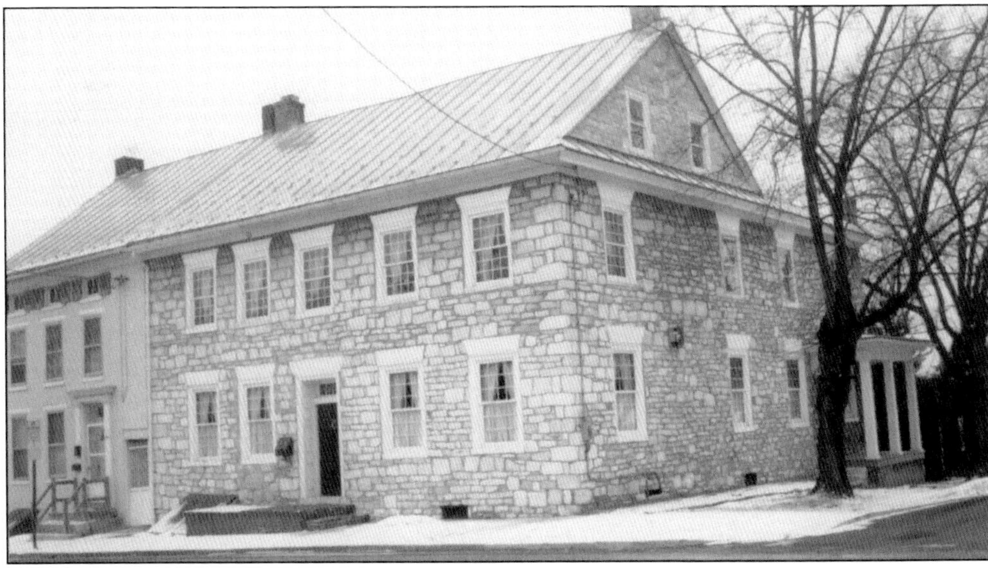

Nos. 142–146 West Main Street. Built by distinguished military man Frank Gruber in 1793, the large home at 146 West Main Street is constructed from a high grade of calcium limestone quarried around Annville that is relatively light and easily broken. The iron rings on the stone steps were used to help slide large barrels of supplies into the basement, which were perhaps sold from a small store once housed in the red building in back of the main house. The Greek Revival house next door at 142 West Main, built around 1840, is distinguished by its classical doorway and eye-winker windows just under the roof.

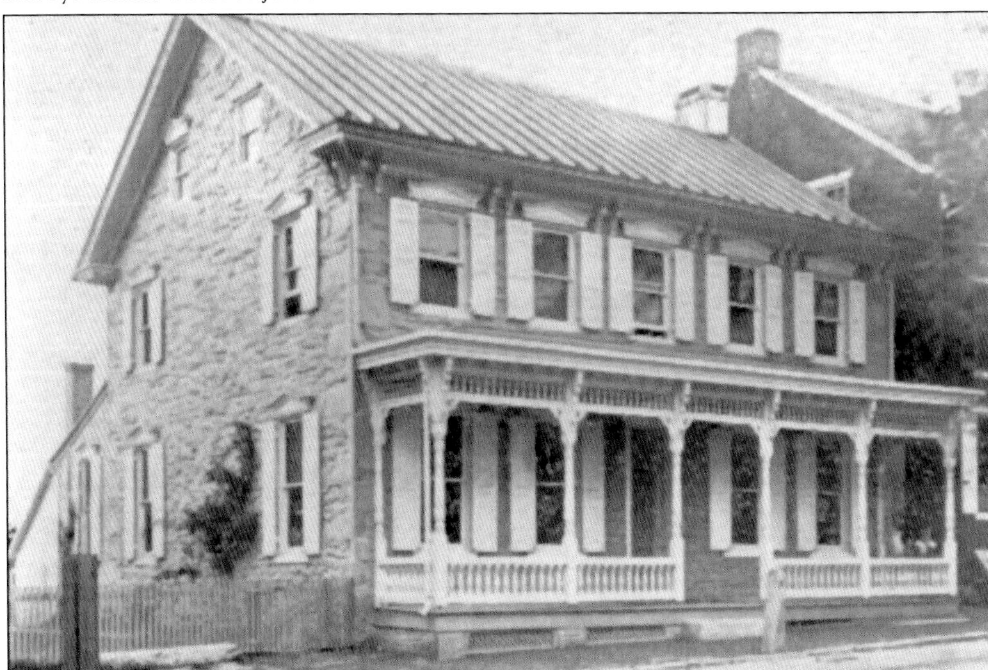

No. 140 West Main Street. Commonly known as the Louis Gilbert Inn, the first floor of this hotel, built in the 1790s, had a partition between rooms on the west side that could be drawn up to the ceiling, converting the entire side into one room for dancing and entertainment.

PRESIDENTIAL VISIT. Pres. Martin Van Buren (1782–1862) and party stopped at the Lewis Gilbert Inn on a visit in June 1839. Van Buren served as secretary of state and vice president before becoming the eighth president of the United States, serving from 1837 to 1841.

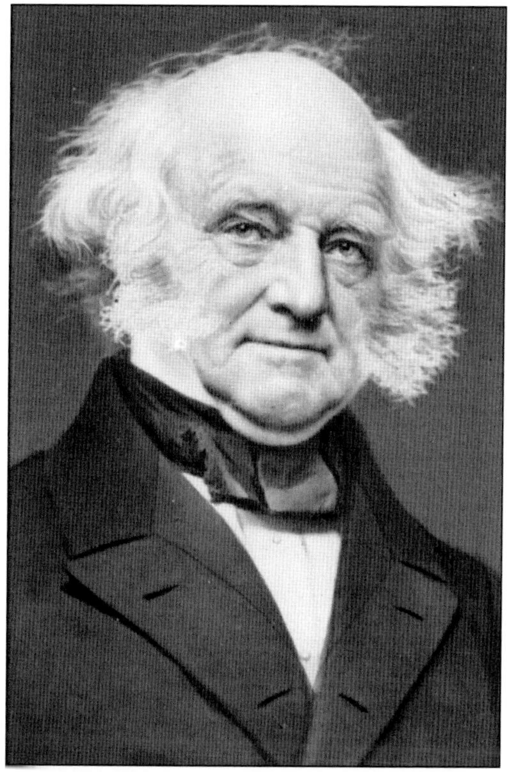

NO. 125 WEST MAIN STREET. This large home was originally built in 1824–1825 for Dr. John G. Marshall (1793–1849), second son of Dr. David Marshall (see 21 West Main Street), shortly after his marriage to Elizabeth Behm. The residence housed Dr. Marshall's medical practice as well as his wife and eight children before it was purchased by Cornelius Smith around 1875 for use, in part, as the town post office. In 1929, Dr. Warren Brubaker returned the use of the building to that of medical offices. Since the Brubaker Family sold the home in 1993, it has served as the site of a flower shop and private residence. A fire at the home on March 6, 2010, revealed the massive logs from which it is constructed. Thankfully, plans are underway for its renovation. (Courtesy of the *Lebanon Daily News*.)

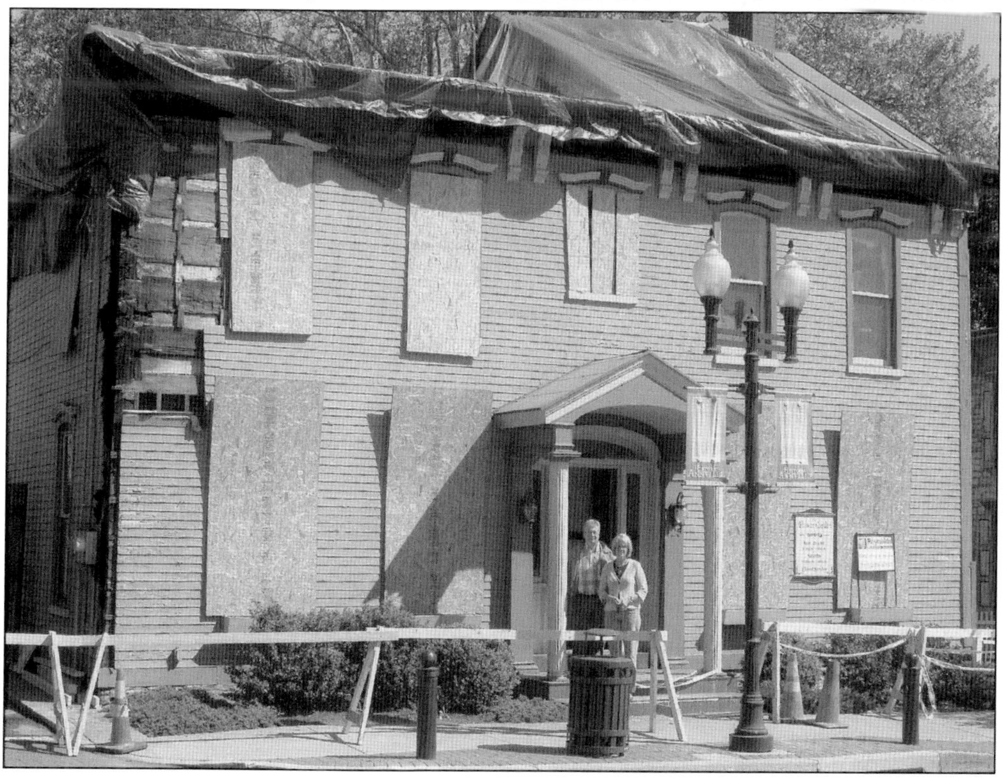

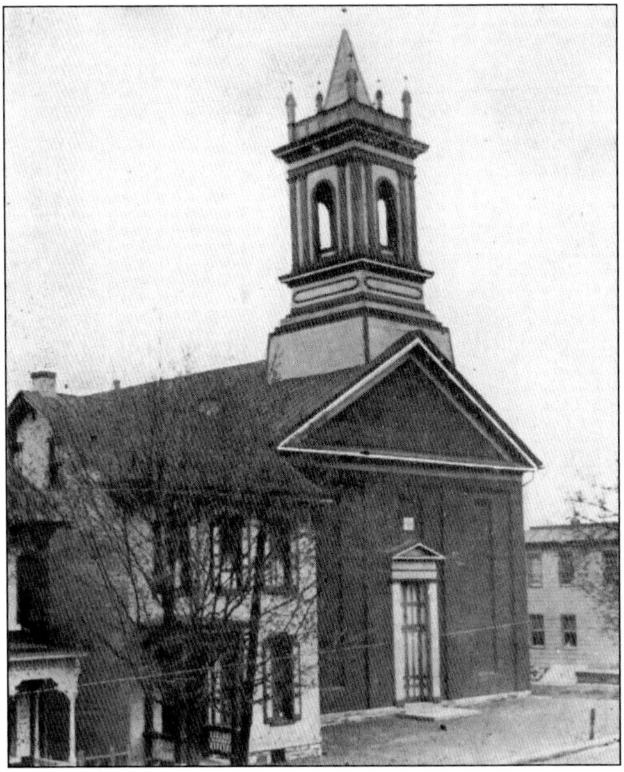

No. 118 West Main Street. This church was built and dedicated in January 1862 by the United Brethren congregation in town. The sanctuary is located on the second level, with a fellowship hall on the first level. In 1867, the congregation attached a single-story frame structure to the rear of the building for use as a Sunday school, and some years later, the handsome parsonage was built to the immediate east of the structure. (Courtesy of Dick and Betty Streicher.)

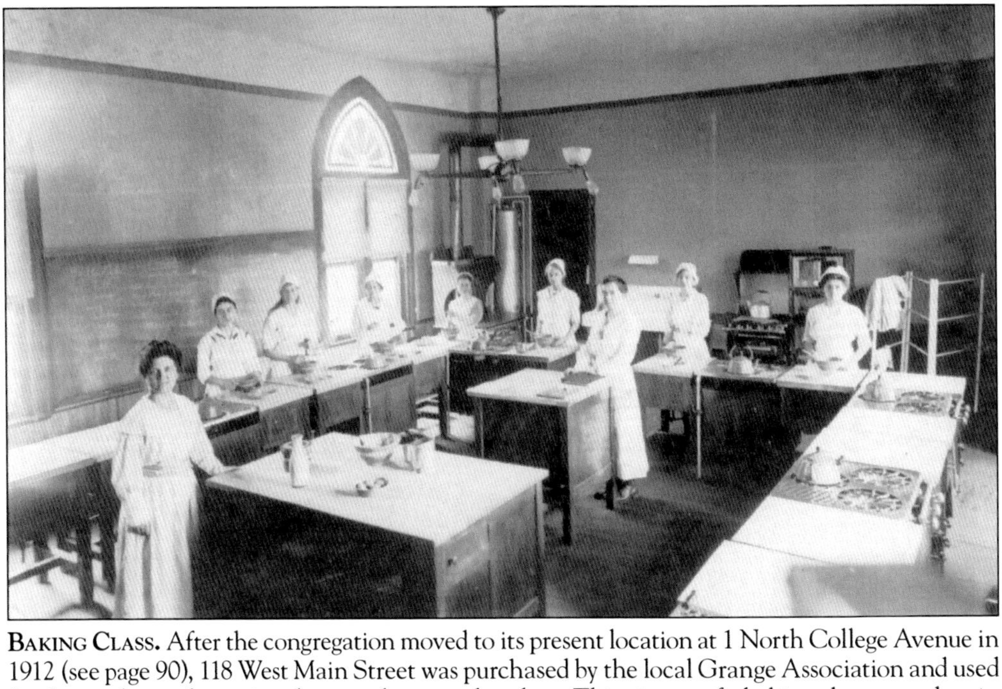

Baking Class. After the congregation moved to its present location at 1 North College Avenue in 1912 (see page 90), 118 West Main Street was purchased by the local Grange Association and used for the teaching of vocational arts and as a marketplace. This picture of a baking class was taken in the back of the first floor of the structure. In 1927, St. Paul the Apostle Catholic Church purchased the building and used it for worship until 1978. (Courtesy of Dick and Betty Streicher.)

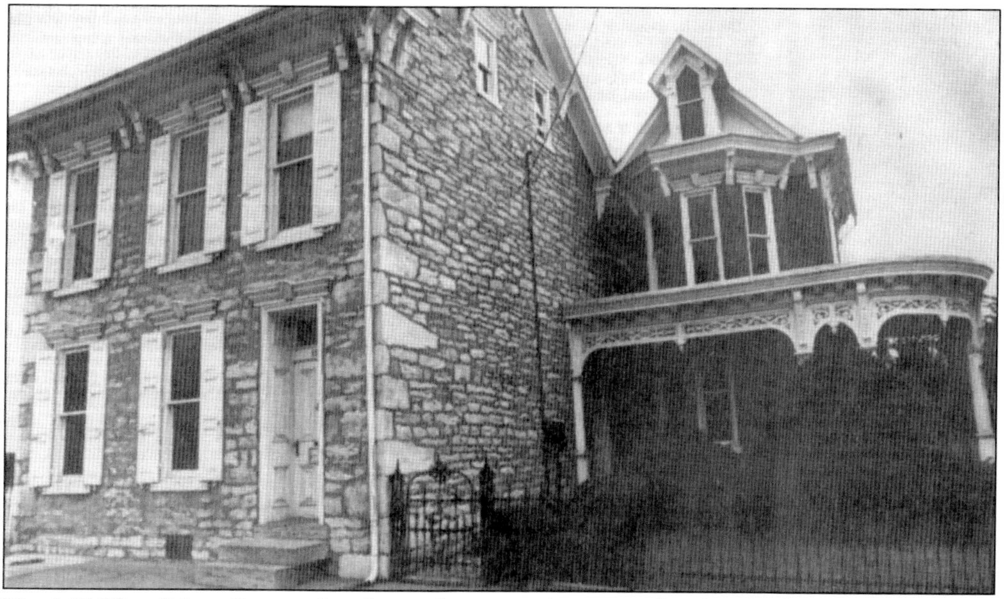

No. 115 West Main Street. Land records suggest that around 1859, Abraham Shenk built the limestone portion of the house that directly borders West Main Street. After the property changed hands to Abraham's son David, it was sold to Abram and Emma Risser, who added the Victorian entrance to the east of the house. Dr. Heilman, a local dentist, made use of both spaces for his practice and family from 1932 to 1972. A set of creative entrepreneurs opened a gourmet restaurant in the house in 1983, but demand did not sustain the business; it is once again a private residence.

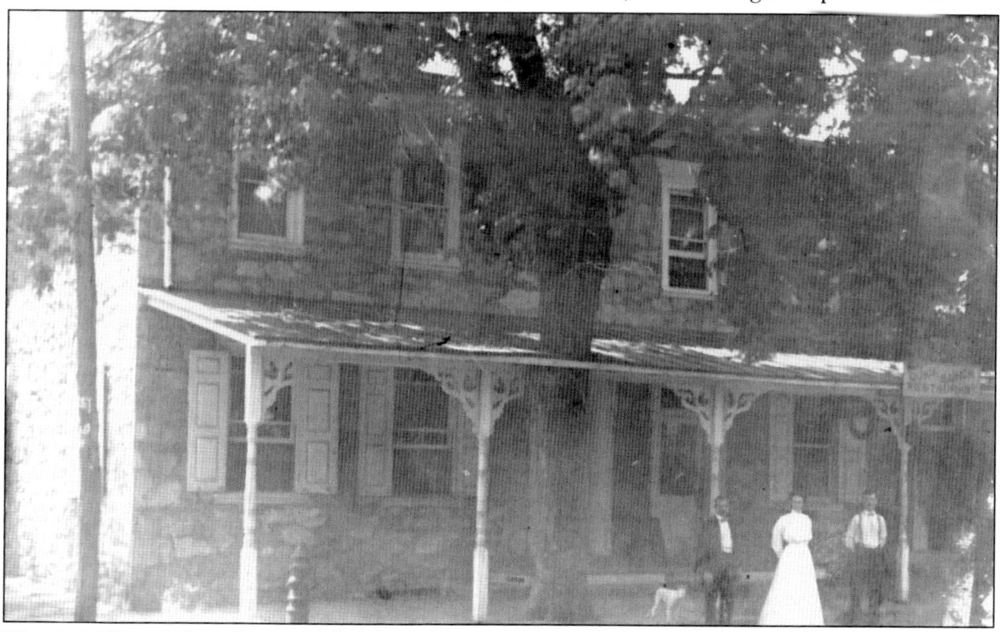

No. 104 West Main Street. This large limestone home was built in the Georgian style around 1780 for the Fleisher family. In the 19th century, the first floor was converted to a storefront. The roof over the sidewalk is a Victorian-era addition to protect customers from the weather. At the time that this picture was taken in the 1890s, the sign at the front of the store welcomed guests to the Quick Lunch Restaurant.

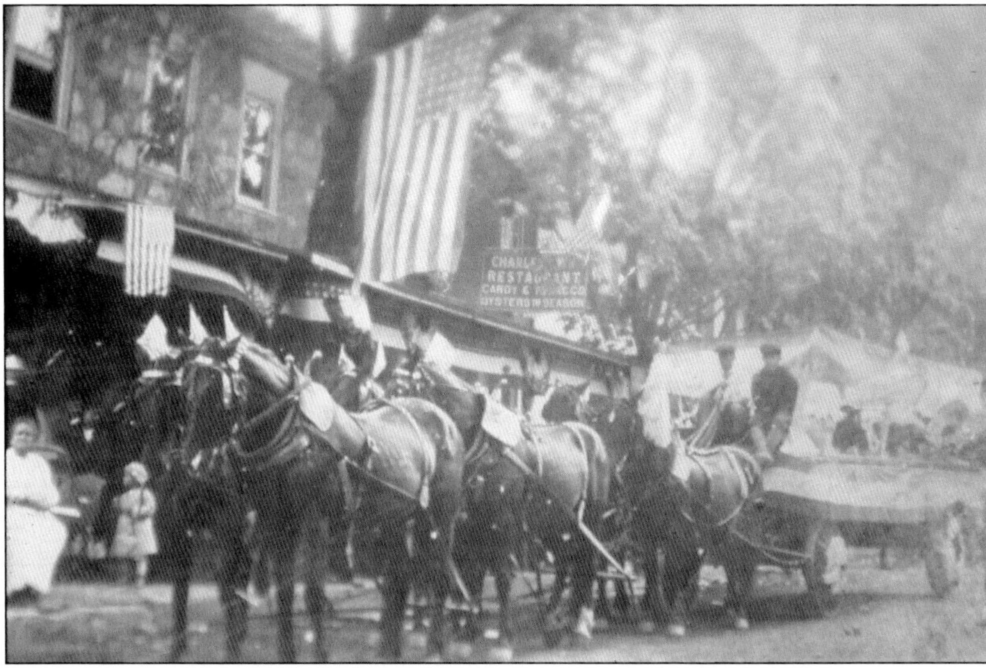

Candy, Tobacco, and Oysters. By the 1900s, the main sign of the store had changed to read, "Charles Wry Restaurant: Candy & Tobacco, Oysters in Season." Charles Wry managed the property through the 1930s.

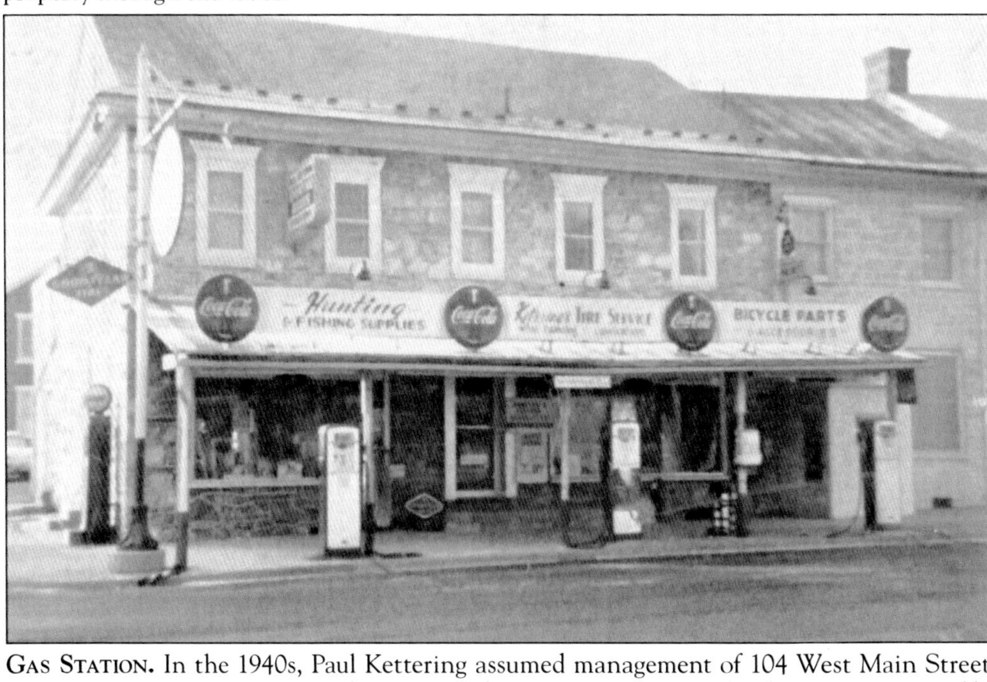

Gas Station. In the 1940s, Paul Kettering assumed management of 104 West Main Street, housing a sporting goods store and gas station there. Kettering Corner has become recognized by many as the "center of town," not only as a result of its heritage but also due to the clock tower and large planters placed on the site, which were part of the Annville Streetscape Project that was completed in 2004. (Courtesy of Paul Kettering.)

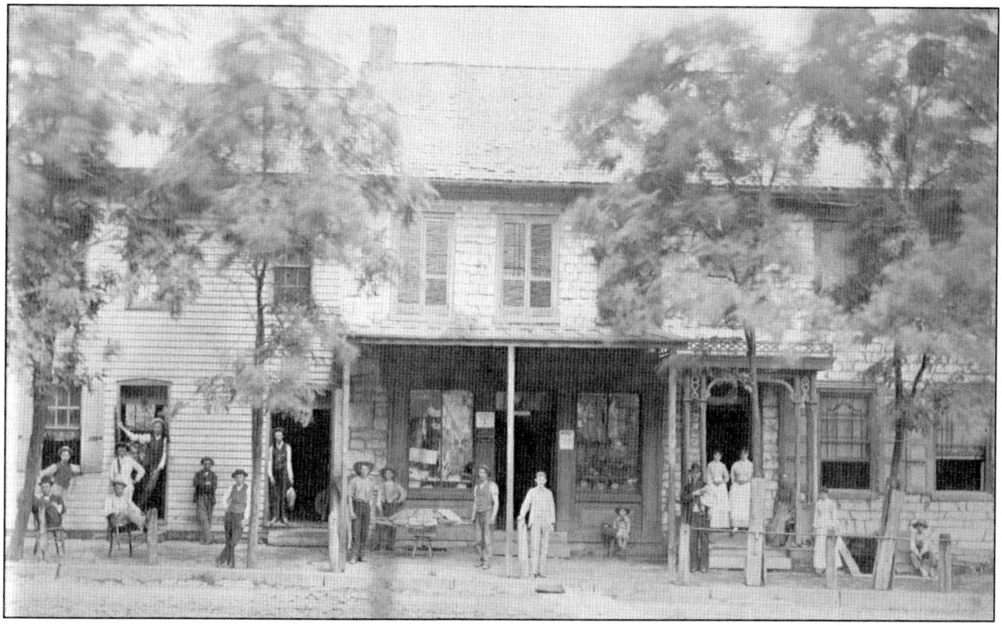

NO. 103 WEST MAIN STREET. This picture from the 1880s shows the Batdorf Building as a two-story structure. Built around 1810, the building has housed many businesses, including the People's Deposit Bank, United Telephone Exchange, and Annville Inn. For more than a century, a barbershop was housed on the west end of the first level. Compare the carefully cut stones on the front wall to the rubble on the side walls. (Courtesy of Dick and Betty Streicher.)

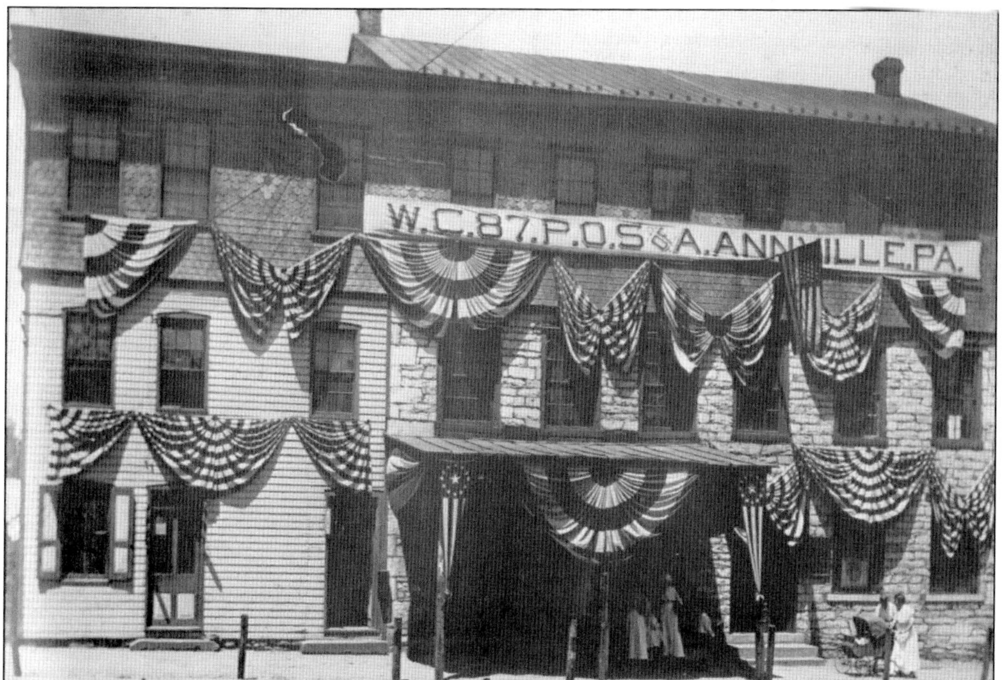

AN ADDITIONAL STORY. In the late 19th century, a third story was added to 103 West Main Street to serve as a meeting place for Washington Camp No. 87 of the Patriotic Sons of America.

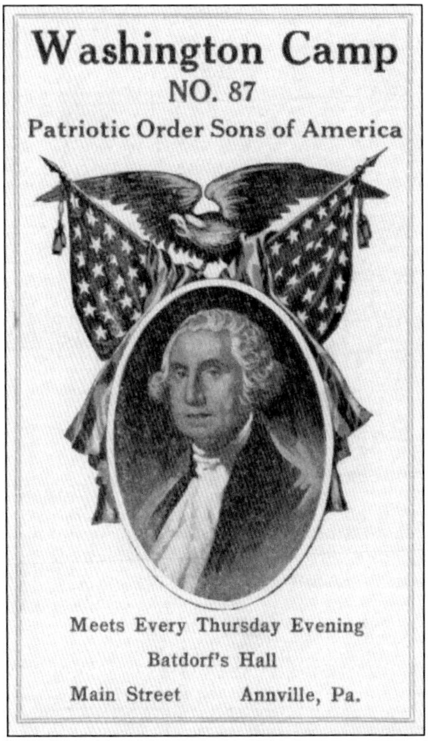

SONS OF AMERICA HALL. Before the popularity of service clubs, social life often centered around lodges, such as the Patriotic Sons of America, the Independent Order of Odd Fellows (see page 46), the Knights of Pythias, and the Daughters of America. There were very few young adults in the late 19th century who did not belong to at least one such group.

PSOA MEMBERSHIP. One of the principle reasons for the popularity of these groups was that they usually paid sick or death benefits to their members or their spouses, providing a form of inexpensive, yet dependable, insurance.

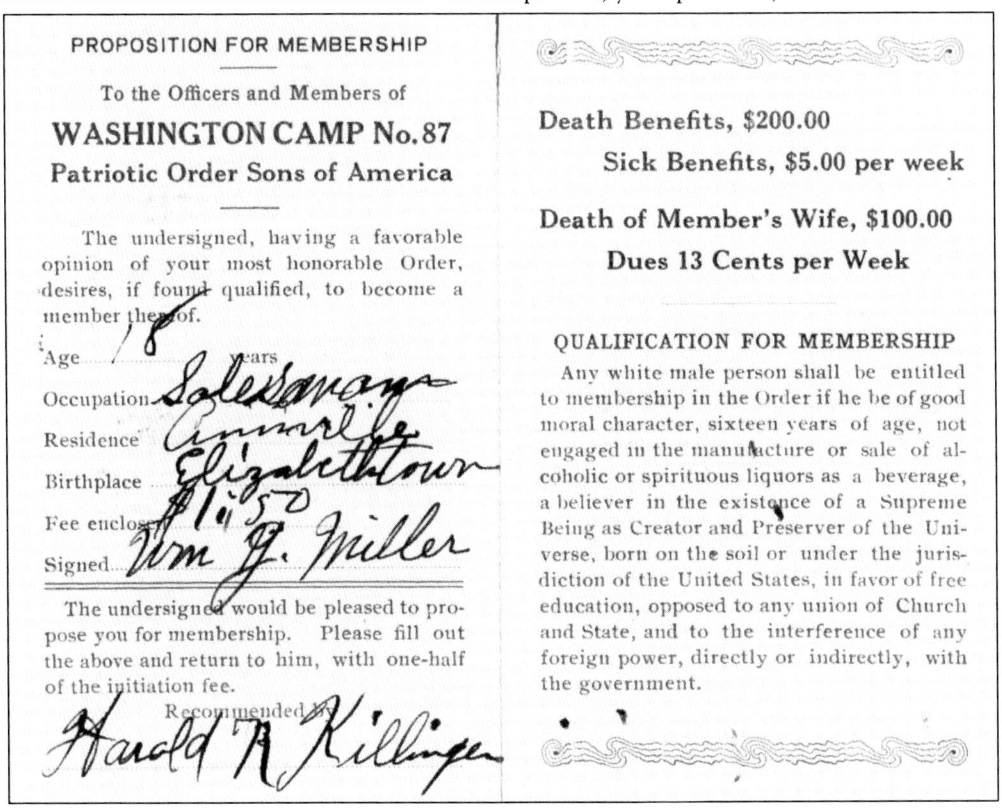

PROPOSITION FOR MEMBERSHIP

To the Officers and Members of

WASHINGTON CAMP No. 87

Patriotic Order Sons of America

The undersigned, having a favorable opinion of your most honorable Order, desires, if found qualified, to become a member thereof.

Age 18 years

Occupation Salesman

Residence Annville

Birthplace Elizabethtown

Fee enclosed $1.50

Signed Wm J. Miller

The undersigned would be pleased to propose you for membership. Please fill out the above and return to him, with one-half of the initiation fee.

Recommended by Harold R Killinger

Death Benefits, $200.00

Sick Benefits, $5.00 per week

Death of Member's Wife, $100.00

Dues 13 Cents per Week

QUALIFICATION FOR MEMBERSHIP

Any white male person shall be entitled to membership in the Order if he be of good moral character, sixteen years of age, not engaged in the manufacture or sale of alcoholic or spirituous liquors as a beverage, a believer in the existence of a Supreme Being as Creator and Preserver of the Universe, born on the soil or under the jurisdiction of the United States, in favor of free education, opposed to any union of Church and State, and to the interference of any foreign power, directly or indirectly, with the government.

Five

THE FIRST BLOCK OF WEST MAIN STREET

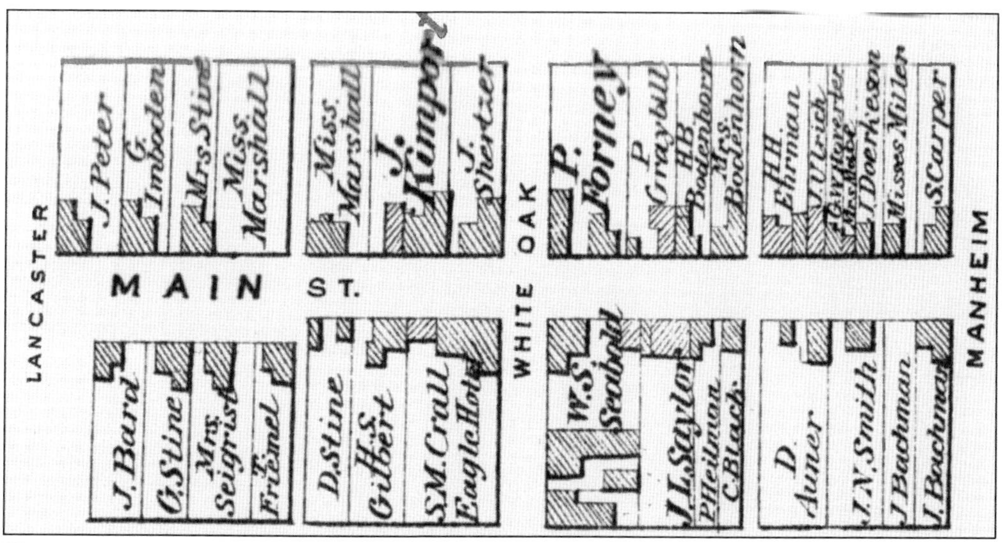

WEST MAIN'S FIRST BLOCK, 1875 VIEW. This portion of the *County Atlas of Lebanon, Pennsylvania* details the building footings and the residents' surnames from the first block of West Main Street through the first block of East Main Street as they existed in 1875.

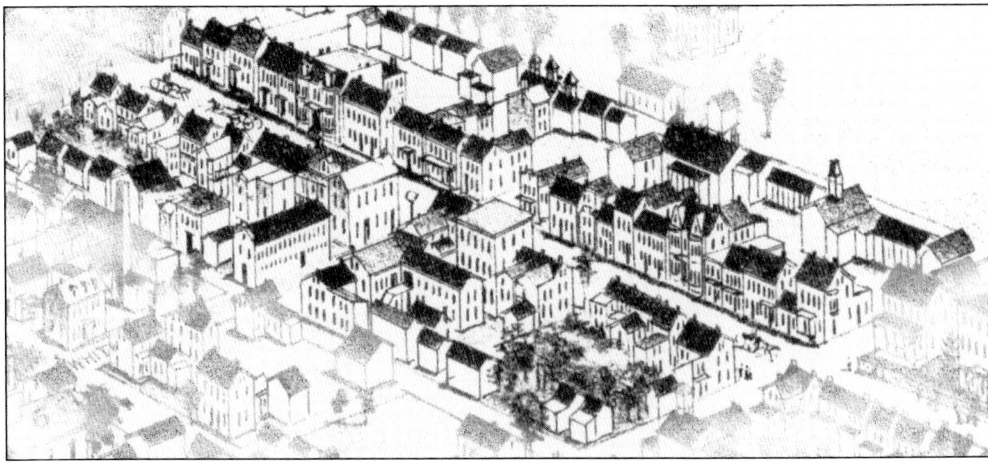

WEST MAIN'S FIRST BLOCK, 1888 VIEW. T.M. Fowler's panoramic view of Annville portrays the buildings of the first block of West Main Street through the first block of East Main Street as they appeared from the southeast in 1888.

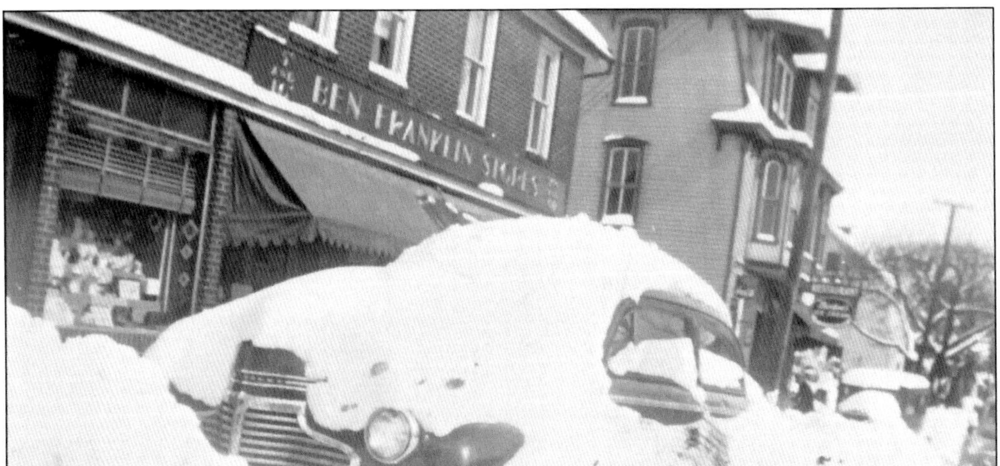

NO. 37 WEST MAIN STREET. Behind an automobile buried by the storms of 1947, one can see the front of Ben Franklin's 5¢ and 10¢ store, now Annville Natural Foods, with the former Hotel Annville to the east.

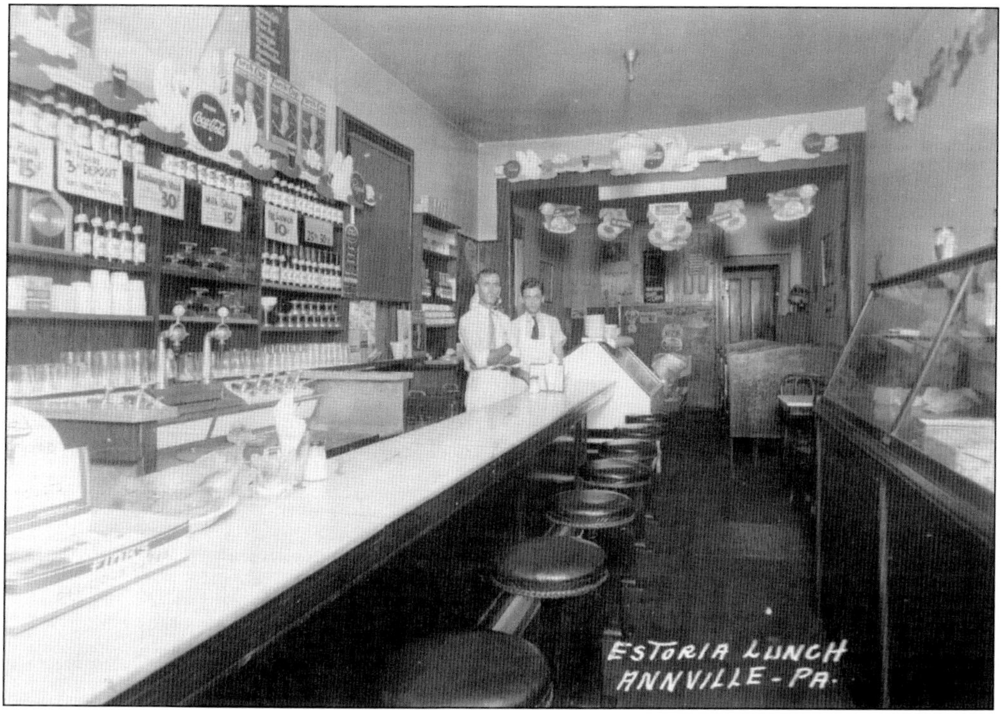

No. 35 West Main Street. From the 1920s to the 1940s, owners William and Frances Theodore made creative use of this long, narrow building as the Astoria Restaurant. The building has also housed Loser's Steak House and Suds Your Duds Laundry, among other businesses.

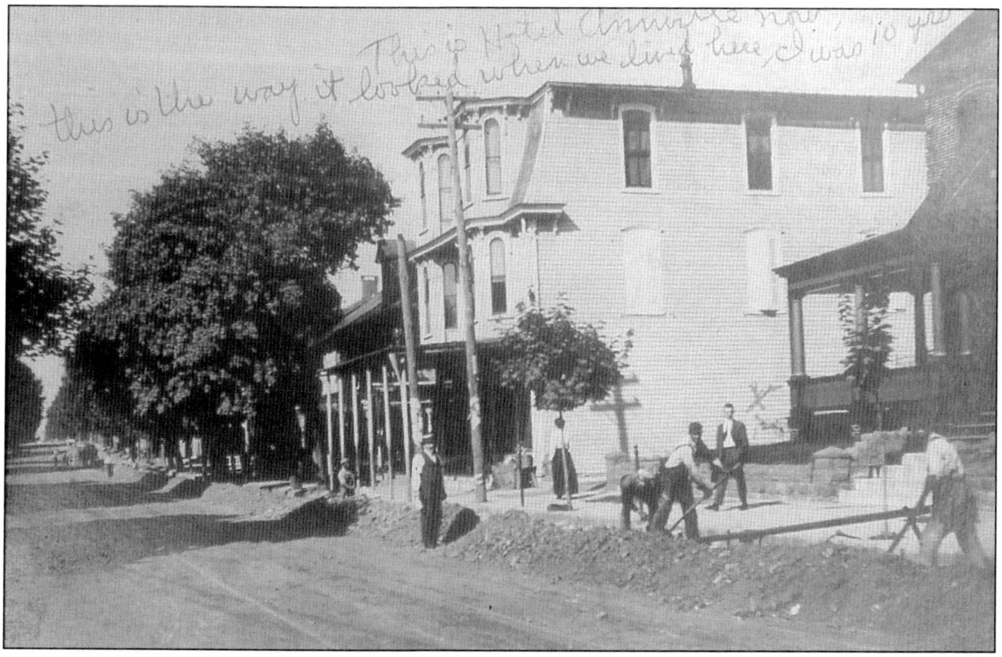

No. 31 West Main Street. Originally built in 1880 by local entrepreneur Solomon R. Light (1824–1905), Hotel Annville housed a variety of businesses on the first floor and as many as 30 residents on the upper floors. (Courtesy of Dick and Betty Streicher.)

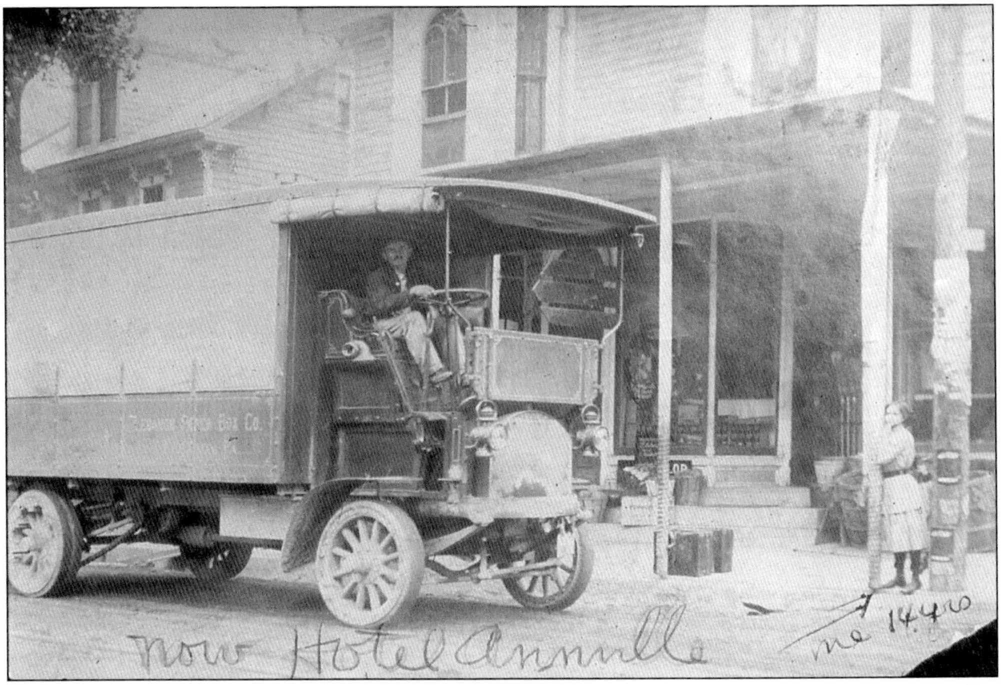

HOTEL ANNVILLE, 1900S. This business thrived until August 4, 1948, when it was destroyed by a fire. (Courtesy of Dick and Betty Streicher.)

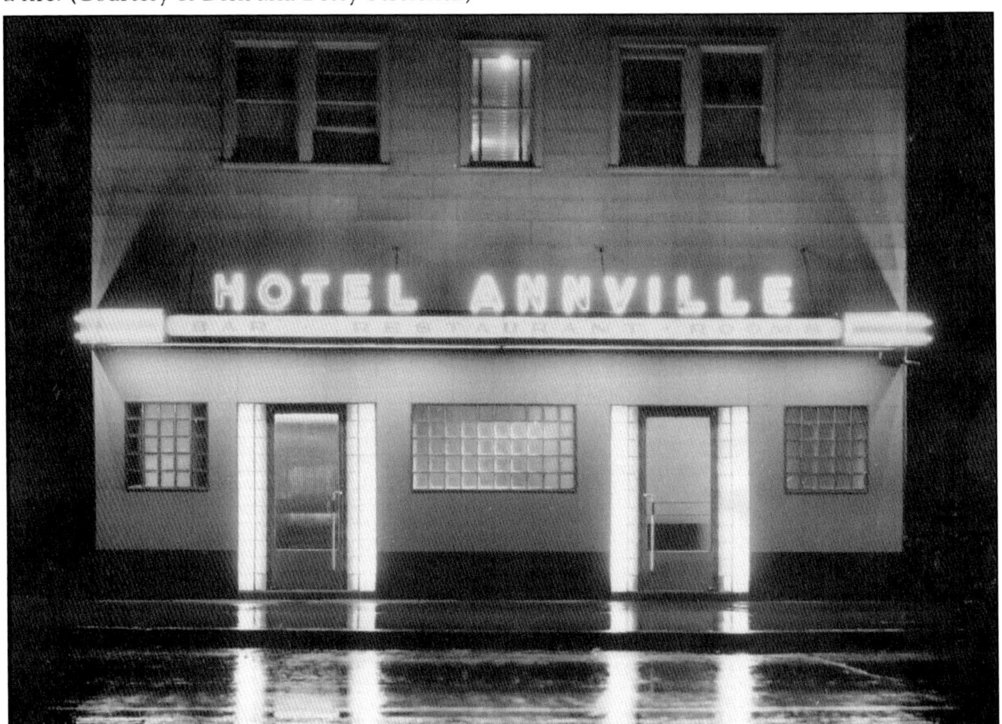

LIGHTS OF ANNVILLE, 1950S. In 1952, Peter Rappoli rebuilt Hotel Annville at the same location. Over time the hotel fell into a general state of disrepair and was abandoned by December 1983.

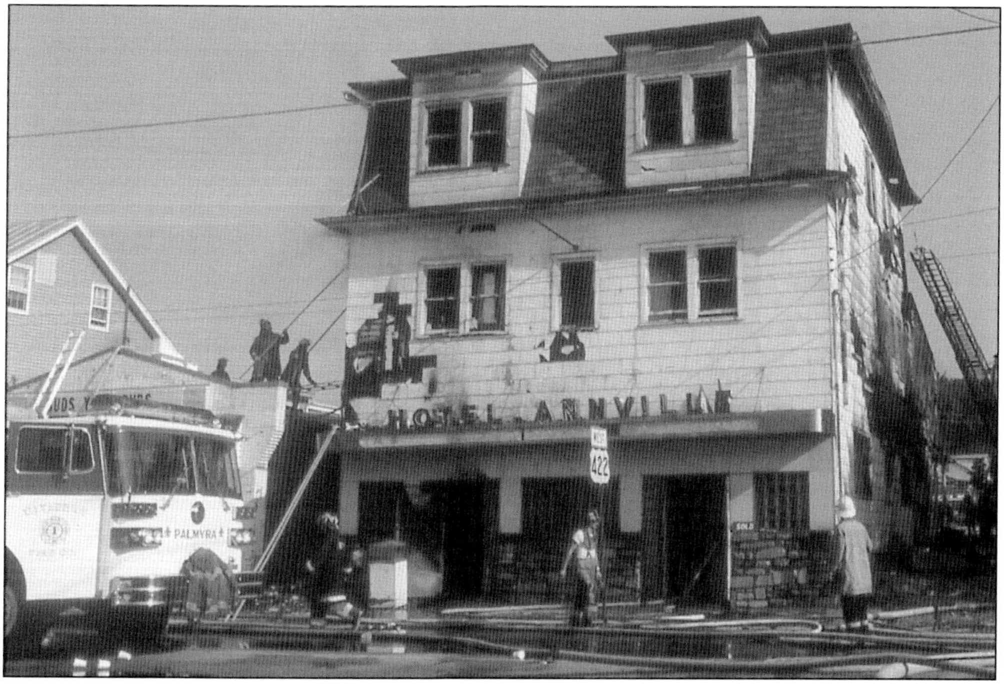

ANOTHER FIRE. On August 5, 1985, the vacant hotel was destroyed by fire. Peter Rappoli sold the land, and in 1986, a pizza restaurant was built at the site.

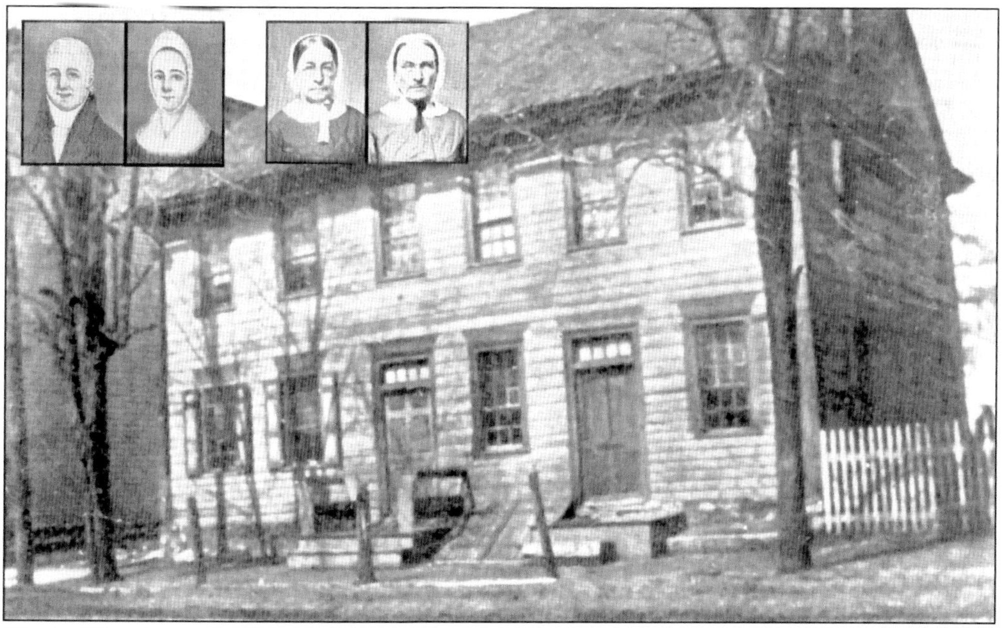

NO. 21 WEST MAIN STREET. The frame building originally erected on this site was home to Dr. David Marshall (1749–1832) and his wife, Elizabeth Gloninger (1769–1841), top left, before becoming home to their daughters "Aunt Polly" (1790–1867) and "Aunt Betsy" Marshall (1798–1877), top center. In 1850, the daughters adopted an orphan girl of six, Jane Fleming, whom they cared for through her young adulthood. Around 1890, this building was removed to make way for the brick residence of the John H. Kettering family, which would house the medical practices of David M. Rank from 1902 to 1943.

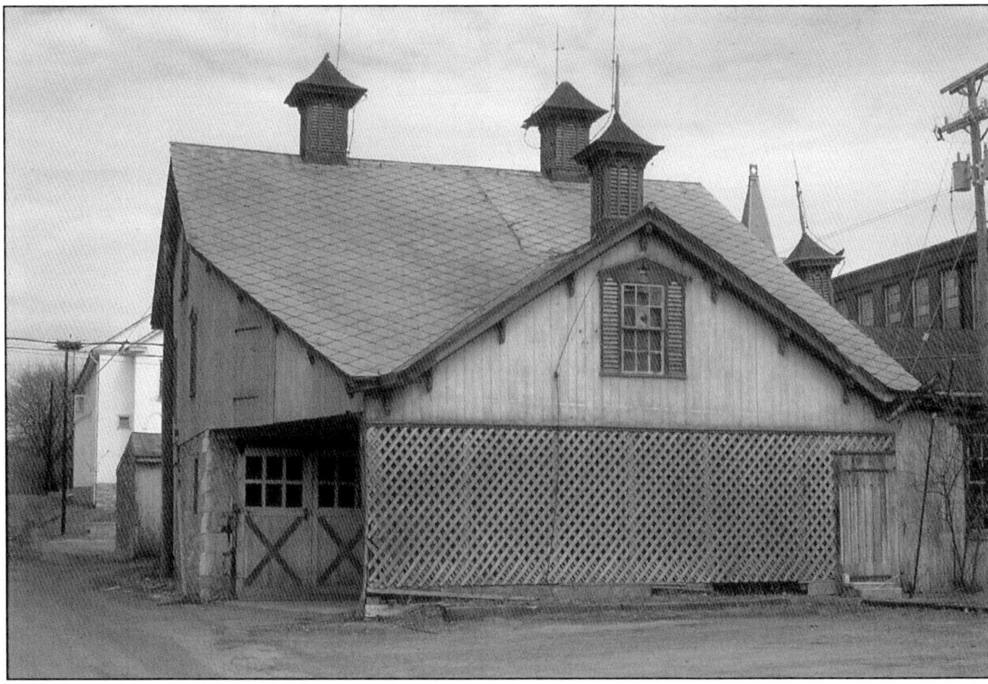

Carriage House. The two-story frame building that stands behind 21 West Main Street was built in 1875 as a carriage house for the property. The three cupolas that crown the roof are a source of ventilation and decoration. A cupola brings in cooler air while allowing warm air to escape. The removal of stagnant hot, moist air from the attic also promoted longevity for the roofing structure. The US Capitol building in Washington, D.C., features a particularly prominent cupola that is now a symbol of democracy around the world. There are several different types of cupolas in American architecture. Cupolas with windows that serve primarily to illuminate a building's interior are known as "lanterns." A cupola that can be reached through a stairway inside the main building became known as a "widow's walk" as a result of the popular belief that it was originally designed for wives of mariners so that they might watch for the return of their spouses. If a cupola contains bells, as is often the case in American churches and cathedrals, it is called a "belfry." A small, low-lying cupola that doesn't extend very far above the roofline is called a "monitor," perhaps due to its possible use as a lookout. The height of the three "vent cupolas" on these rooflines would provide an effective means of drawing stale or hot air out of the carriage house. Today the structure houses residential apartments.

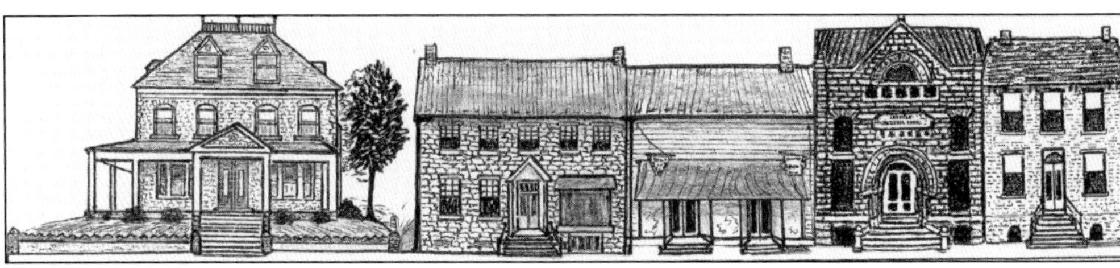

Nos. 1, 3, 7, 11, 13, and 21 West Main Street. Local historian and artist Doris Flory sketched the buildings of the northern side of the first block of West Main Street as they looked at the turn of the 20th century. To the east of the Rank Home stands the Kinports store, a pharmacy, Annville National Bank, and the post office. Between 1956 and 1976, all four properties to the east of the Rank Home were purchased by Lebanon Valley National Bank. They are currently occupied by the bank and its drive-through.

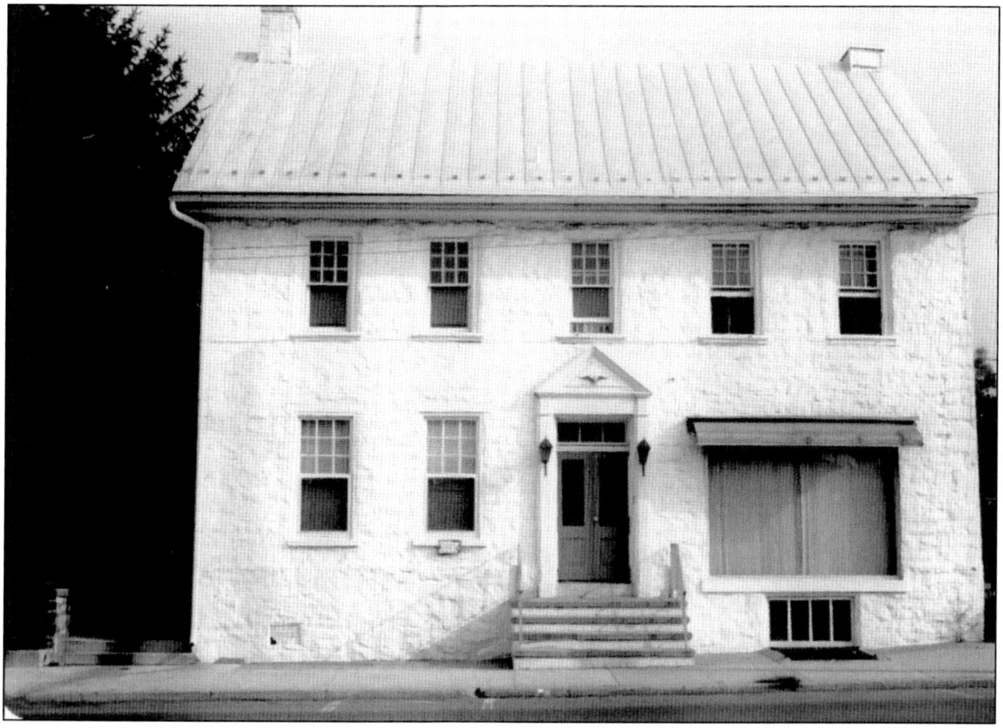

No. 13 West Main Street. This building, which once stood where the drive-through for the bank is presently located, was originally constructed in 1798 for John Shertzer Sr. (1766–1847), a prominent merchant and manufacturer of pianos in Annville prior to 1800. (See page 51.) Judge John Kinports (1821–1893) later acquired the building for his "merchandising store," which served the community from 1864 through the early 1920s. The razing of this structure in May 1978 was a significant factor in the formation of the Friends of Old Annville the following year.

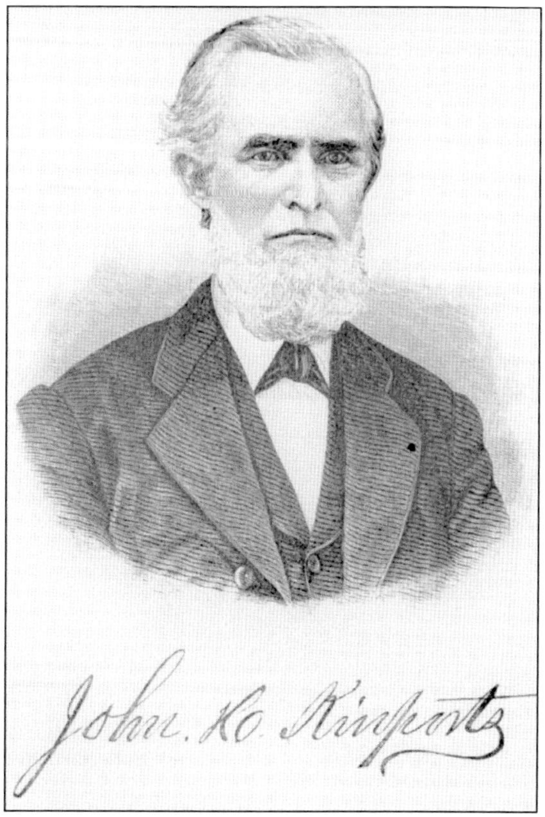

John Kinports. Judge Kinports (1821–1893), who owned and operated the store at 13 West Main, was honored in the 1917 yearbook of Lebanon Valley College for his civic engagement, which included participation in the founding of the college, as well as Annville National Bank.

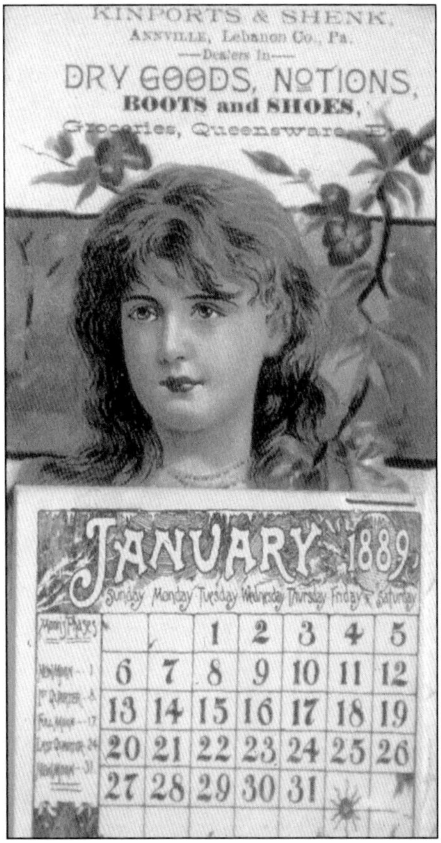

KINPORTS CALENDAR. This novelty calendar details some of the goods to be found upon a visit to the Kinports store. Kinports partnered with C.H. Killinger and H.H. Kreider before working with D.O. Shenk, whose name is noted on this 1889 calendar. In the 19th century, the term "notions" most often designated small personal articles of clothing or sewing items such as buttons and needles. Queensware is a light, cream-colored pottery, much like China, developed in England in the 1730s by Joseph Wedgwood and named in honor of Queen Charlotte, patron to Wedgwood. (Courtesy of Dick and Betty Streicher.)

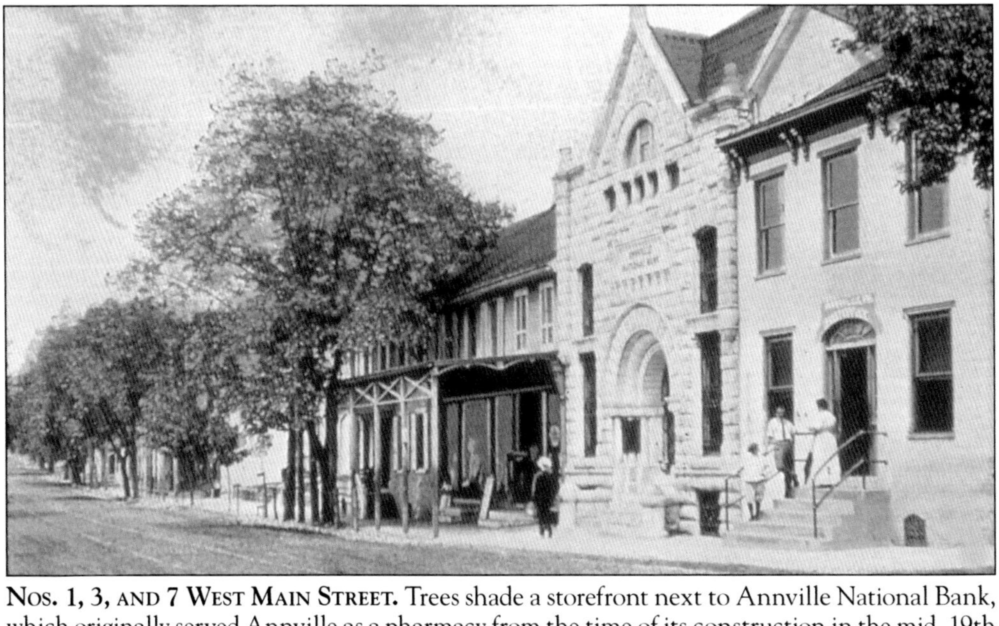

NOS. 1, 3, AND 7 WEST MAIN STREET. Trees shade a storefront next to Annville National Bank, which originally served Annville as a pharmacy from the time of its construction in the mid–19th century through the 1970s. Two doors down, community members greet one another on the steps of the former Post Office Building, popularly rumored to be the place where couples met.

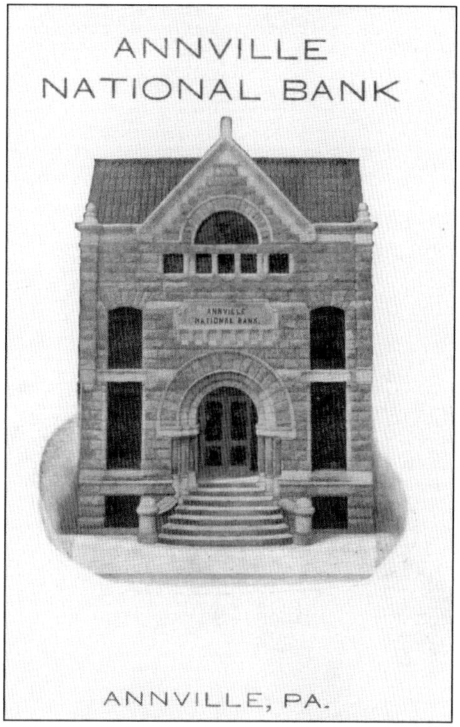

No. 3 West Main Street. When Annville National Bank was founded in the 1870s by a group of well-to-do citizens, it was housed in the home of John Kinports at 13 West Main. Kinports served as its first president. The formal bank building, pictured here, was completed in 1894. (Courtesy of Dick and Betty Streicher.)

A 1900s Advertisement. This early advertisement for Annville National Bank seeks to appeal first to farmers, then to merchants and personal bankers. When the bank merged with Lebanon Valley National Bank in 1956, the smaller stone building was replaced by the current building. The business merged with Lebanon Valley Farmers Bank in 1999, which in turn merged with Fulton Bank in 2007. (Courtesy of Dick and Betty Streicher.)

Safe deposit boxes in steel vaults for rent.

THE
ANNVILLE NATIONAL BANK

invites attention to its financial statement and asks you to note particularly the marked increase in its earnings as well as its strong condition.

Its equipment and conservative management insures to farmer, merchant and banker the prompt and careful transaction of their banking business.

It solicits the accounts of corporations and individuals, granting the utmost liberality of treatment consistent with prudent banking methods.

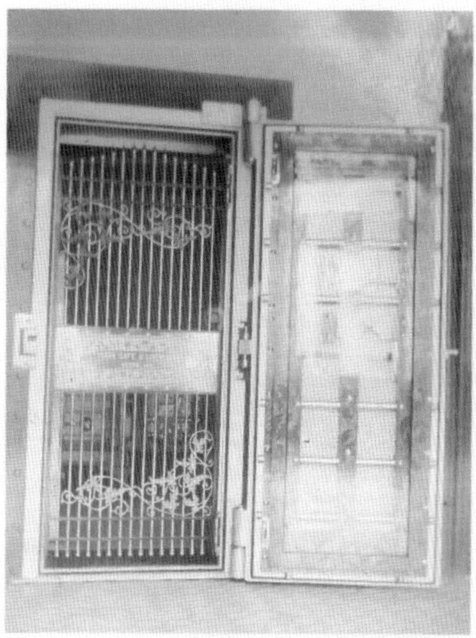

3 per cent paid on special deposits.

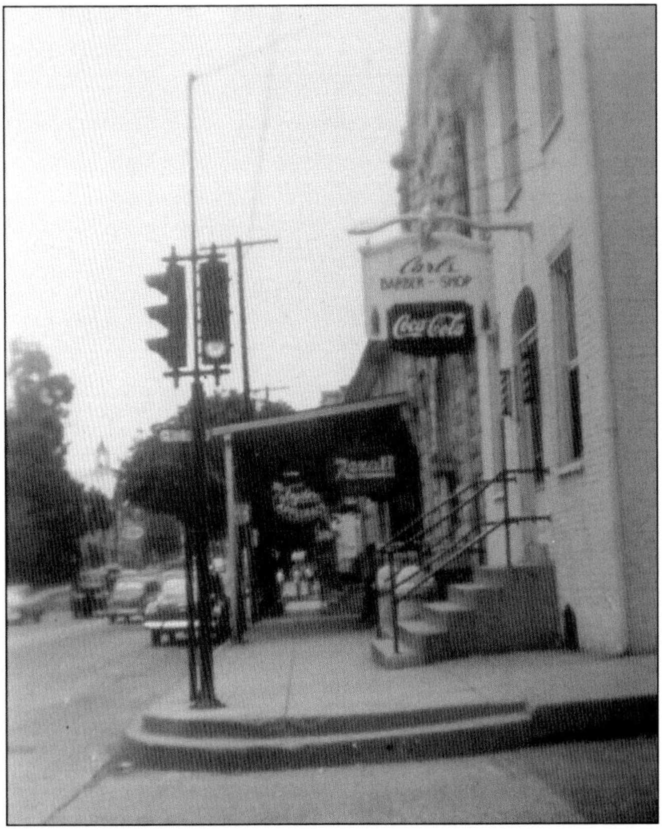

No. 1 West Main Street. Originally constructed in 1829 as the home of merchandiser John Shertzer Jr. (1799–1854), this building became the post office in 1898 before housing a barber in 1928. It was torn down in 1956 for the construction of Lebanon Valley National Bank. (Courtesy of Dick and Betty Streicher.)

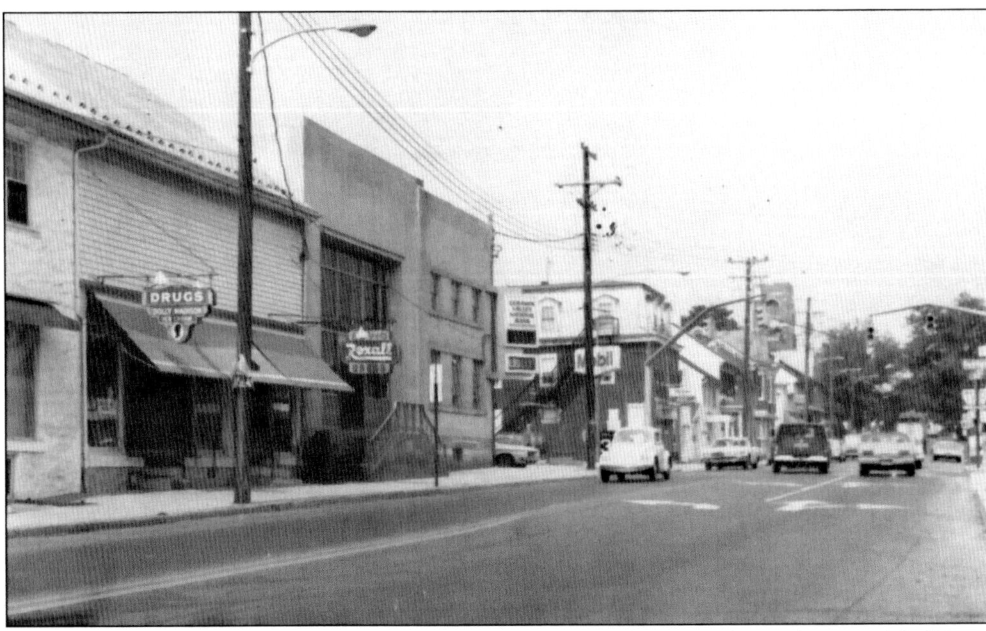

Nos. 1, 3, 7, and 11 West Main Street. This picture from the 1960s shows the remodeled Davis Pharmacy, as well as other businesses to the east. The pharmacy was razed in 1978 to develop lanes for drive-through service at Lebanon Valley National Bank. (Courtesy of John Weaber.)

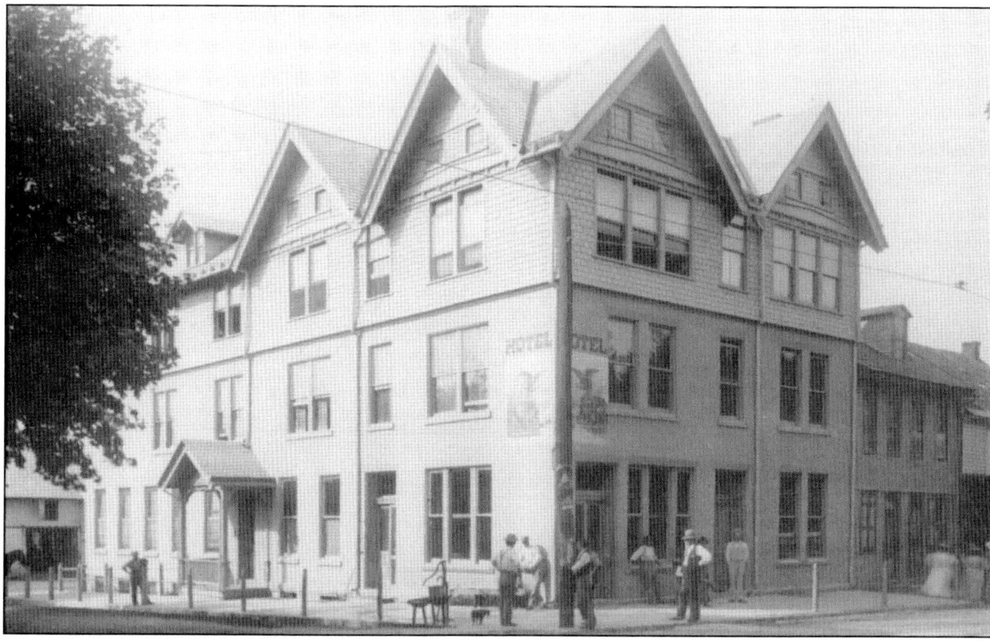

No. 2 West Main Street. The first building on the southwest corner of the center of town—where the Sunoco station now stands—was an inn built by Daniel Henning in 1790, known as Henning's Hotel. In 1845, Charles Kuhule replaced the smaller inn with a large stone restaurant and hotel managed by Jacob Fink in the 1860s, but it was perhaps best known as the Eagle Hotel from the 1870s through the 1890s, under the management of Simon Krall. Following Krall's death in 1899, the hotel was owned and operated by George Imboden and his son-in-law, Charles F. Saylor.

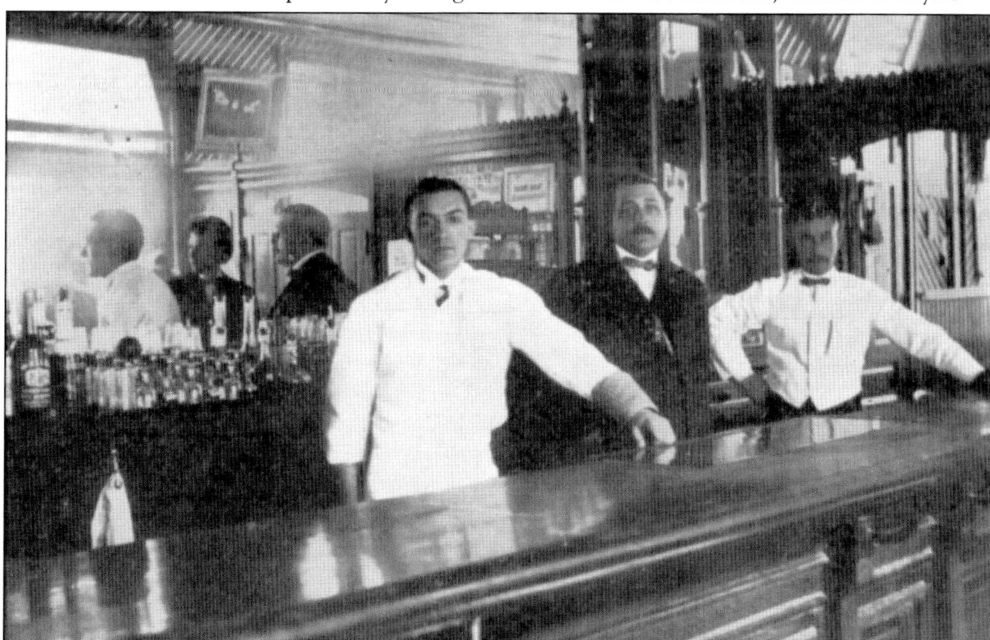

Interior Bar. The hotel provided a comfortable atmosphere for weary coach travelers. Inside, one found a bar with comfortable chairs and cuspidors (spittoons).

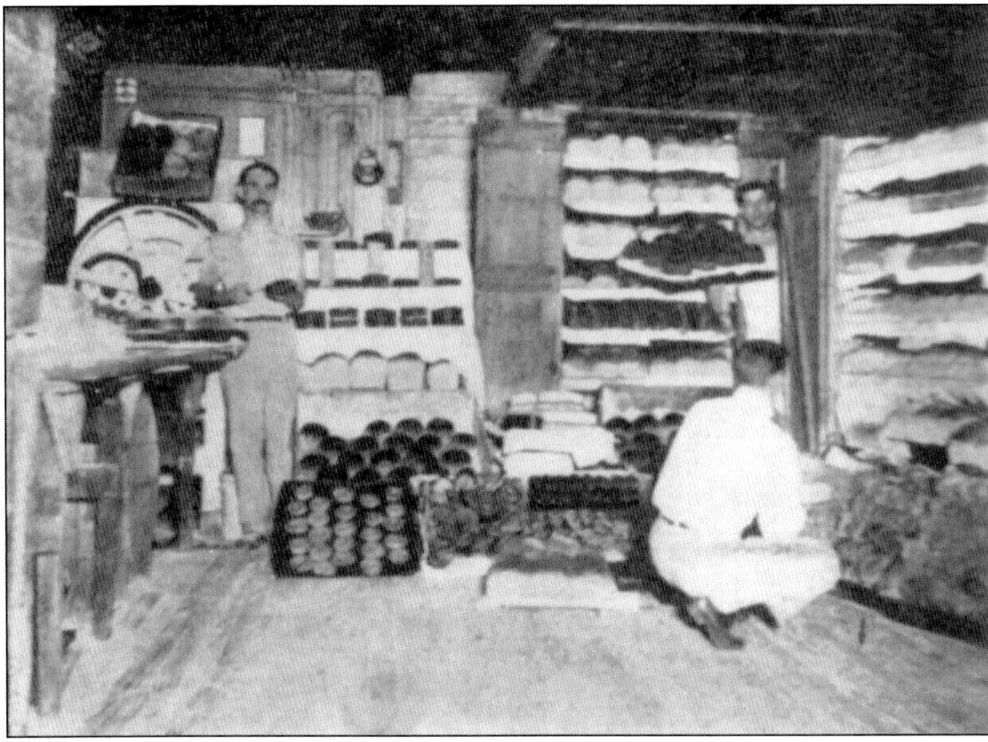

Bakery. The rear of the building housed many businesses through the years, including the Model Vienna Bakery. (Courtesy of Blanche Schaeffer.)

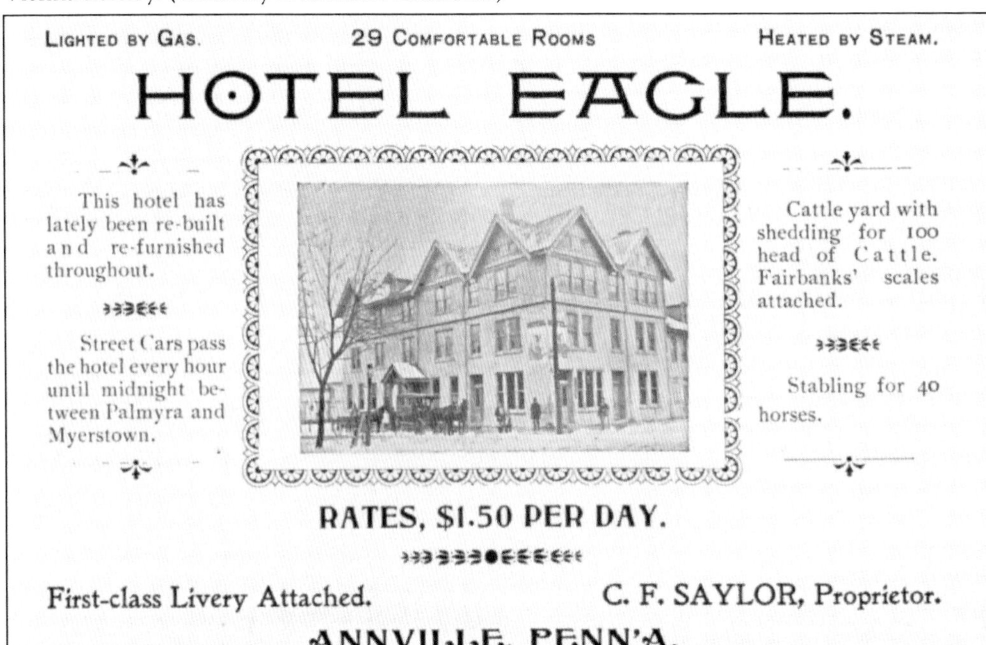

A 1901 Advertisement. In addition to the amenities listed in this advertisement, there were carriage stepping stones, horse-hitching posts, and a large watering trough. (Courtesy of Lebanon Valley College.)

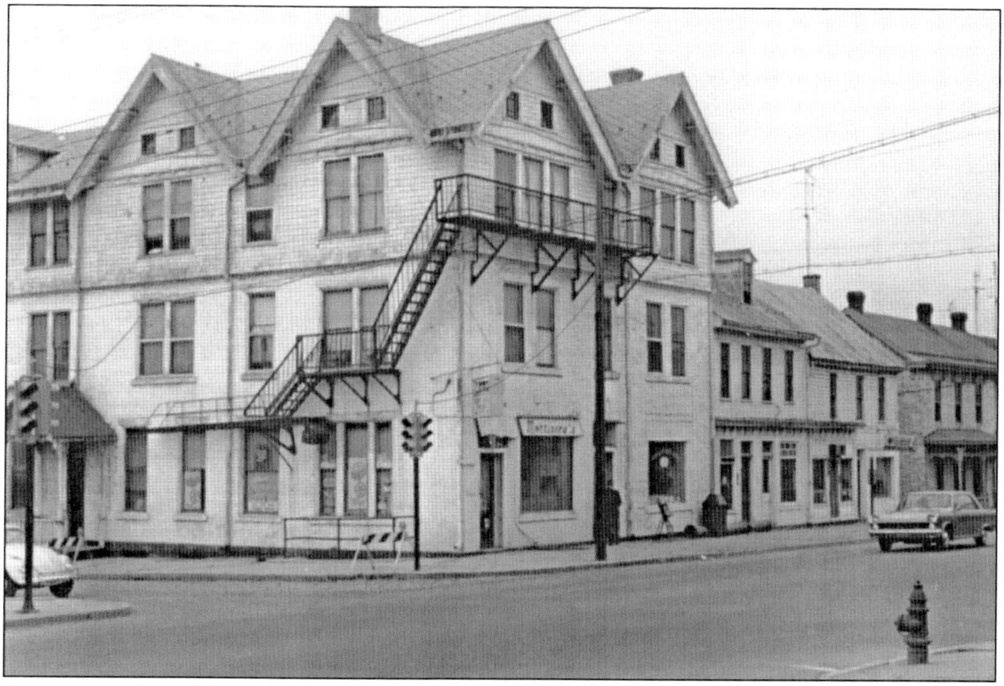

Before the Fire. When Isaac Bowman assumed management of the property in the 1910s, he changed its name to the Pennway Hotel and Bakery. The bakery occupied three floors at the back of the building. Dough that was mixed on the second or third floor was sent down a chute to the ovens on the first floor. The Pennway sold bakery products under the trade name "Aunt Betty's." (Courtesy of Nancy Darkes.)

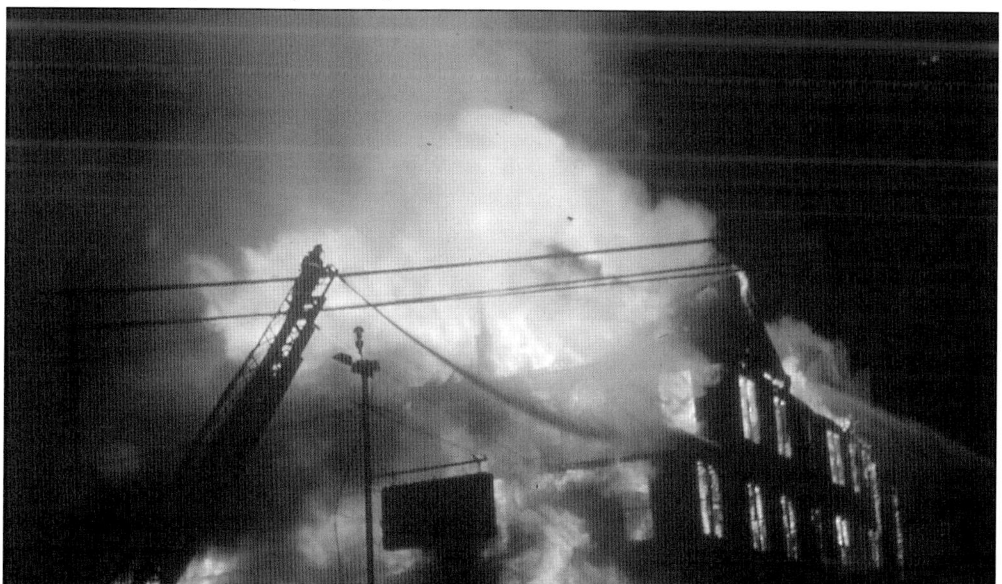

Fire, 1970. On April 13, 1970, the hotel burned down in a massive conflagration. The building was vacant at the time. The owner, Clayton Risser, was in the process of selling it to the Atlantic Richfield Oil Company. It took eight fire companies and more than 80 firemen to bring the blaze under control. The cause of the fire was never determined.

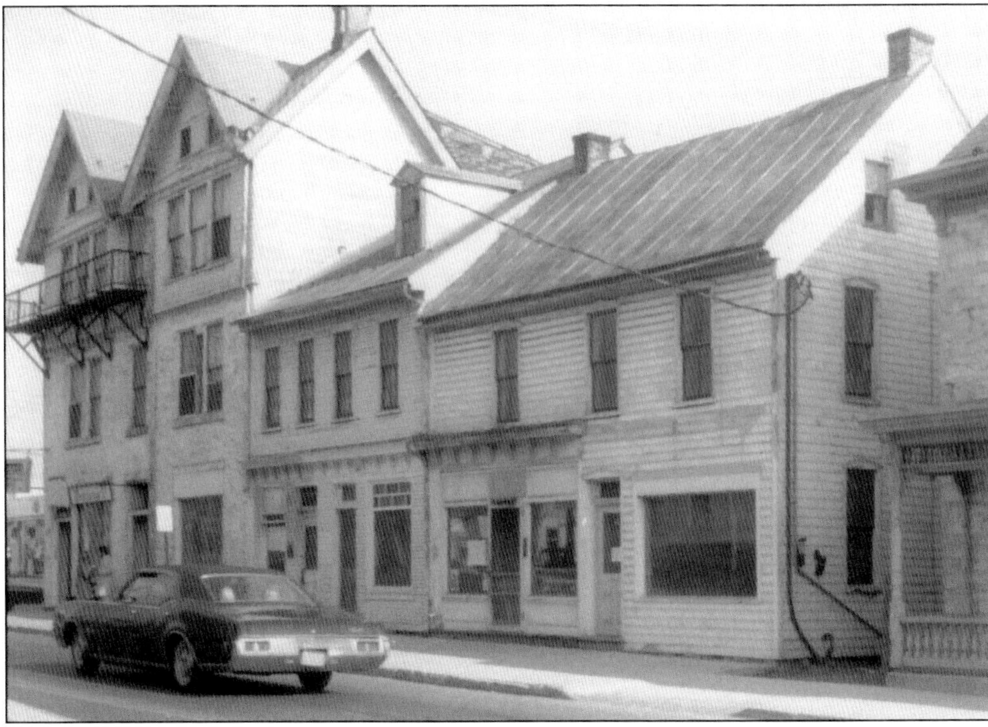

NOS. 2–16 WEST MAIN STREET. The south side of the first block of West Main Street used to be lined with small shops, all of which burned with the Pennway. Pictured here from east to west are the Pennway Hotel, Rauch's Barbershop, Wornas's Shoeshine Shop, Bowman's Bakery, and the offices of insurance agent Isaac M. Long.

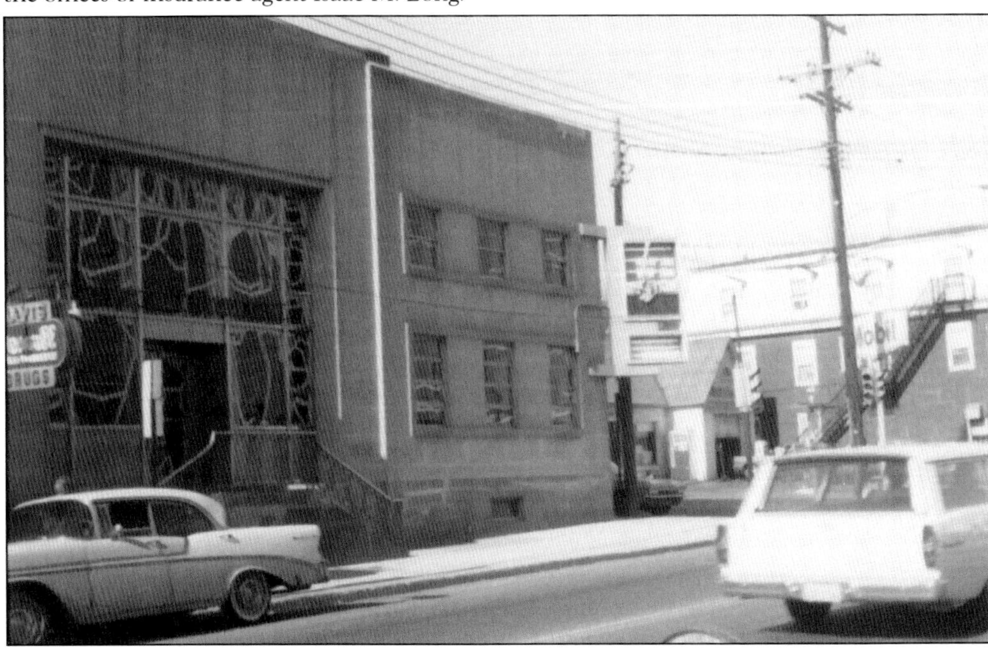

NOS. 13 WEST MAIN STREET. So intense was the heat of the fire that all of the glass on the front of the bank across the street was melted.

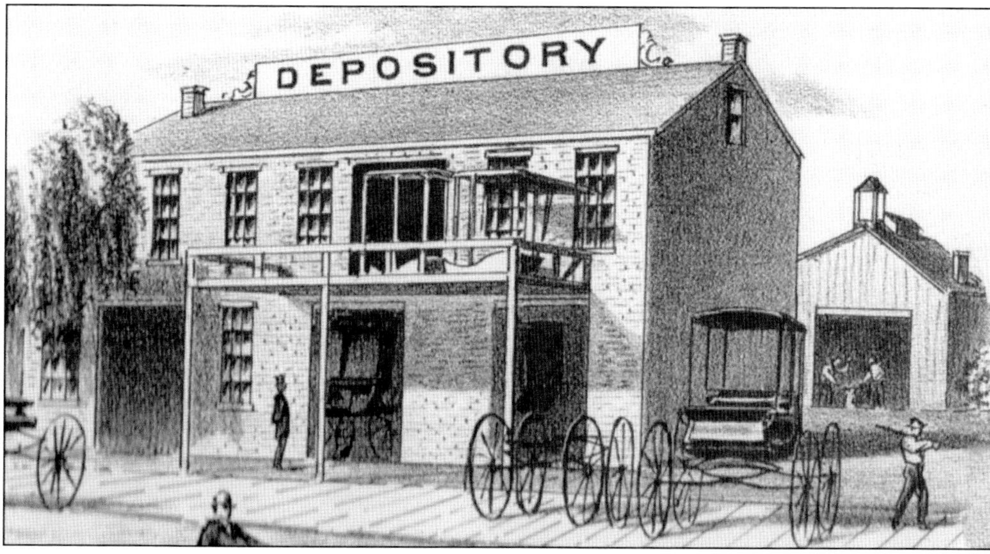

No. 16 South White Oak Street. Originally constructed around 1840 for carriage maker John Allwein, this building served as part of a carriage shop complex that extended behind this property to the back of 18 East Main Street. The complex was purchased by John L. Saylor in the early 1870s. A large sign on the front of Miller's Hardware Store announced the presence of Saylor's Carriage Shop in the back. (See page 79.) Carriages were built or repaired on the upper level and lowered to the first floor via a pulley that still hangs in the rafters of the house. Note the three large openings in the building for carriages and supplies.

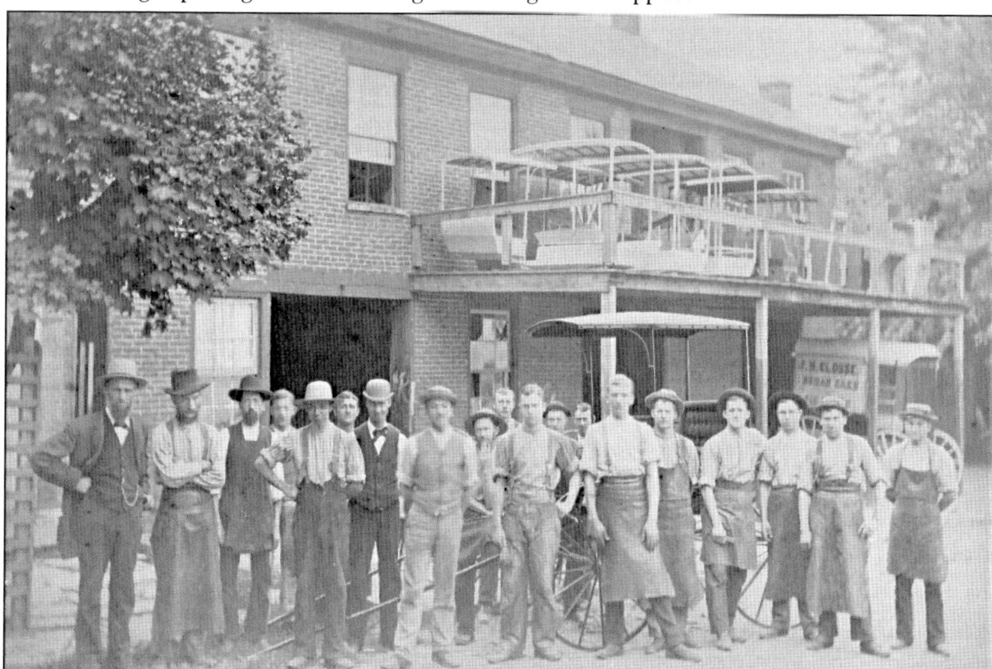

Carriage Crew. In the 1890s, John L. Saylor (far left) stands at 16 South White Oak Street with his work crew. The three large openings on the lower level of the building are visible. (Courtesy of Scott Saylor.)

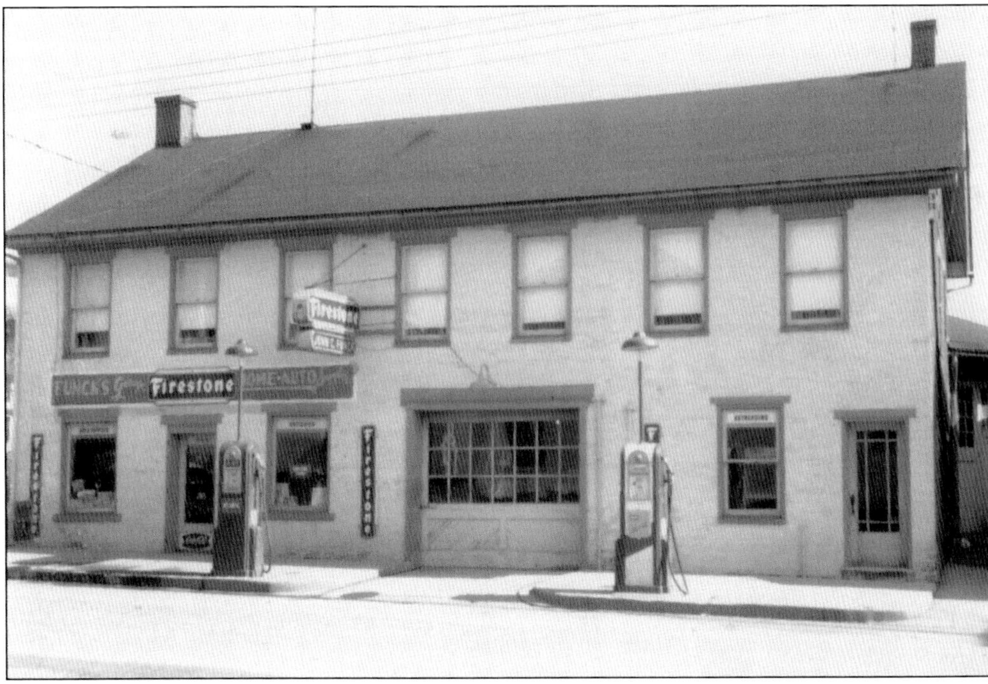

Funk's Garage. Following the advent of the automobile, an auto repair shop replaced the carriage factory. Only the large door in the center of the first floor has been retained. Eventually, that door was also removed when the business was remodeled into a private residence with cedar siding.

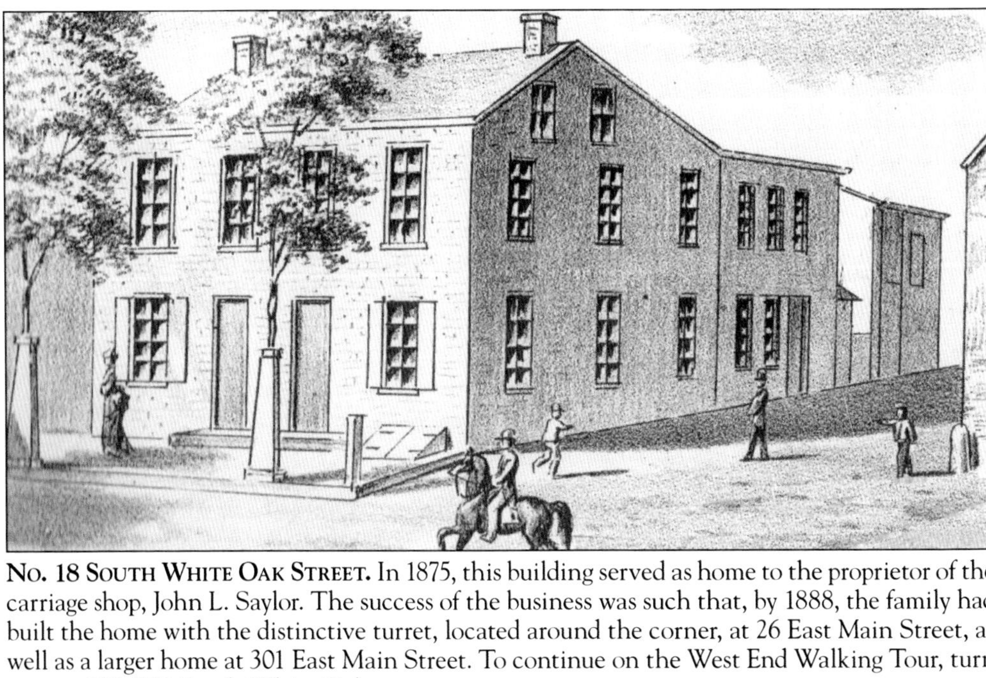

No. 18 South White Oak Street. In 1875, this building served as home to the proprietor of the carriage shop, John L. Saylor. The success of the business was such that, by 1888, the family had built the home with the distinctive turret, located around the corner, at 26 East Main Street, as well as a larger home at 301 East Main Street. To continue on the West End Walking Tour, turn to page 125, 200 South White Oak.

Six

The First Block of East Main Street

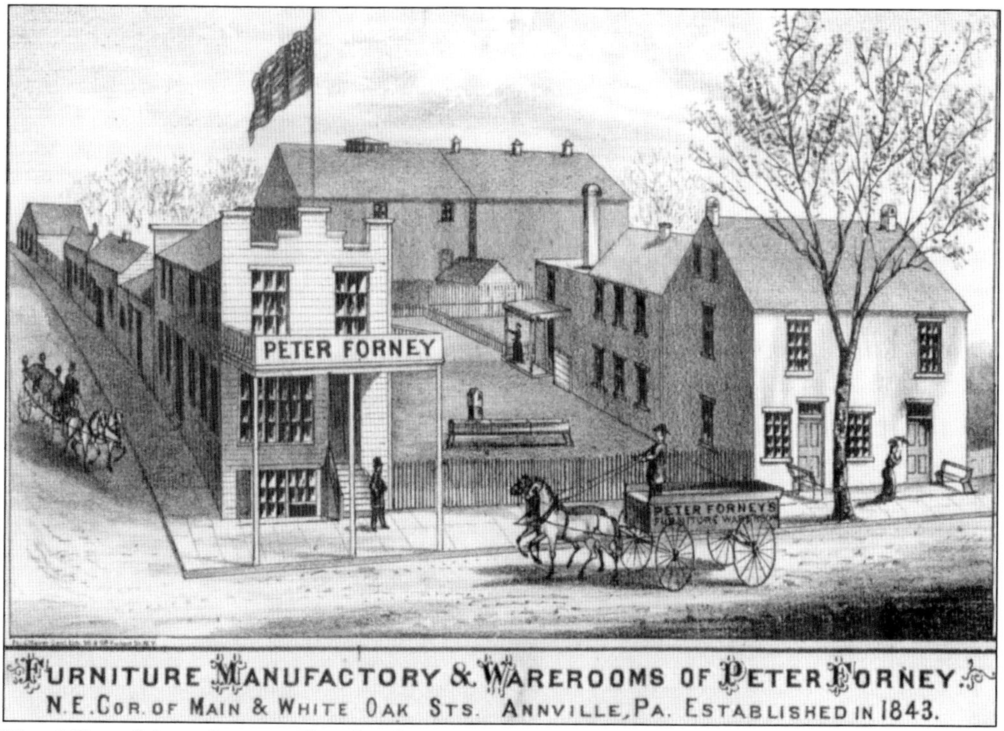

No. 1 East Main Street. Shortly after Peter Forney, carpenter and mortician, married Maria Henning in 1842, the family began to manufacture furniture on the northeast corner of the center of town. As was common at the time, the furniture business also provided coffins and the services of an undertaker. (See page 38.) Peter would eventually have three wives and 12 children here before building a home for his retirement at 441 East Main Street in 1880.

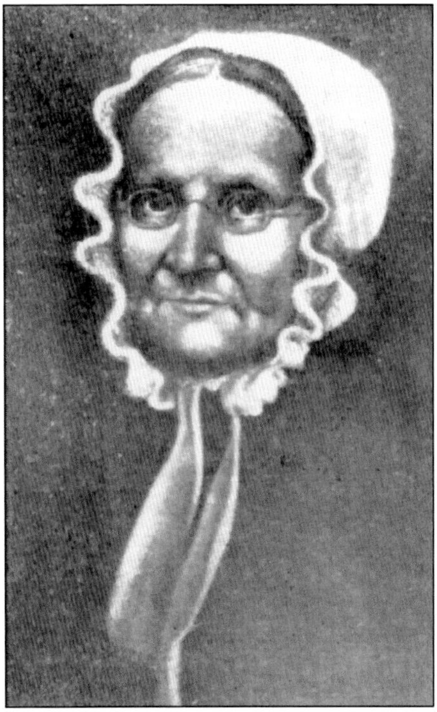

GRANNY FORNEY. Mary Martin "Granny" Forney (1794–1872) used the front room of a house to the east of Forney's furniture store for her cake and beer shop. Her stock included moshy (candy made from molasses), mintsticks (a hard confection), lebkuche (bars made with molasses, sugar, and honey, associated with funeral gatherings), ladyfingers (stiff ginger cake), sweetbeer (made from molasses, non-intoxicating), and mead (made from honey, fermented). For a full-length treatment of the life of Granny Forney, see Professor Stein's 1927 article listed in the bibliography of this volume.

GAS STATION. By 1882, Forney's furniture and caretaking business transferred to Harvey Sheffy, who eventually rented the corner building to J.B. Frey Grocery, Tobacco, and Oyster Bar (1916–1933) and an additional building to Lutz's Butcher Shop. (See page 76.) In 1933, these buildings were removed for the development of a Mobil Gas Station, which was operated for several decades by members of the Shearer family. (Courtesy of Aaron Shearer.)

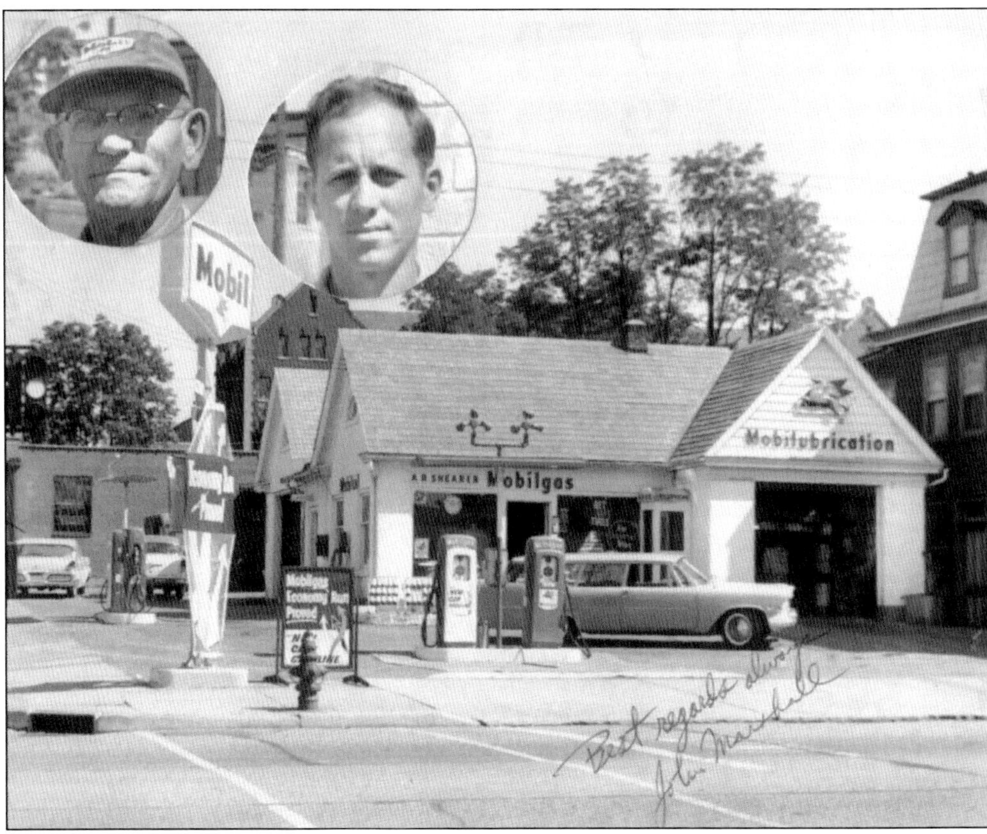

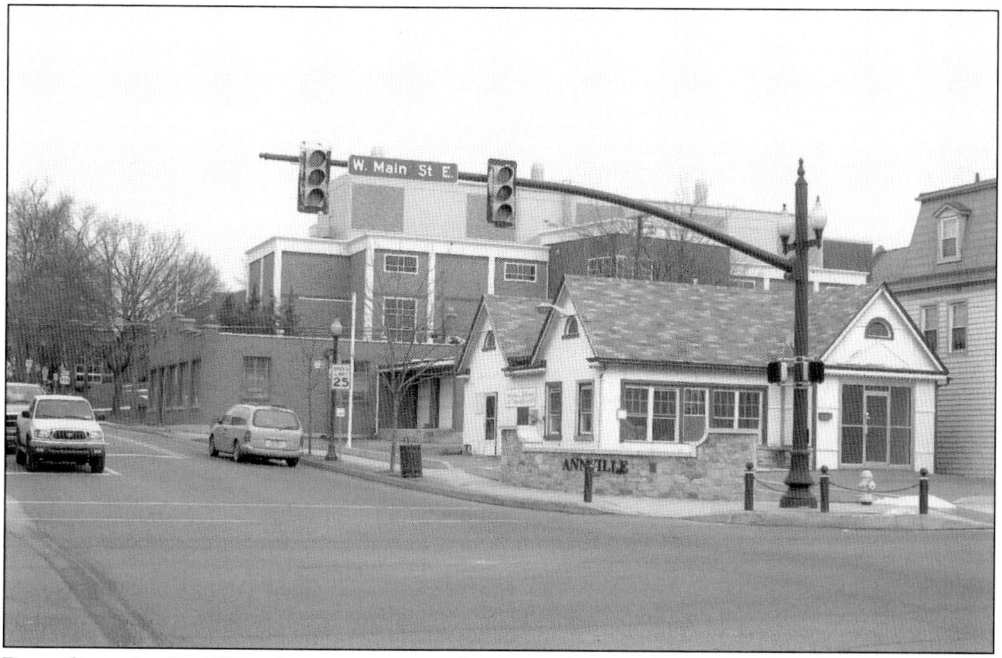

PIZZA SHOP. In the 1980s, the gas station on the corner became home to Shirk's Auto Sales before being remodeled into Roma Pizza. Both the pizza shop and the post office to the north were removed in 2010 as the initial step in an effort to revitalize business along this block. (Courtesy of the *Lebanon Daily News*.)

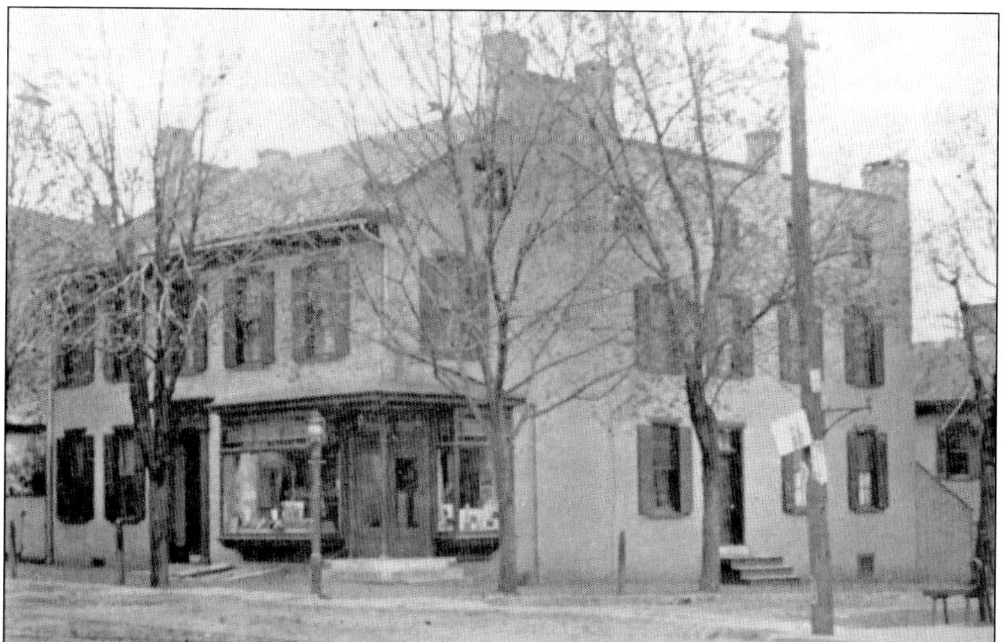

NO. 2 EAST MAIN STREET. As early as 1875, the corner of the property currently owned by Turkey Hill was home to the Seabold family and Seabold's Drugstore, pictured here in 1907. Extremely large and colorful apothecary jars filled the front windows for most of its history. (Courtesy of Dick and Betty Streicher.)

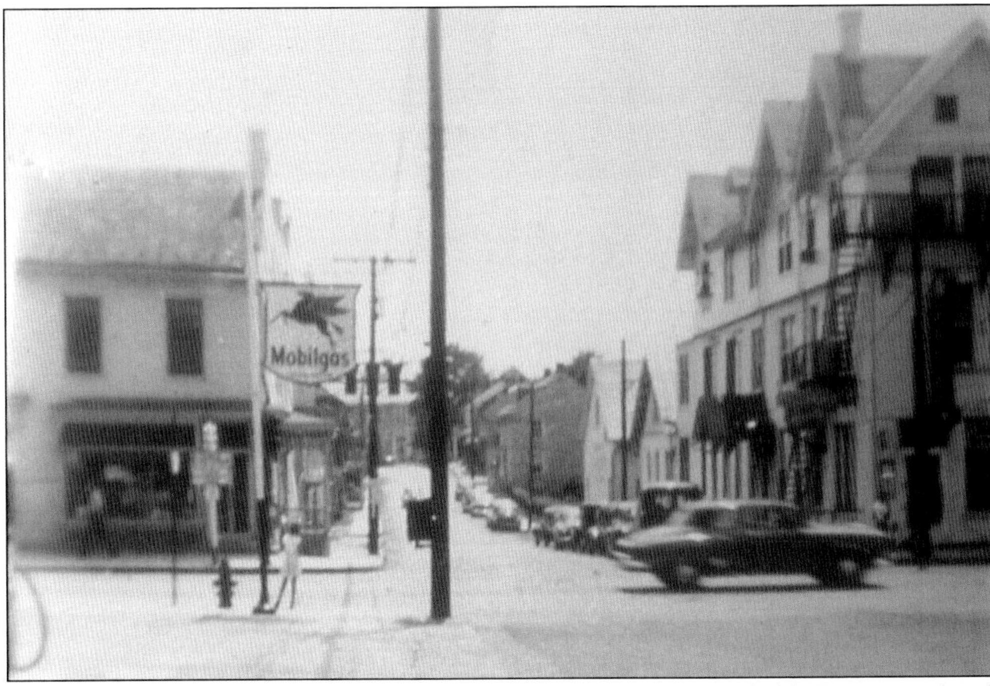

A 1940s View. Shortly after this picture was taken in the 1940s, Seabold's Drugstore closed. Eventually, the residence was torn down to meet the needs of the service station to the east of the building. (Courtesy of Dick and Betty Streicher.)

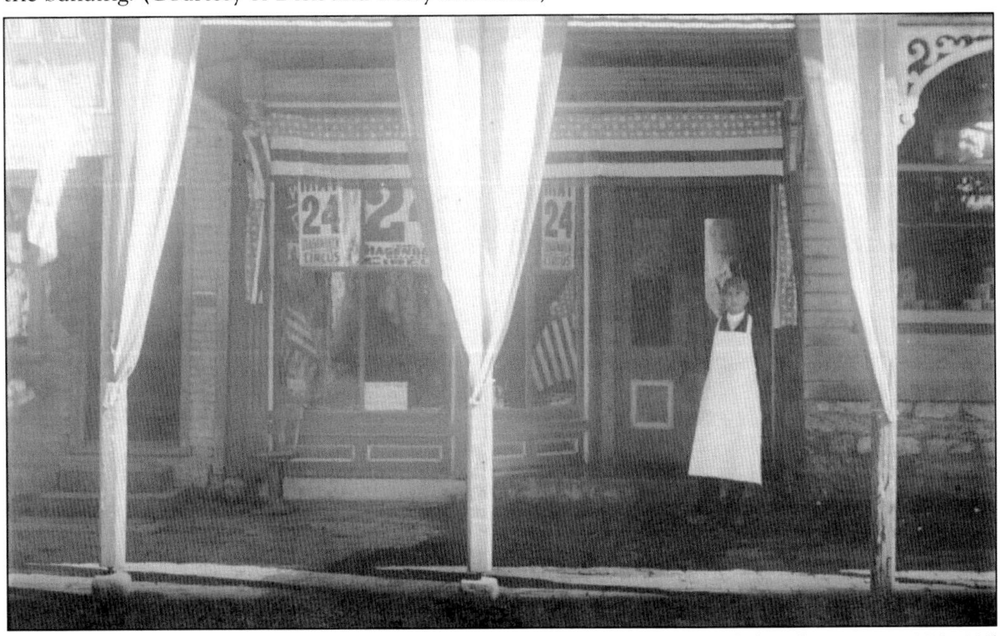

No. 3 East Main Street. In 1904, butchers Spangler and Lutz expanded their business at 223–225 West Main Street by building a new storefront on this corner. Lutz sold the shop to his son-in-law William M. Rohland in 1911. Over the course of the next two decades, Rohland would befriend and support two young immigrants from Greece, Frank and Mary Aftosmes, as they established a business next door. (Courtesy of Blanche Schaeffer.)

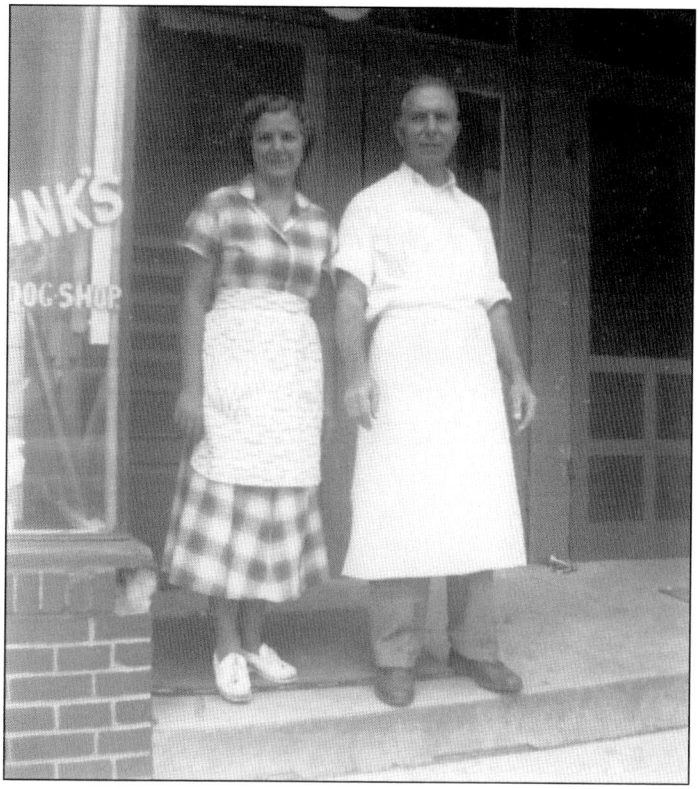

Nos. 7, 9, and 11 East Main Street. With the backing of the Rohland family, in 1928 Frank and Mary Aftosmes took out a lease to rent the Gruber family's store and restaurant at 7 East Main Street for $35 a month, establishing Hot Dog Frank's Restaurant. The adjoining store at 11 East Main first housed Harvey Sheffy's Paper Goods and a pinochle parlor in the back room—a popular place to roll a cigar and enjoy the newspaper—before becoming home to Hostetter's TV, as well as a series of other businesses. The Aftosmeses rented space above the restaurant at 9 East Main Street. (Courtesy of Peter and Jane Aftosmes.)

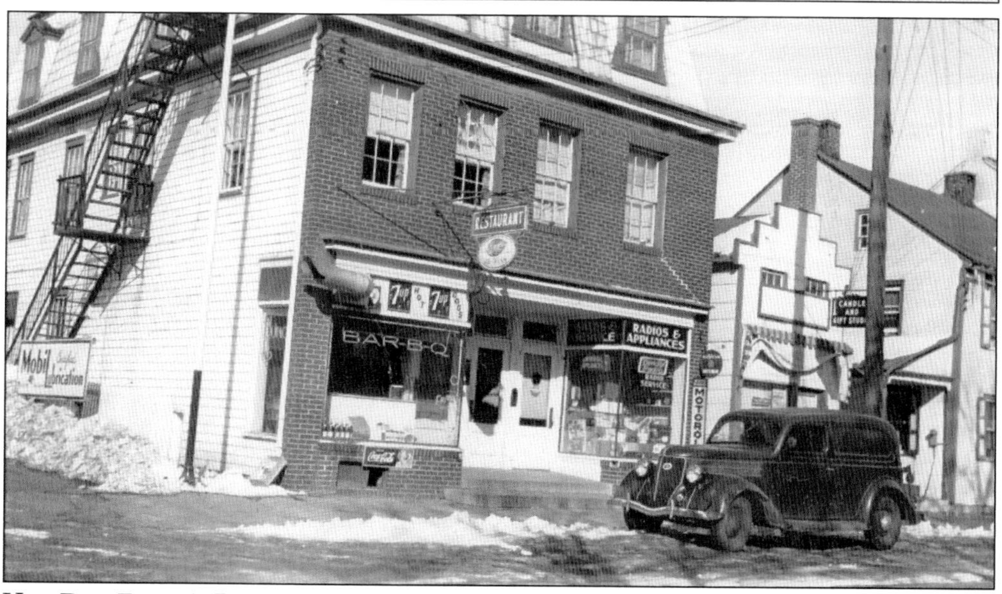

Hot Dog Frank's Restaurant. In 1943, Frank and Mary's popularity among LVC students and servicemen from Fort Indiantown Gap eventually afforded them the ability to purchase the historic residence at 15 East Main Street, which had been home to the Peter Bachman family in the early 19th century and to cobbler Peter Graybill and family since the mid-19th century. At the same time they also obtained Detweiler's Shoe Store at 13 East Main Street, a small cobbler shop between the restaurant and the home.

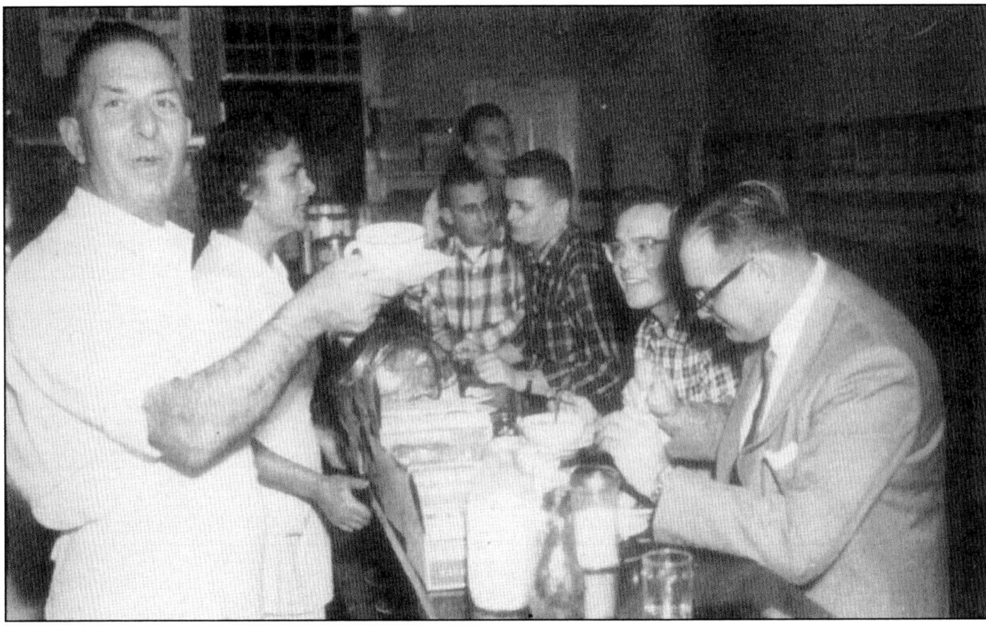

FRANK AND MARY. The influence of Frank and Mary's personal care has been noted by those who knew them (see the bibliography), so much so that a bronze statue of Frank has been placed in the Peace Garden of Lebanon Valley College. (Courtesy of Peter and Jane Aftosmes.)

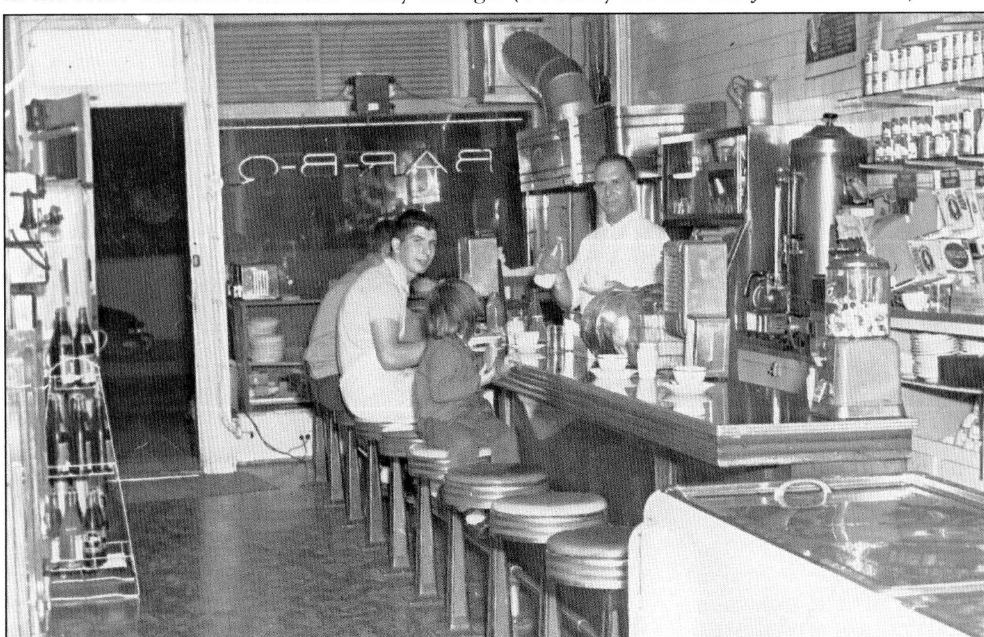

THE SODA COUNTER. Mary and Frank Aftosmes served the community until the 1970s, at which time their son John purchased the business. Two restaurants (including an early manifestation of Schwalm's Restaurant now in Cleona) and a beauty shop would take up residence here before the building was purchased by Lebanon Valley College along with 13–15, 17, 21, and 25 East Main Street between 1993 and 1995. In 2009, these buildings were purchased by Annville Township for use in a redevelopment project. (Courtesy of Peter and Jane Aftosmes.)

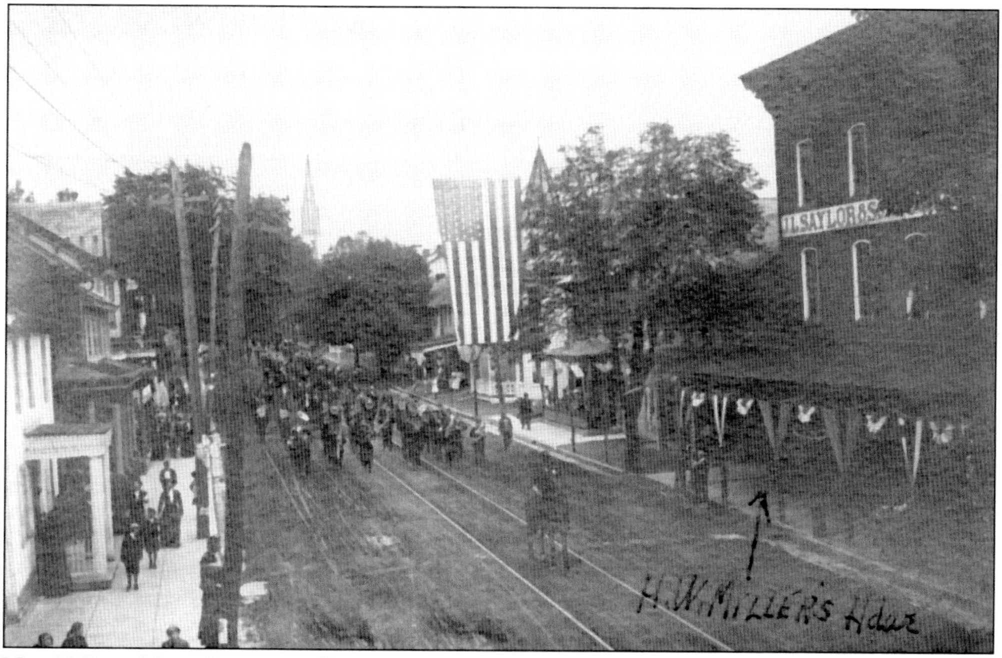

No. 18 East Main Street. Miller's Hardware, pictured on the right in the early 1900s, was owned and operated by H.W. Miller, who lived at 301 East Main at that time. Note the advertisement for Saylor's Carriage Shop above the store. (See page 71.) (Courtesy of Blanche Schaeffer.)

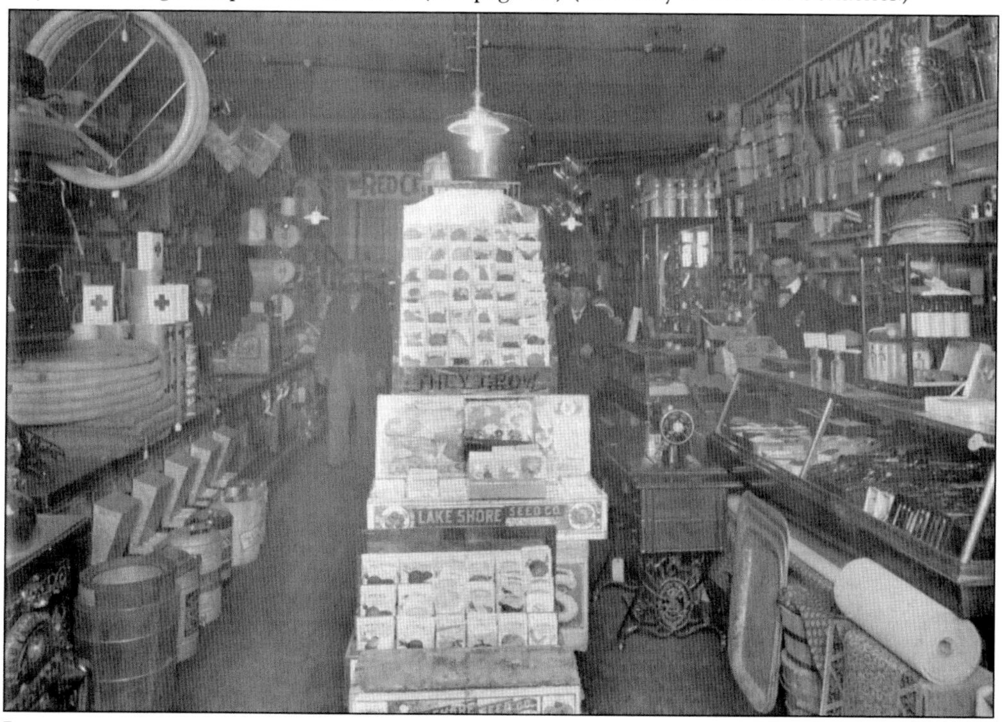

Interior, 1910s. Given the practice of referring to people by their occupations, such as Cobbler Graybill and Butcher Rohland, local children who visited the store often wondered whether proprietor H.W. Miller's initials stood for "Hard Ware Miller." (Courtesy of Dick and Betty Streicher.)

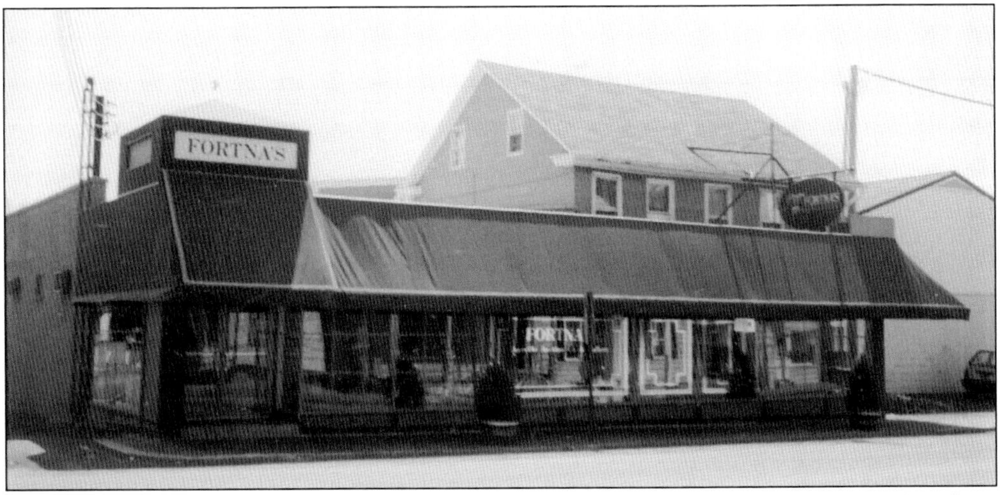

Fortna's Auction. After the closing of Miller's Hardware, the property housed Miller's Grocery Store and then Fortna's Auction Gallery from the 1970s. Michael Fortna's website would be named the best auctioneering website in Pennsylvania in 2005. As a result of his effective online business, Fortna closed his storefront in 2008, making way for the current Chinese restaurant.

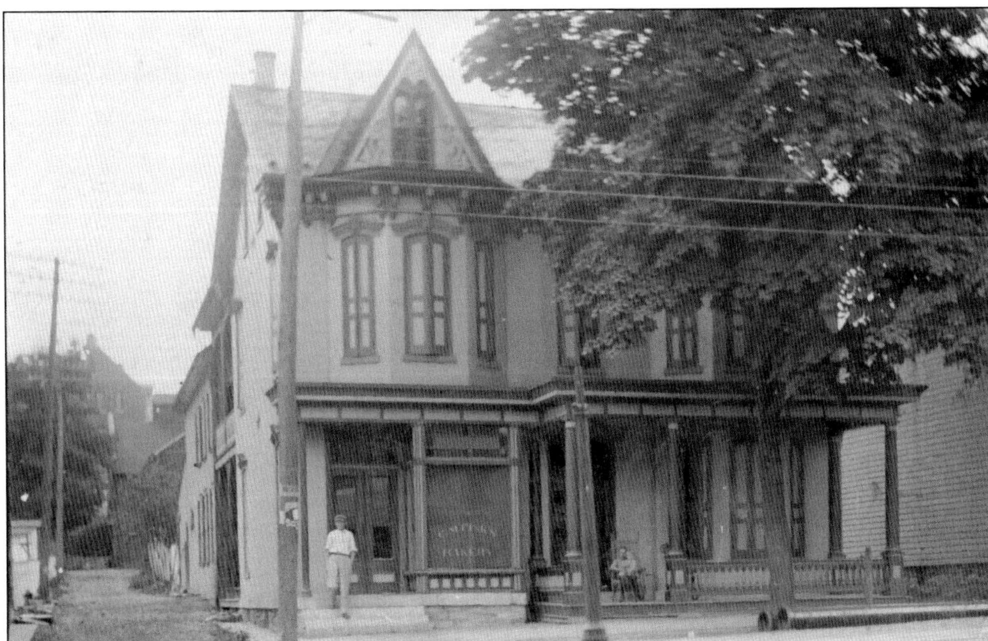

No. 25 East Main Street. The smell of freshly baked bread and rolls drew the people of Annville and the broader community into Fink's Bakery, but it was the cream puffs that sold at high volume to those who were enticed through the front doors. The building, as well as several additions to the back of the property, is now owned by Annville Township, which plans to use it as the centerpiece of a redevelopment plan. (Courtesy of Dick and Betty Streicher.)

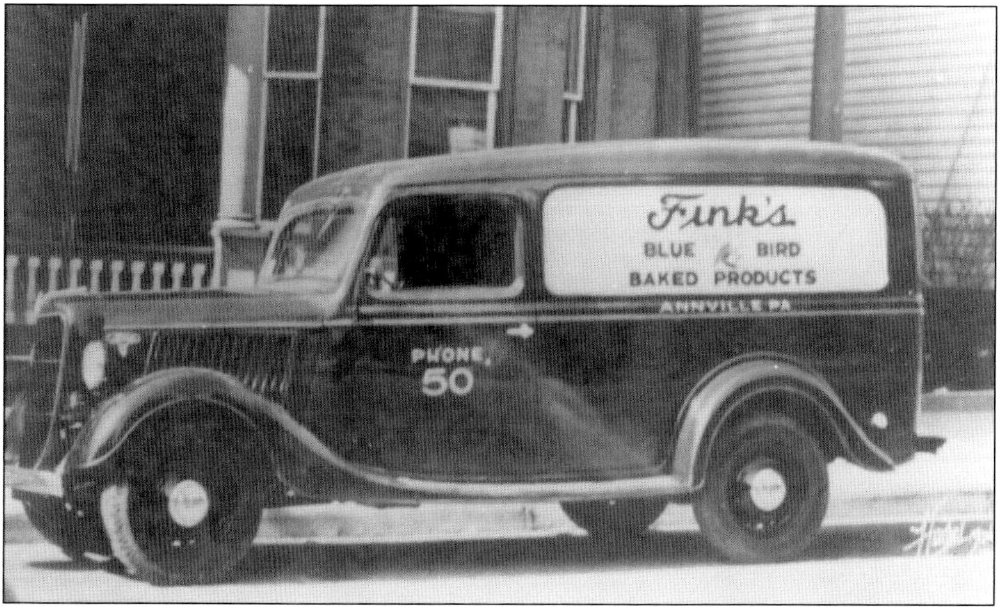

COMPANY CAR. Fink's Bakery served the neighboring community through an extensive delivery system. (Courtesy of Blanche Schaeffer.)

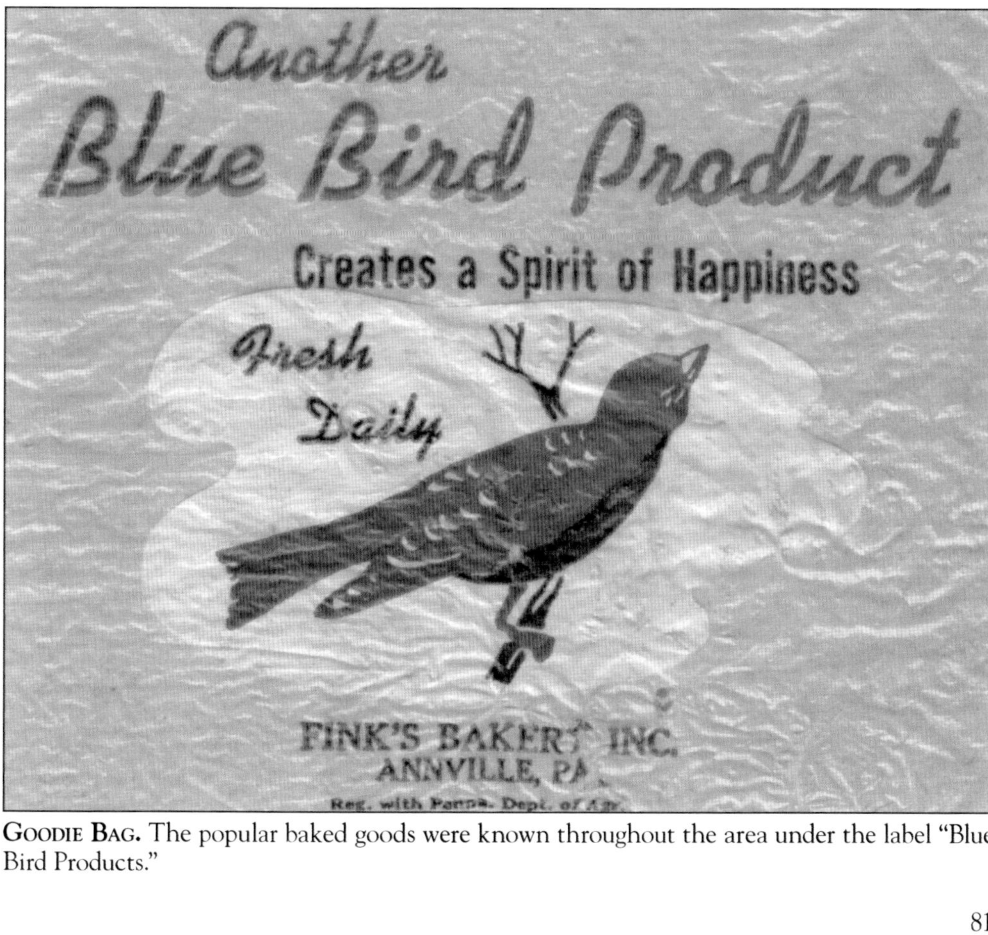

GOODIE BAG. The popular baked goods were known throughout the area under the label "Blue Bird Products."

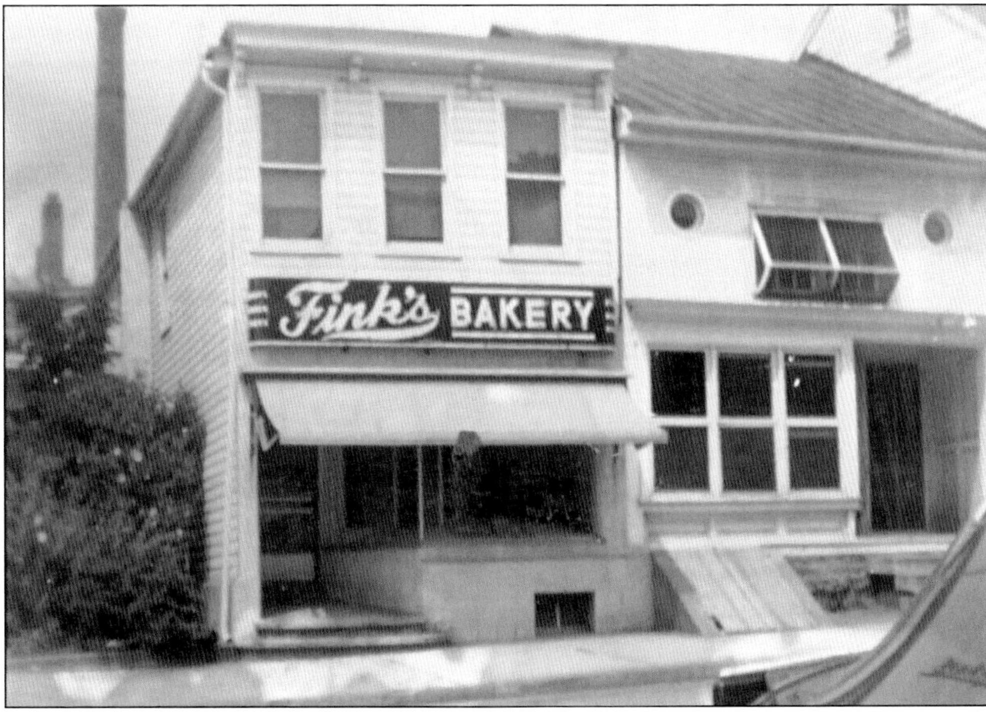

No. 29 East Main Street. In 1936, Fink's Bakery opened a sales shop directly east of their main facility. The company remained in operation until 1960. It was purchased by Capital Bakery, which closed in 1968. (Courtesy of Ron and Doris Flory.)

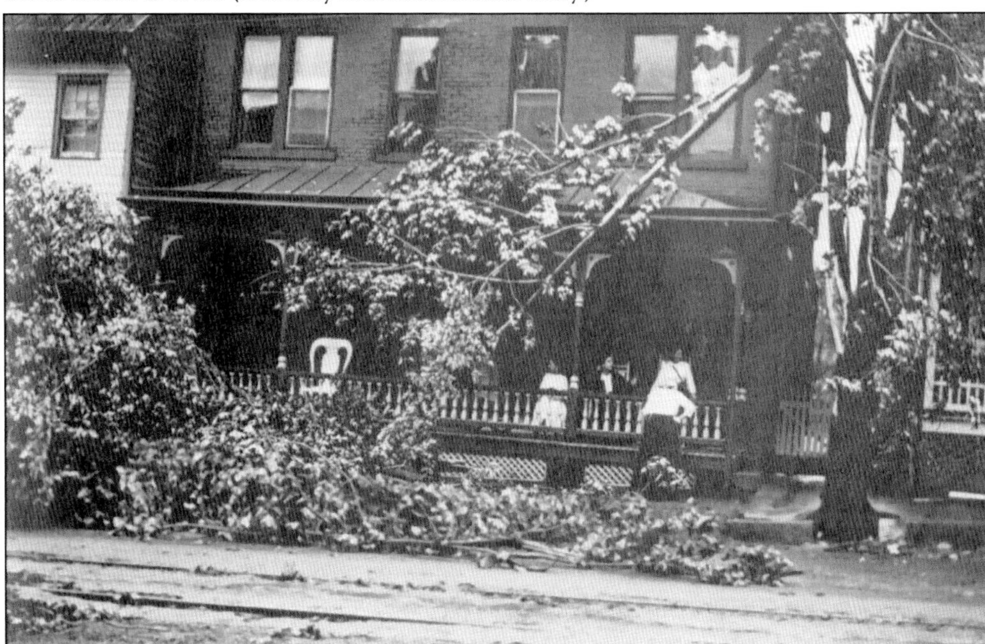

Nos. 35 and 37 East Main Street. The storm accompanying the cyclone of 1915 took down several trees along Main Street. See page 13 for an overview of the cyclone's path. (Courtesy of Dick and Betty Streicher.)

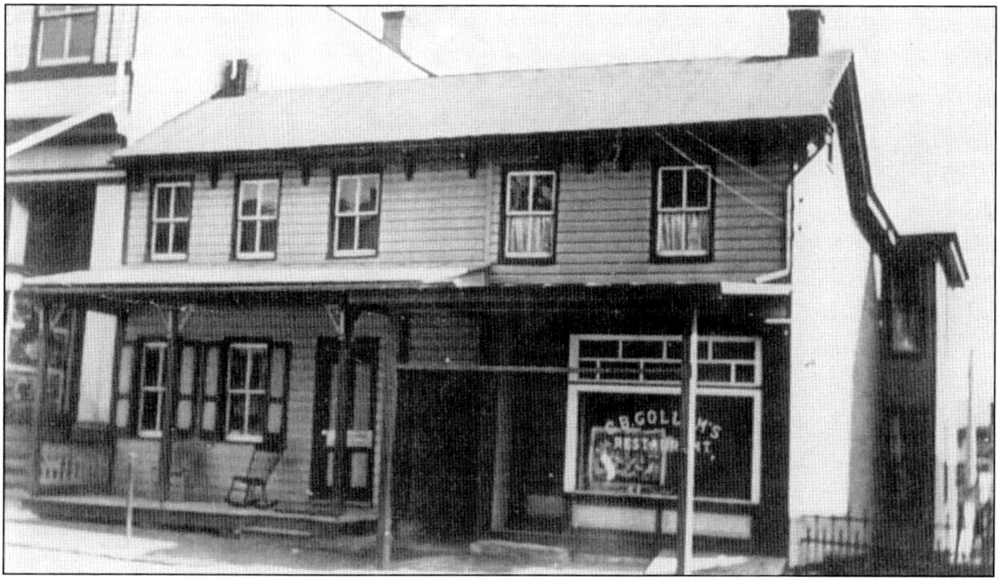

No. 30 East Main Street. Annville resident Christian B. Gollam (see page 108) opened this restaurant in the 1900s before deciding a few years later to specialize in ice cream at a new facility at 308 West Penn Street in Cleona. After Gollam's departure, the building housed a variety of restaurants at different times, including Roemig's, The Brunners's, The Edwards's, and The Stones's. A menu dated July 29, 1945, when Reedy's occupied the space, offered a full-course T-bone steak dinner for just $1.25. (Courtesy of Howard Starry.)

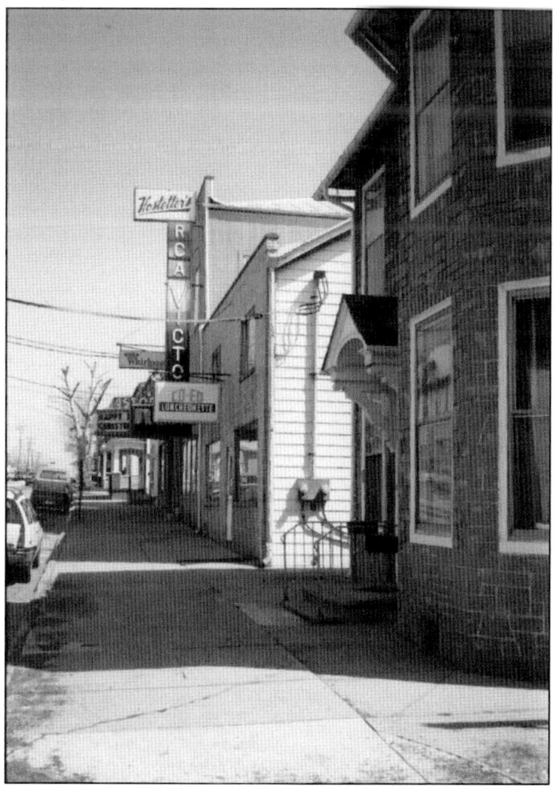

The Co-Ed. This building, which has also served a variety of businesses, became most well known in the late 1950s as the Co-Ed Luncheonette, owned and operated by Della (Mariani) and Frank Marino. The Co-Ed was a popular spot for high school students and their teachers, but LVC students preferred to eat at Hot Dog Frank's. (See page 77.) Hostetter's TV moved next door to this location from 9 East Main Street in the 1950s.

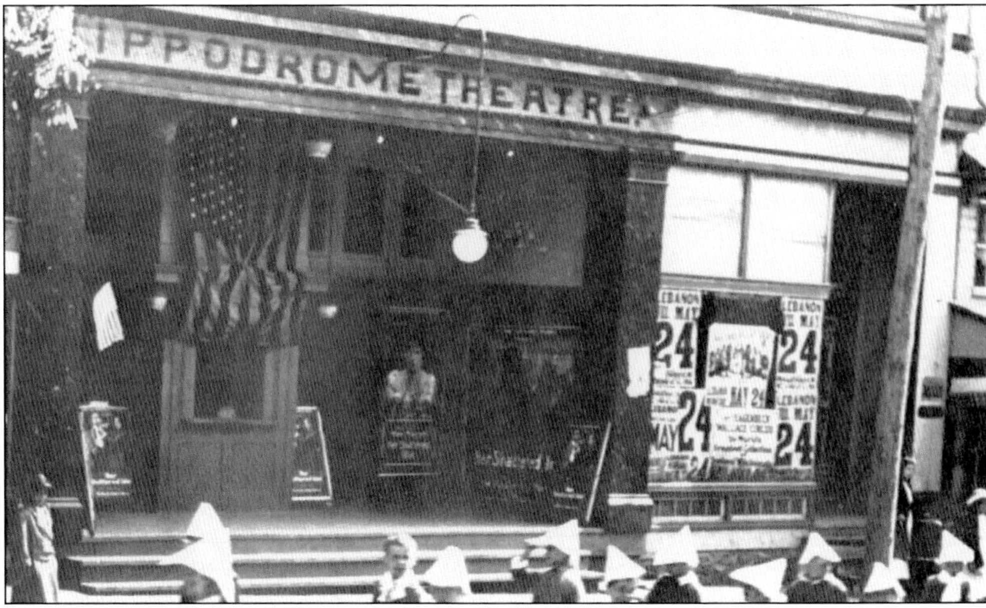

No. 36 East Main Street. The earliest manifestation of the movie theater at this site was known as the Hippodrome, shown here in the 1900s. The seating capacity of the Hippodrome was somewhat smaller than the Astor or the Allen that followed, occupying the front portion of the present building. Even in its earliest days, the business was operated as a "second-run" theater, showing movies at discounted rates after they left first-run theaters.

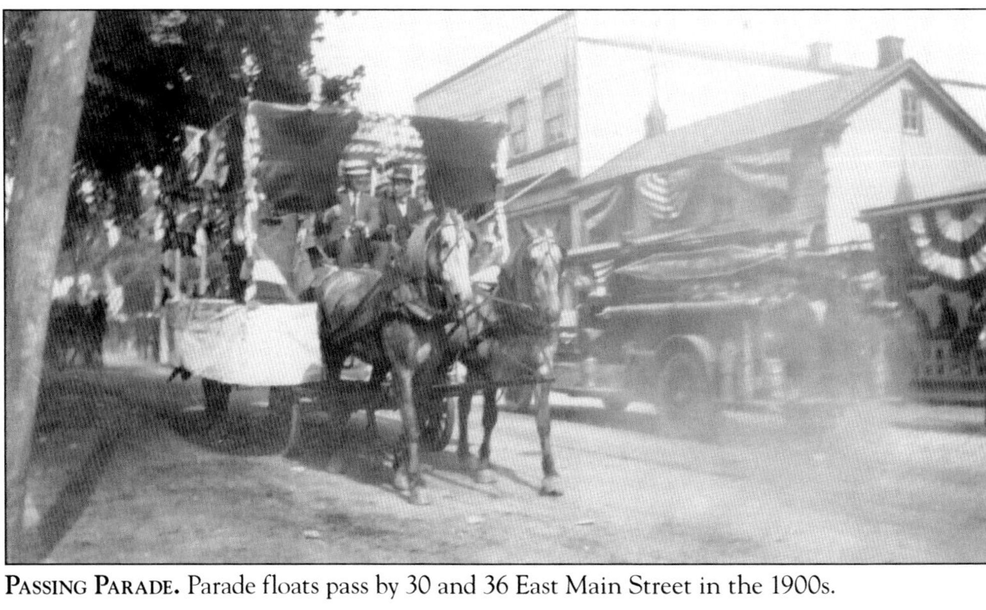

Passing Parade. Parade floats pass by 30 and 36 East Main Street in the 1900s.

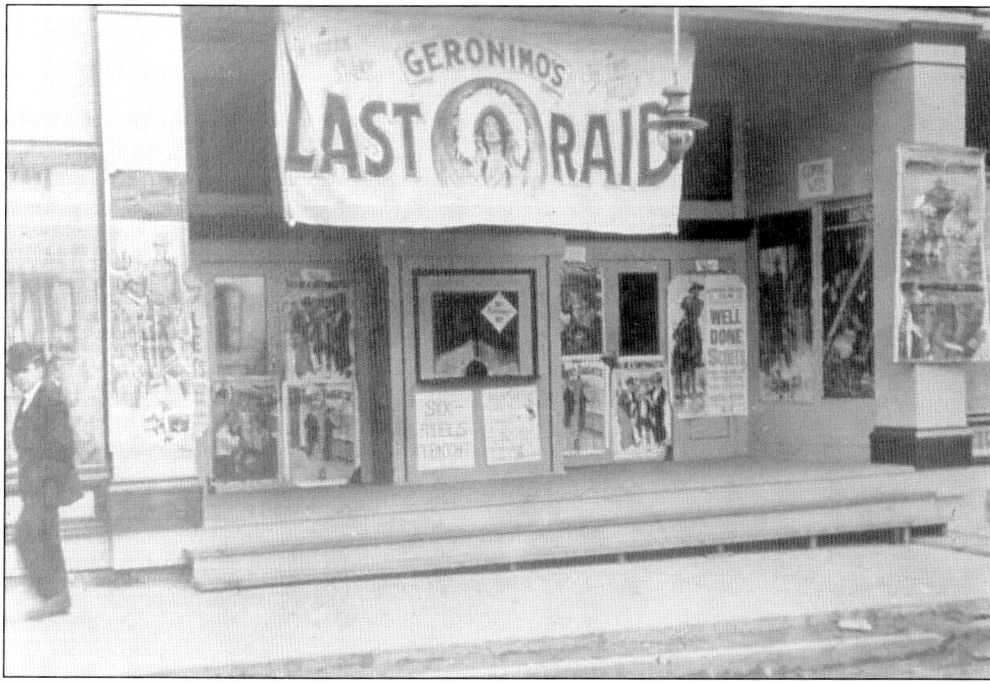

GERONIMO. As a second-run theater, the headlining of the feature film, *Geronimo's Last Raid*, suggests that this picture dates from a year or so after the movie's initial release in 1912. (Courtesy of Dick and Betty Streicher.)

NOS. 36, 38, 40, 42, AND 44 EAST MAIN STREET. Around the 1930s, new management changed the name of the theater from the Hippodrome to the Astor and expanded the seating capacity to 400 in 1942. Financial struggles in the early 1970s led theater management to resort first to pornographic films, then to religious productions. Eventually, the Astor closed in the early 1980s.

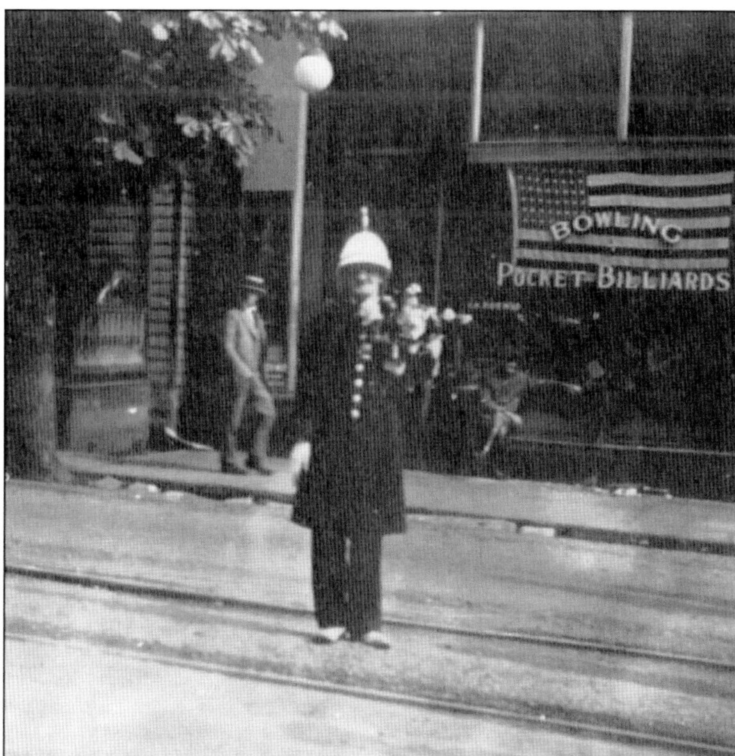

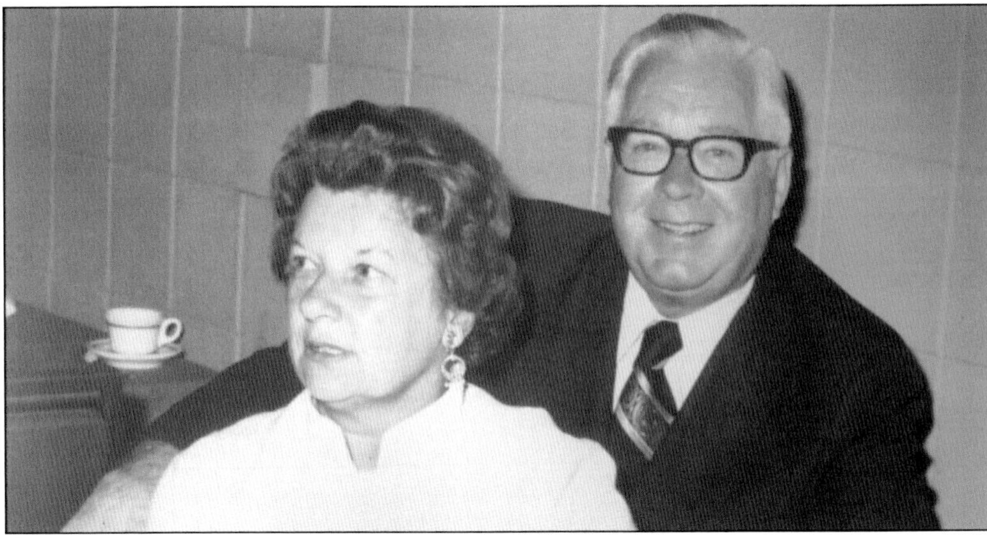

Allen and M.J. Hicks. When Mary Jane Hicks (1915–2006) won the Pennsylvania State Lottery, fortunes changed for the theater. Mary Jane funded the reopening of the facility under the direction of her son Skip Hicks. Its rededication on September 21, 1995, as the Allen (named in memory of Skip's father, Allen Hicks [1914–1981]), with the adjacent MJ's (Mary Jane's) Coffeehouse, is noted by many members of the community as the turning point in Annville's current renaissance. Under the continued personable management of Skip Hicks, the Allen was named one of the 12 best local movie theaters in the nation by www.moviefone.com in 2010. (Courtesy of the Hicks family.)

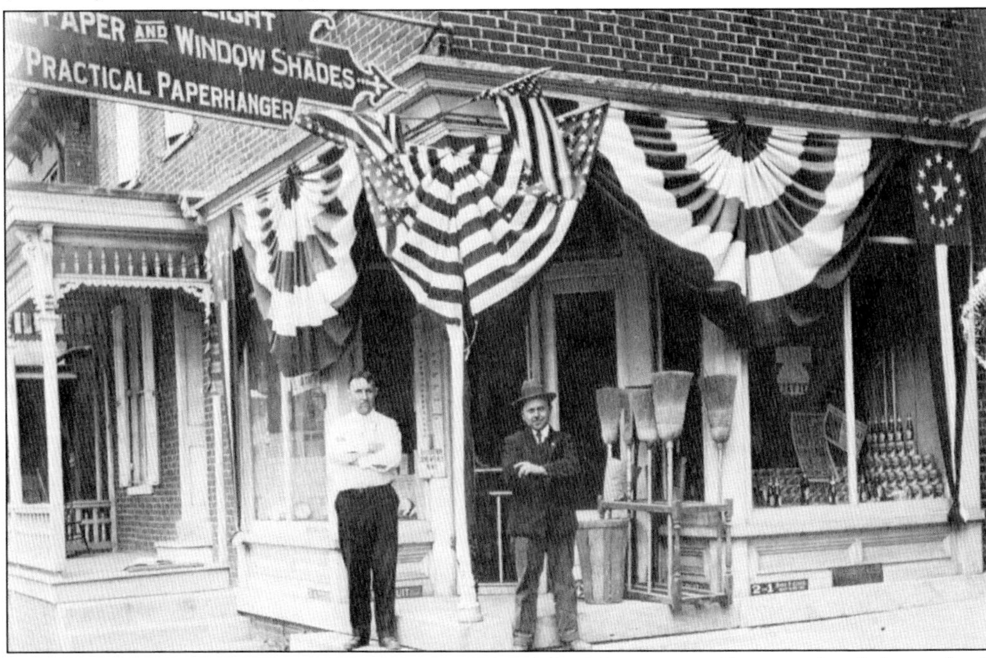

Nos. 44 and 45 East Main Street. At 44 East Main Street is a 13-room, brick house built around 1830 that served for many years as home and office to Dr. E.B. Marshall (1853–1931). Across from this house is the last building on the north side of the block, 45 East Main Street. Roy Light managed a successful business as a "paperhanger" here in the first half of the 20th century.

Seven

Nos. 100–200 East Main Street

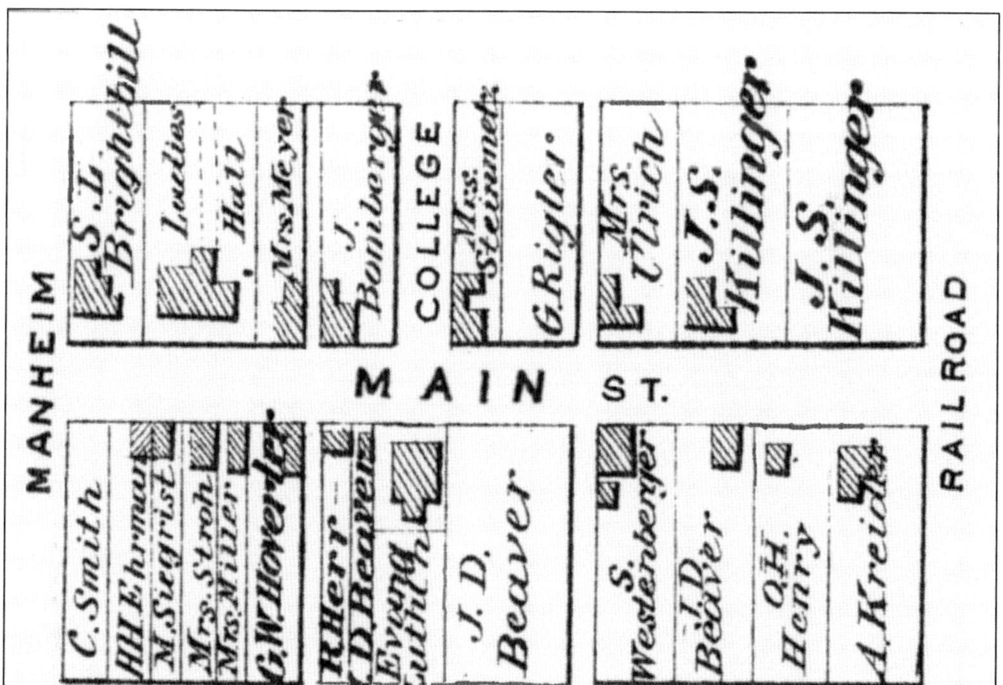

East Main's 100 Block, 1875 Map. This portion of the *County Atlas of Lebanon, Pennsylvania* details the building footings and residents' surnames from the 100 block through the 200 block of East Main Street as they existed in 1875.

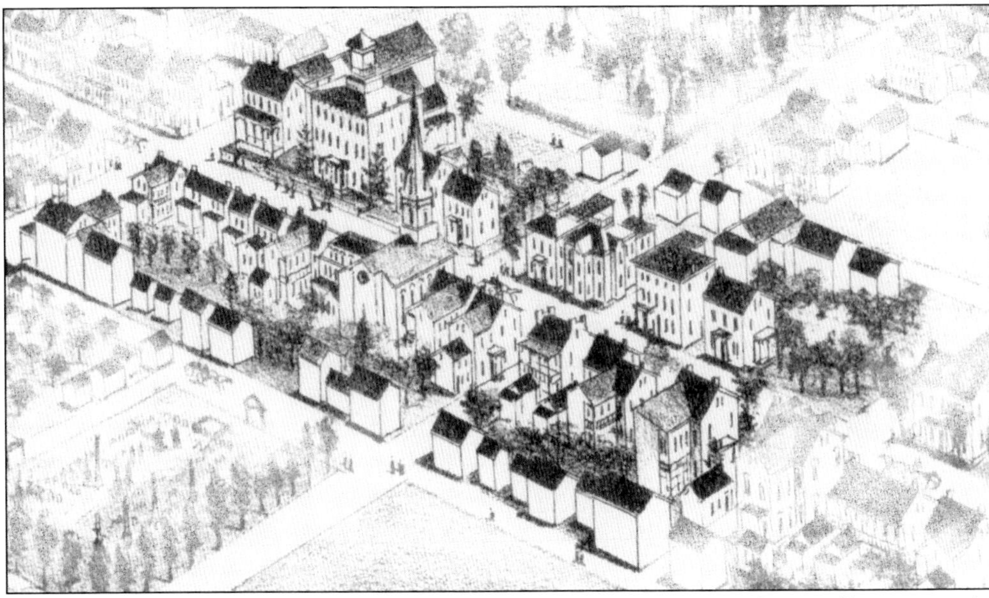

EAST MAIN'S 100 BLOCK, 1888 VIEW. T.M. Fowler's panoramic view of Annville portrays the buildings of the 100 block through the 200 block of East Main Street as they appeared from the southeast in 1888.

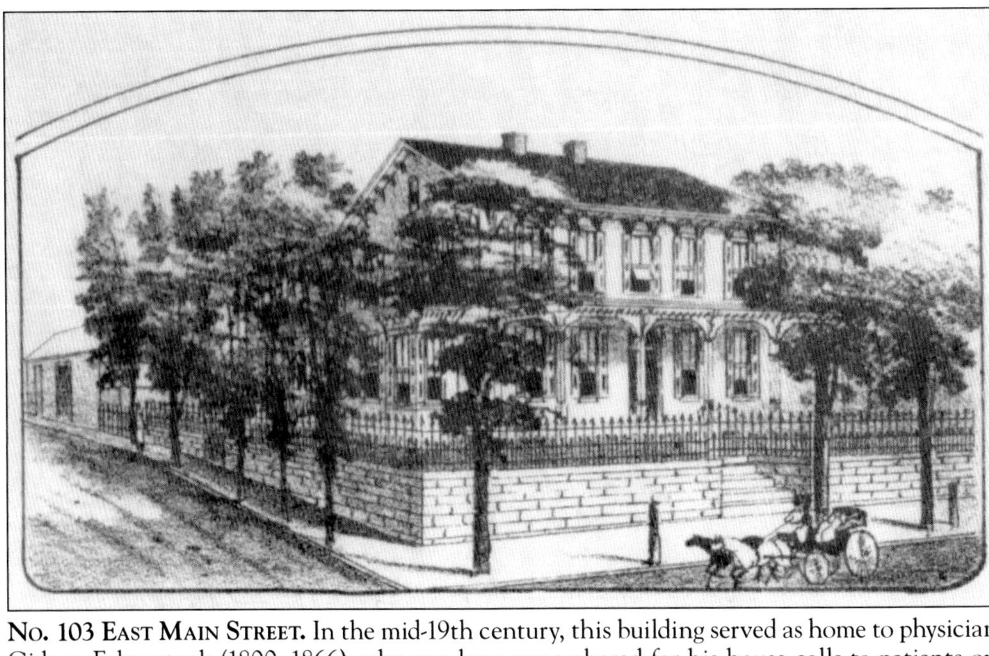

NO. 103 EAST MAIN STREET. In the mid-19th century, this building served as home to physician Gideon Fahnestock (1800–1866), who was long remembered for his house calls to patients on horseback. By 1875, the home belonged to Samuel L. Brightbill (1841–1898). Brightbill had made a comfortable living from his dealings in coal and lime.

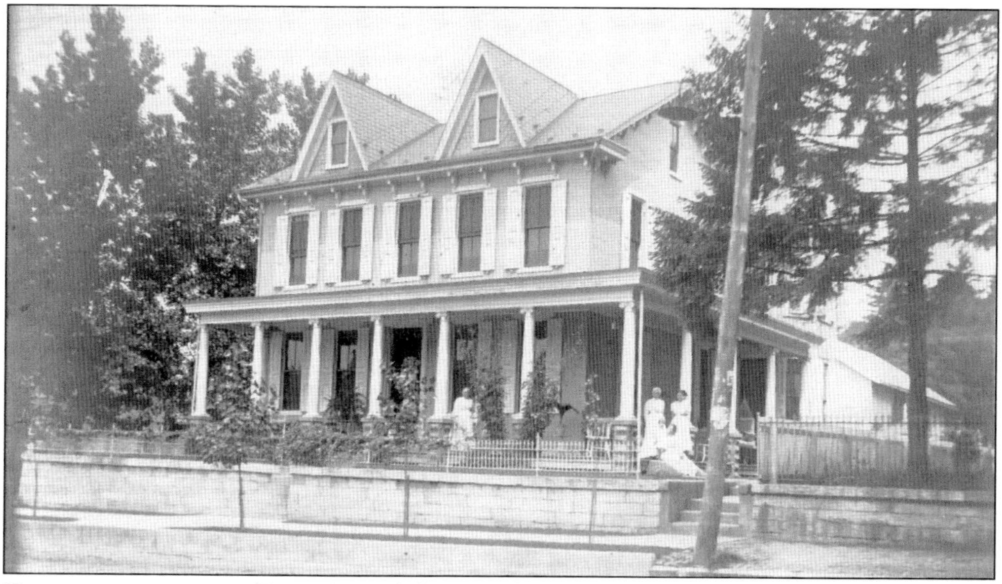

Transitions through Time. Around the time that the Sprague family lived at 103 East Main Street from the 1910s to the 1930s, the house was painted white, the porch was replaced, and two dormers were added to the third floor of the building. Rathburn Sprague earned his money as owner and manager of sugar plantations in Chapena, Cuba. Clyde Lynch, the president of Lebanon Valley College, moved into the home in 1949, but died the following year. The building was then used by the college to house students. After a significant renovation in 1990 that included a symmetrical addition to the northern end of the building, several administrative offices of the college were located here. (Courtesy of Robert and Suanne Long.)

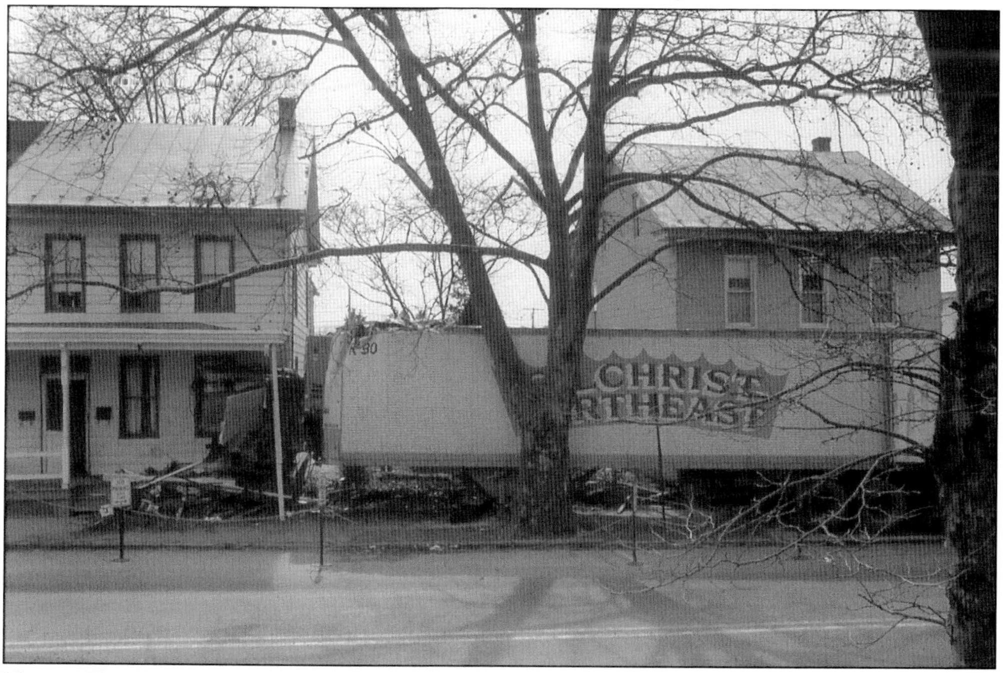

No. 108 East Main Street. In 1985, a truck drove into the porch of this home. A parked car and several other buildings were also struck in the accident, resulting in more than $200,000 total damage.

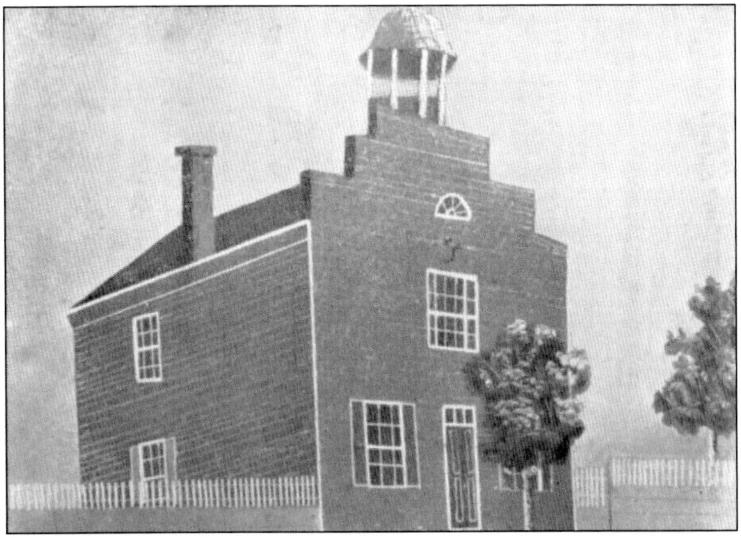

BOLLINGER PLAZA. The Annville Academy was established in this plaza as an educational institution in 1834. This sketch from Shenk's 1904 article on the academy details the building that served the institution at this location from 1836 to 1858. (See Bibliography.)

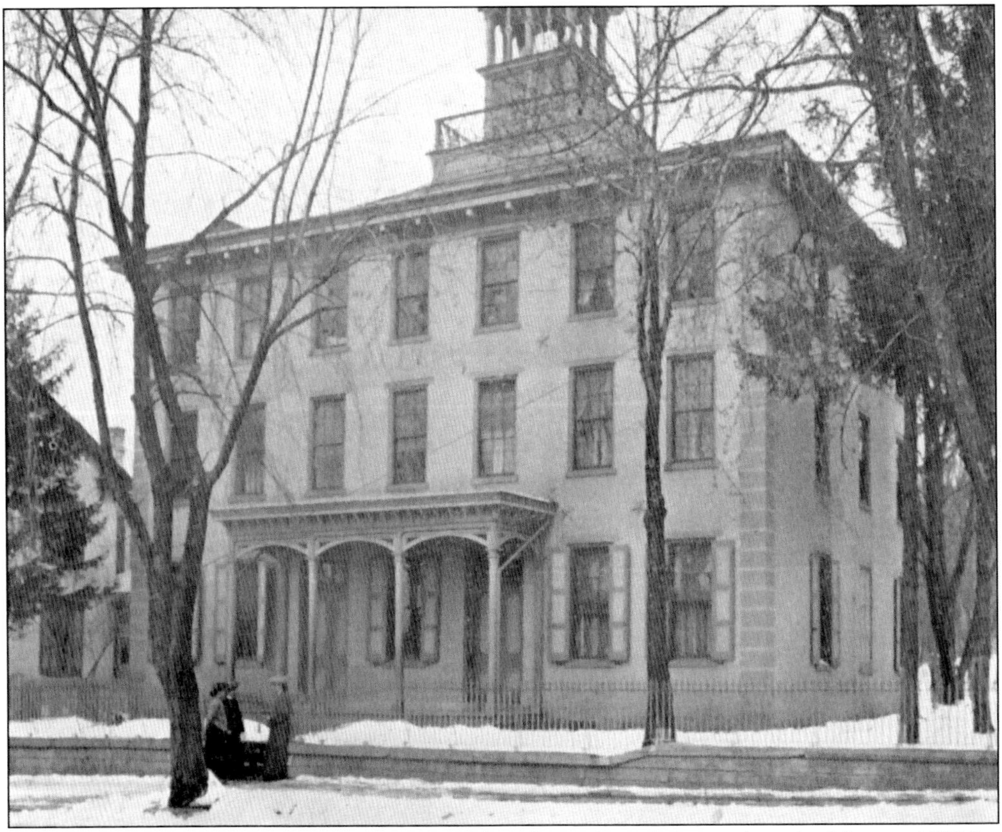

SOUTH HALL. Two years after Prof. Daniel Balsbaugh purchased the academy building in 1855, he razed the school and built the facility pictured here in its place. Balsbaugh called his school the Lebanon Valley Institute. In 1865, the new building was purchased by leaders of the United Brethren Church to "maintain there forever an institution of learning of higher grade," which would be called Lebanon Valley College. This structure was initially designated as Ladies' Hall and later as South Hall. The building was torn down in the early 1970s. (Courtesy of Dick and Betty Streicher.)

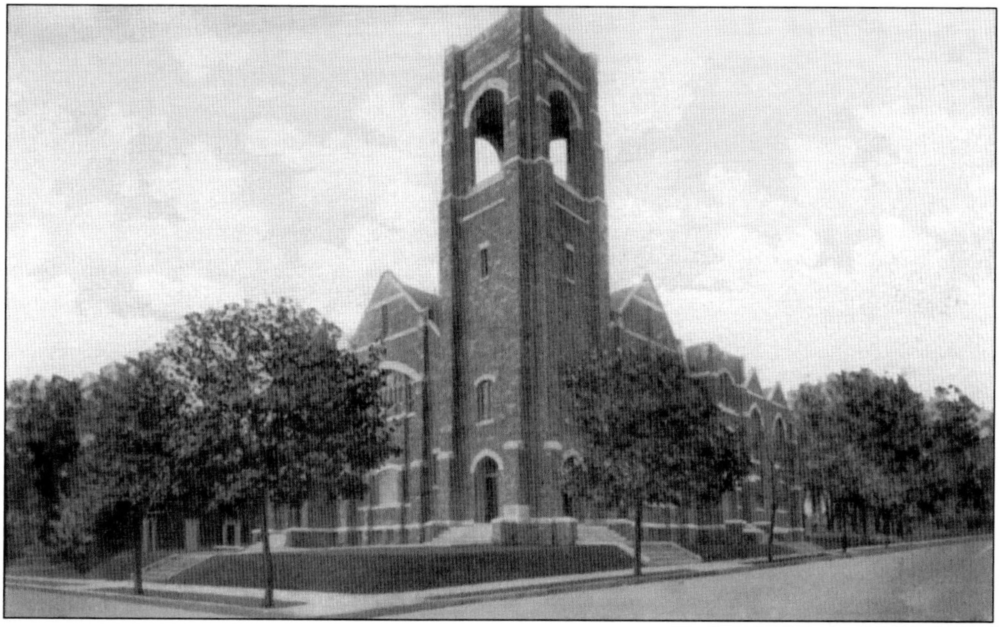

No. 1 North College Avenue. The congregation that built this church first worshipped at 49 South Mill Street, then at 118 West Main Street. (See pages 12 and 52, respectively.) The structure was dedicated as Annville United Brethren Church on November 7, 1912, to be a church for Lebanon Valley College, as well as for the community. In April 1968, a denominational merger led to the name Annville United Methodist Church (but note the inscription on the exterior wall facing East Main Street). The exterior of the building is constructed of King of Prussia Marble, also known as Pennsylvania Blue Marble. The interior utilizes the Akron Plan, employed by many Protestant churches at the turn of the century, which incorporates dividers into the sanctuary balcony such that separate classrooms could be utilized during the Sunday school hour. (Courtesy of Hughey May.)

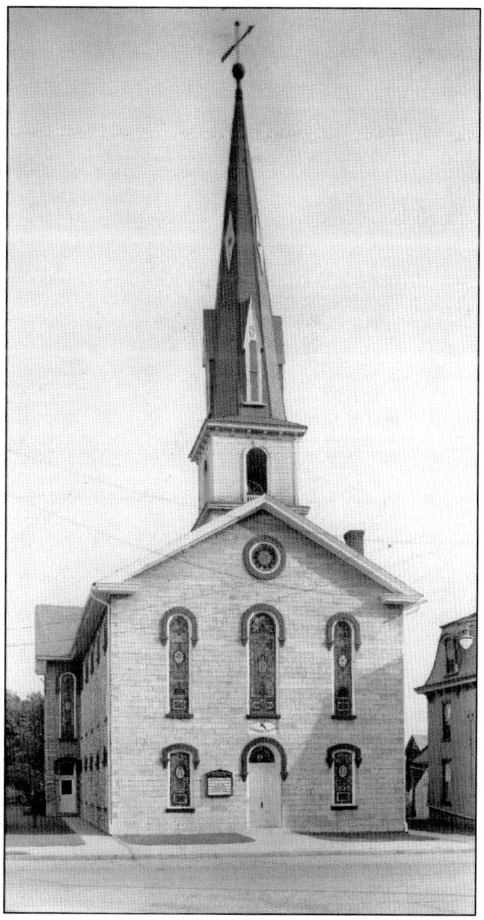

No. 200 East Main Street. In 1872, the Lutherans sold their share of the Jerusalem Church at 200 South White Oak Street (see page 10) to the Reformed Congregation and erected First Evangelical Lutheran Church at this site. The lot for the building, as well as a two-story sexton's house and the parsonage on the east side, was donated by John D. Beaver Jr. (See page 12.)

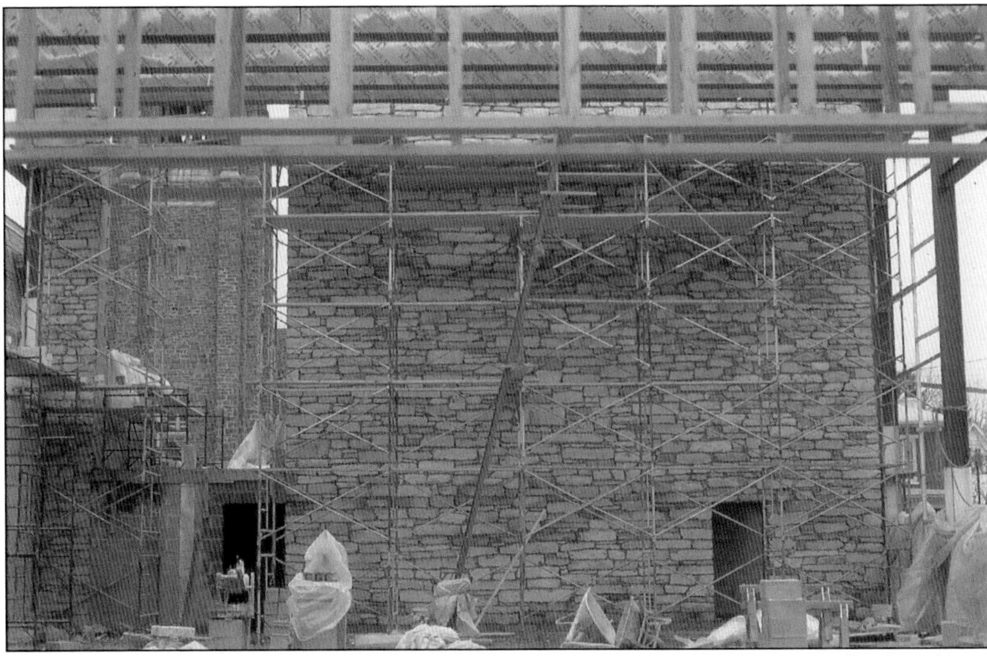

NEW FROM THE OLD. Shortly after merging with members of St. Paul's Evangelical Lutheran Church in 1968, the decision was made to raze the first structure and to build a new church on the site, dedicated in 1972. Stones from the old church were used to construct the east wall of the new sanctuary, which was named St. Mark Evangelical Lutheran Church. An observance of the 200th anniversary of Lutheranism in Annville on October 31, 2004, was marked by the dedication of a tower with three new bells, as well as the bells from First Lutheran and St. Paul's Lutheran, completing the merger visually and symbolically.

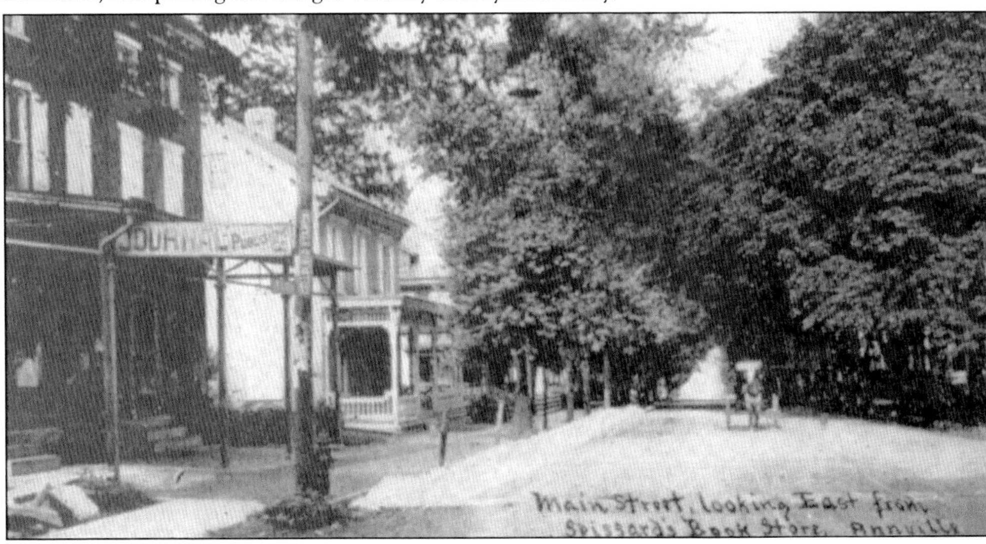

NO. 215 EAST MAIN STREET. At this location in 1887, Joseph Kreider established the *Annville Journal*, a newspaper that was "independent in politics" and issued every Saturday morning until 1938. Gilman's East End Grocery was also housed in this building. The sign on the post advertises that "celluloid starch," popular for shirts and collars at the turn of the century, could be purchased there.

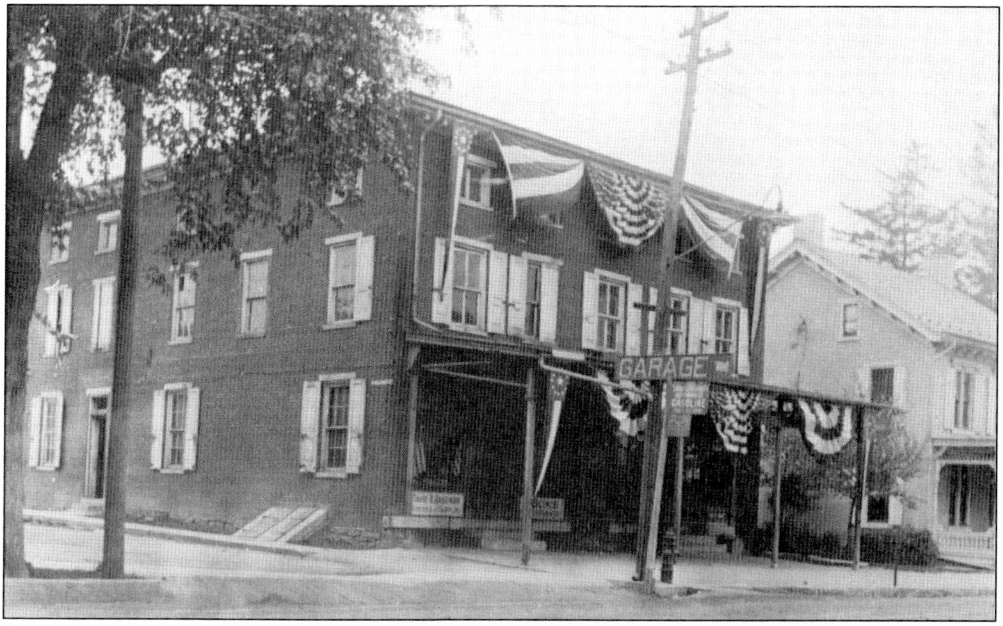

BOOKSTORE AND GARAGE. This picture of the Journal Building in the 1910s reveals Harnish and Smith Bookstore at the front west side (previously Spissard's Bookstore and David Basehore's Bookstore). Bolton's Garage was located at the same site. The building was razed in the early 1970s for the construction of new facilities for the Union Hose Fire Company, which were dedicated on April 30, 1972.

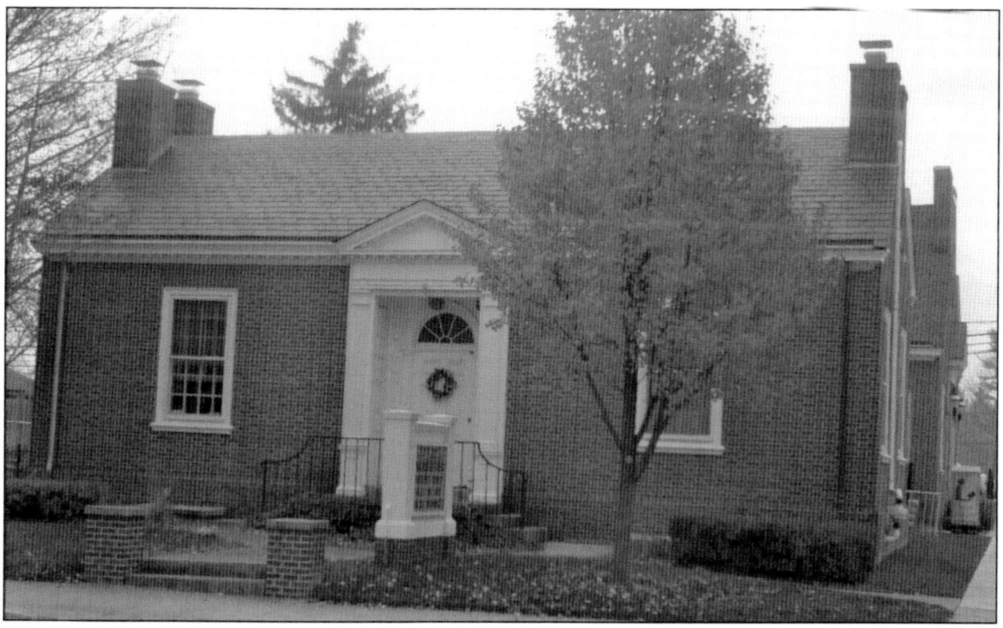

NO. 216 EAST MAIN STREET. In 1939, a group of eight mothers, led by Lillie Struble, started a book club for children in the storefront at 11 East Main Street. On January 23, 1941, the group was established as the Annville Free Library Association. Lacking a permanent home, however, the library was frequently relocated. Recognizing the need, Gideon R. and Alice Kreider financed the construction of this Colonial-style library in 1949.

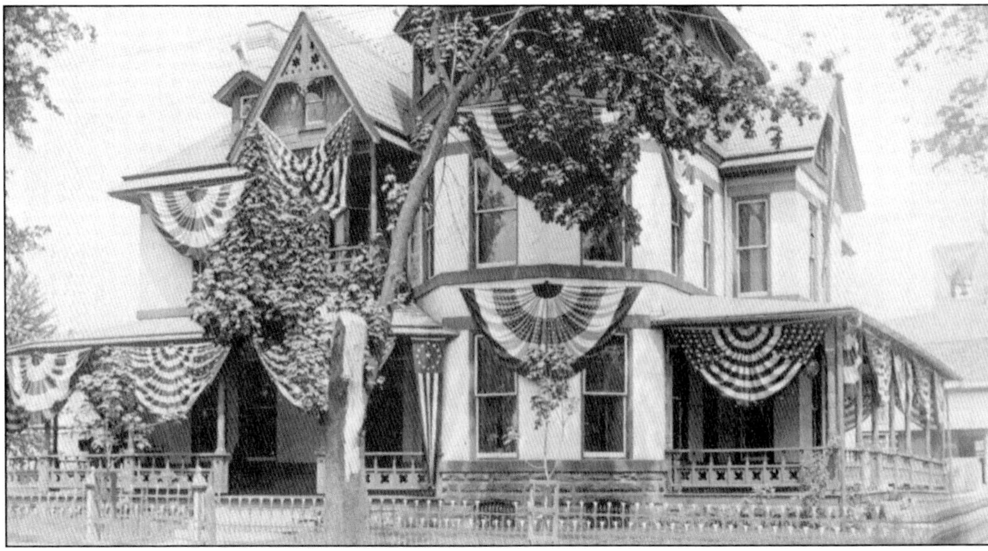

NO. 243 EAST MAIN STREET. This quintessential Queen Anne home was built prior to 1890 by David Saylor, a brother to carriage maker John L. Saylor. (See page 71.) David had developed successful businesses in coal and lumber. His company, David Saylor and Sons, completed the woodwork on many of the homes built in Annville and the surrounding area at the turn of the 20th century. Many innovative ideas were implemented in the construction of this particular home, the most unique, perhaps, being a system of rain spouts that led through the roof into a large tank positioned on its third floor. Rainwater that accumulated in the tank was used for the plumbing system, producing the first indoor bathrooms in Annville!

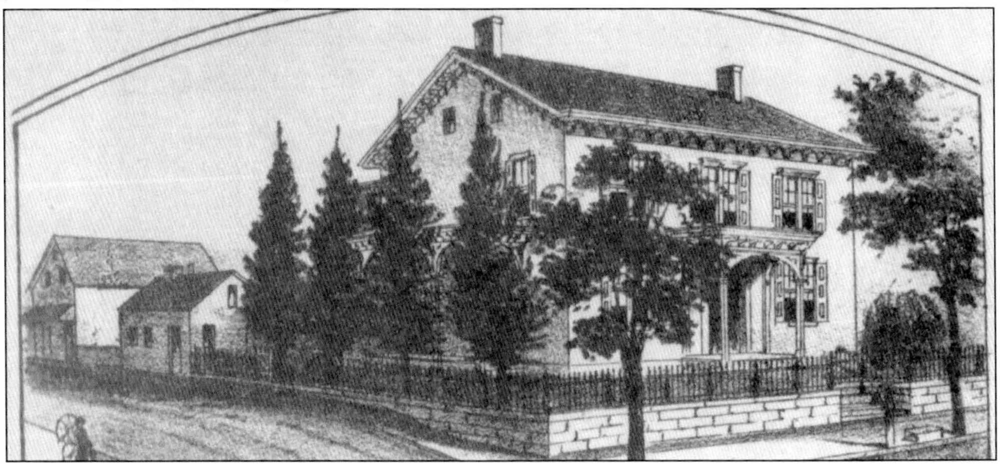

NO. 244 EAST MAIN STREET. As indicated by the inscription in the limestone step at its main entrance, this home was built by Andrew and Emma Kreider in 1867. Members of his immediate family lived here for 99 years until his daughter Anna Kreider retired to assisted living in 1963 at age 90. At some point during that time, ornate stoops at the front and side of the house were replaced by a wraparound porch. The large knob to the right of the front door is the original pull-knob doorbell. The wrought-iron fence that encircles the property is also an original feature of the house. As Ralph and Mildred Shanaman, who purchased the home in 1966, worked to restore the walls of the basement, they discovered that a newspaper from the year 1800 had been tucked between the rocks of the limestone foundation and featured an ode to George Washington (who had recently passed away) and a letter by John Adams.

Eight

Nos. 300–500 East Main Street

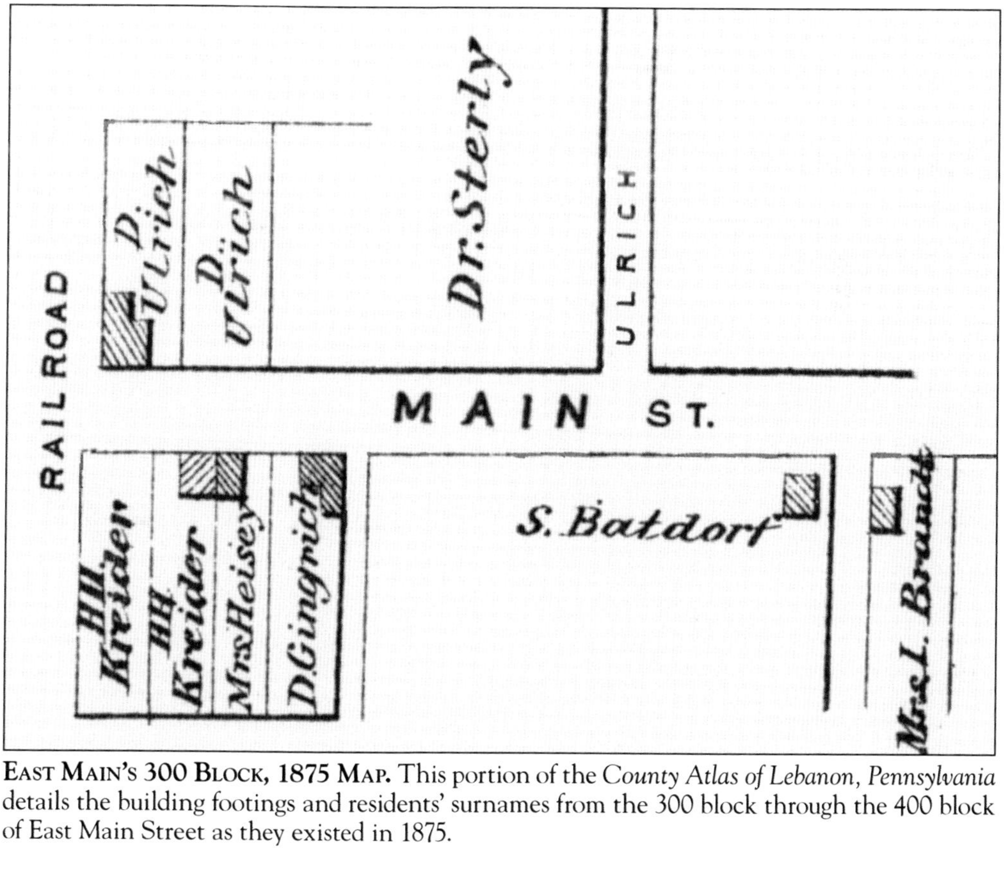

East Main's 300 Block, 1875 Map. This portion of the *County Atlas of Lebanon, Pennsylvania* details the building footings and residents' surnames from the 300 block through the 400 block of East Main Street as they existed in 1875.

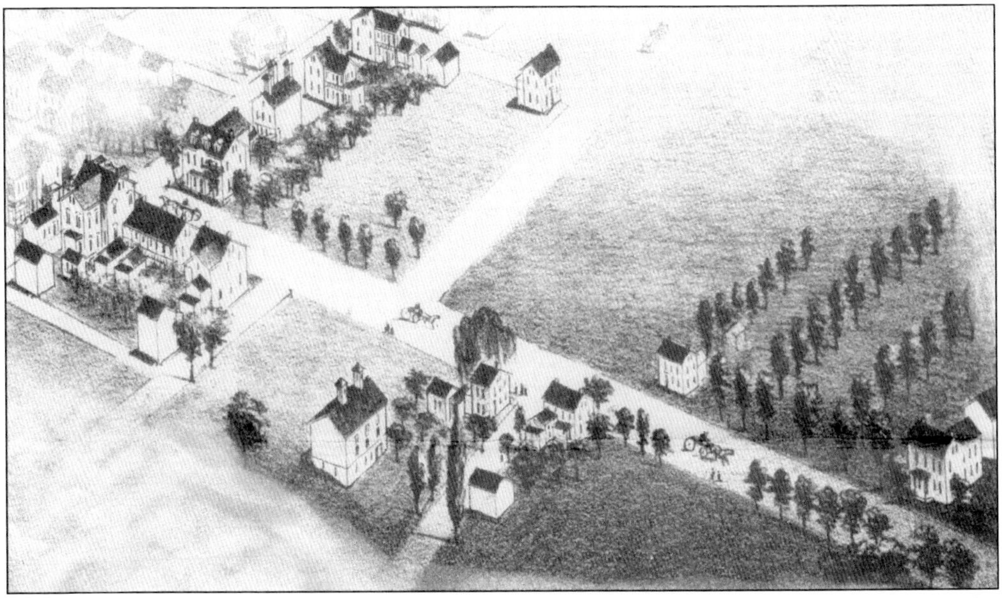

EAST MAIN'S 300 BLOCK, 1888 VIEW. T.M. Fowler's panoramic view of Annville portrays the buildings of the 300 block through the 400 block of East Main Street as they appeared from the southeast in 1888.

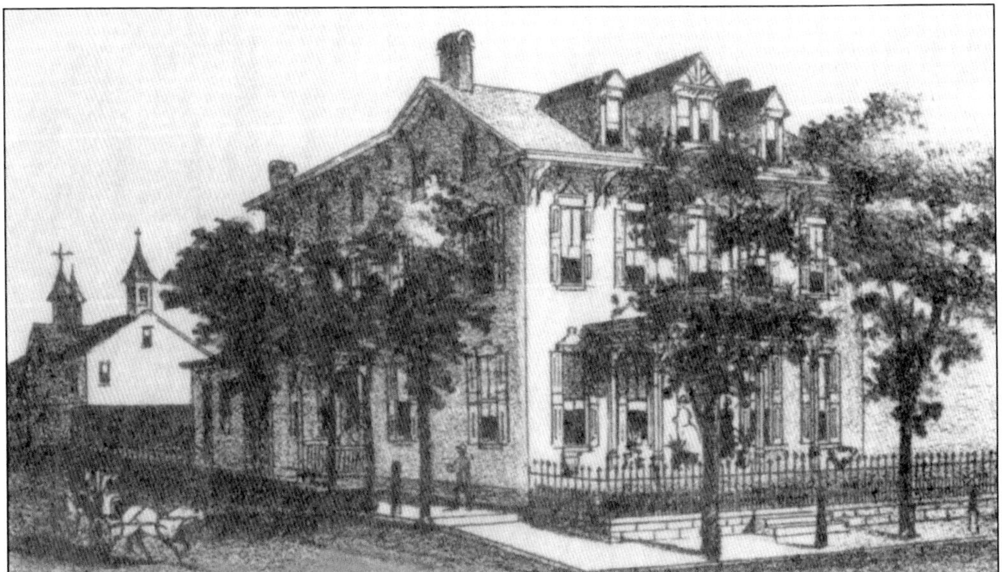

NO. 301 EAST MAIN STREET. This home, built by John L. Saylor sometime before 1875, is constructed of brick that has been covered with siding. (See page 71.) In the early 1900s, H.W. Miller, the owner of the hardware store at 18 East Main Street, lived here with his family. (See page 79.)

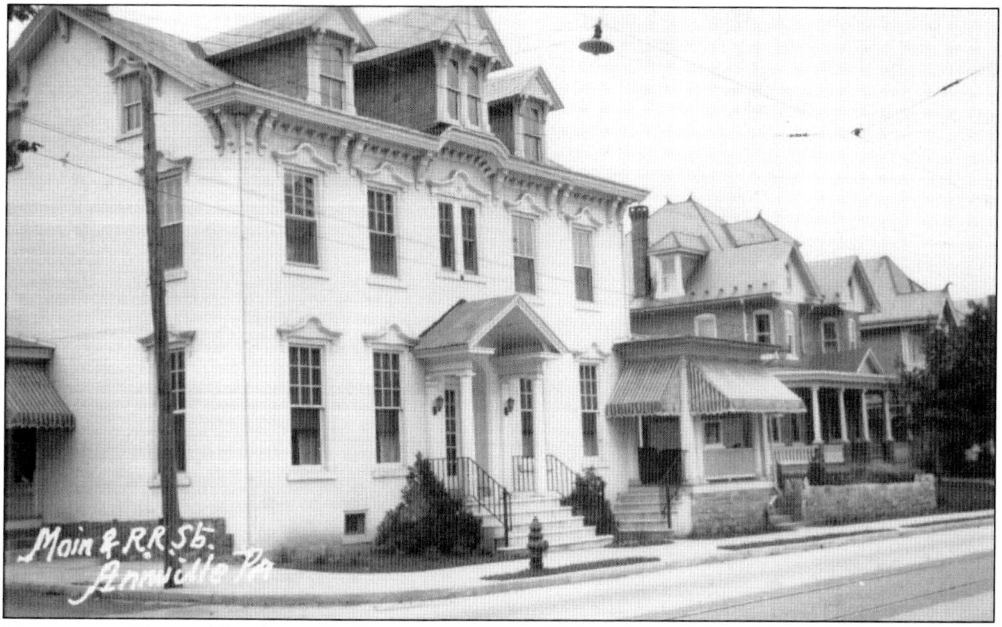

MONTEITH HOME. No. 301 East Main Street was next purchased by local physician James Monteith (1909–1978), then the Stalnecker family. Tom and Julie Tshudy renovated the home as the Patriot House Bed and Breakfast in 2008. (Courtesy of Blanche Schaeffer.)

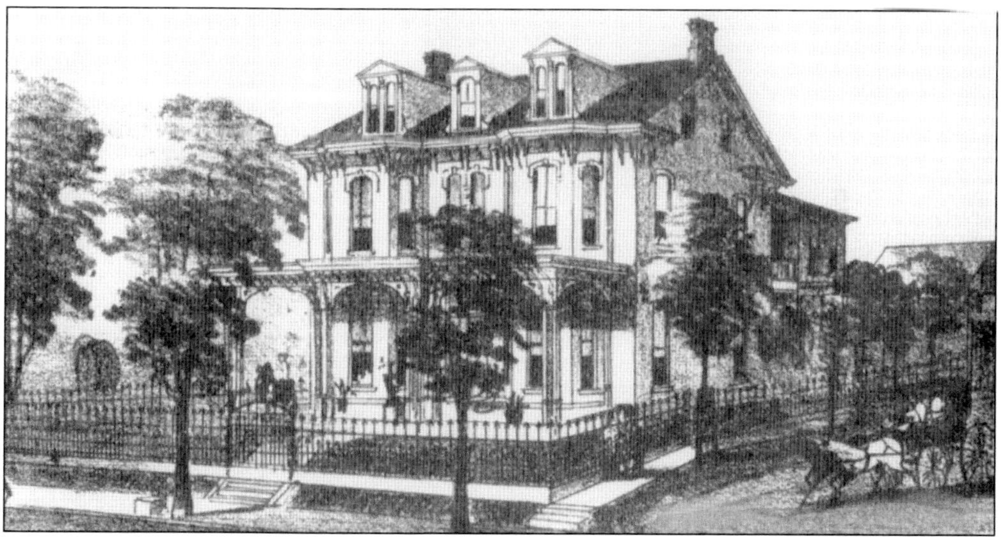

NO. 304 EAST MAIN STREET. Henry H. Kreider, whose older brother Andrew lived across the alley at 244 East Main Street, built a home here sometime between 1875 and 1888. The house was distinguished as one of the first to have electric lighting, which Henry accomplished by connecting the wiring in the house to the trolley lines that ran along Main Street. The lower half of the house was significantly remodeled into apartments in the late 20th century. Somewhat ironically, the house burned to the ground in 2000 as a result of an electrical fire. The current private, Victorian-style residence on this site, built in 2008, utilizes the foundation of the original property. (Courtesy of Blanche Schaeffer.)

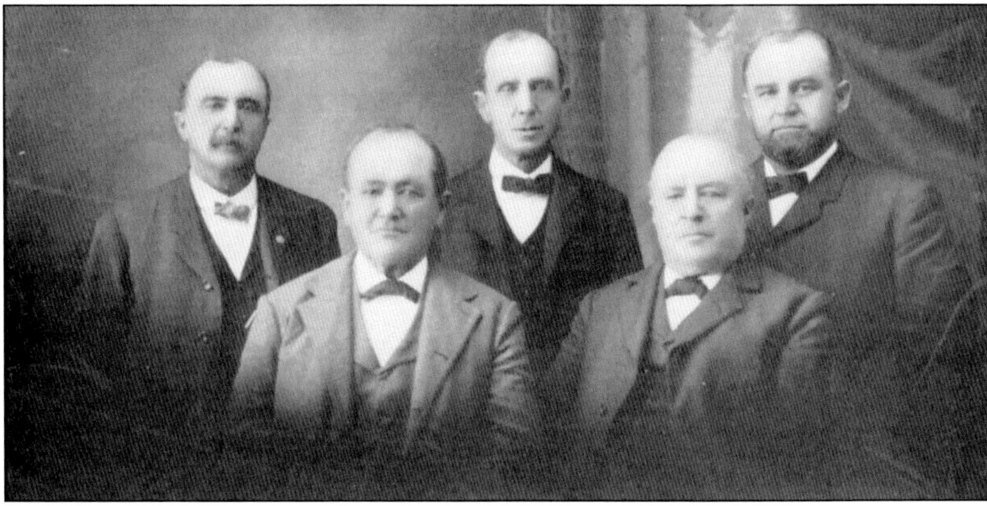

THE KREIDER BROTHERS. Five of the 10 sons of David Kreider, who farmed land on the 300 and 400 blocks of South White Oak Street, all lived within a few blocks of each other in Annville. They are, from left to right, Joseph H. Kreider (206 North College Avenue, see page 117), David Kreider Jr. (83 East Sheridan Avenue, see page 118), Henry H. Kreider (304 and 308 East Main Street), Andrew Kreider (244 East Main Street, see page 94), and Aaron S. Kreider (515 East Main Street, see page 104). Their half-sister Lydia Kreider Kettering lived at 327 East Main Street.

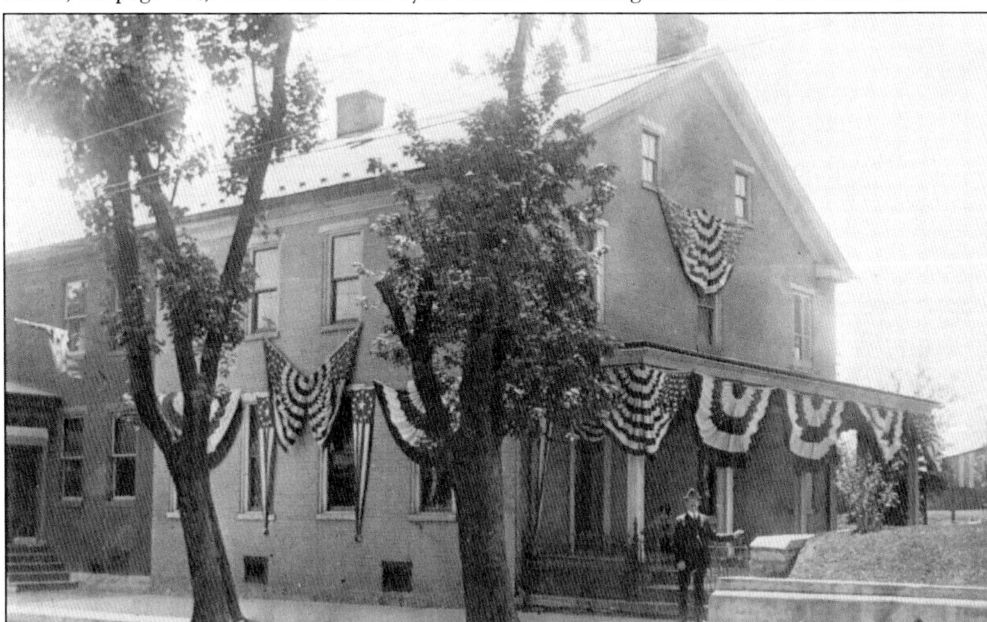

NO. 308 EAST MAIN STREET. Henry H. Kreider built this house in the 1860s as his first private residence. H.H. was an active citizen in Annville, serving as a lumber and coal merchant, treasurer and trustee of Lebanon Valley College, vice president of Annville National Bank, and president of the Annville Water Company, among other roles. When he moved to his second house next door (304 East Main Street), he gave 308 East Main Street to his son Morris, who left the home to his daughter Elizabeth and her husband, Charles Ristenbatt (pictured here). Owen and Kathy Moe purchased the home from the estate of Elizabeth Ristenbatt in 1975.

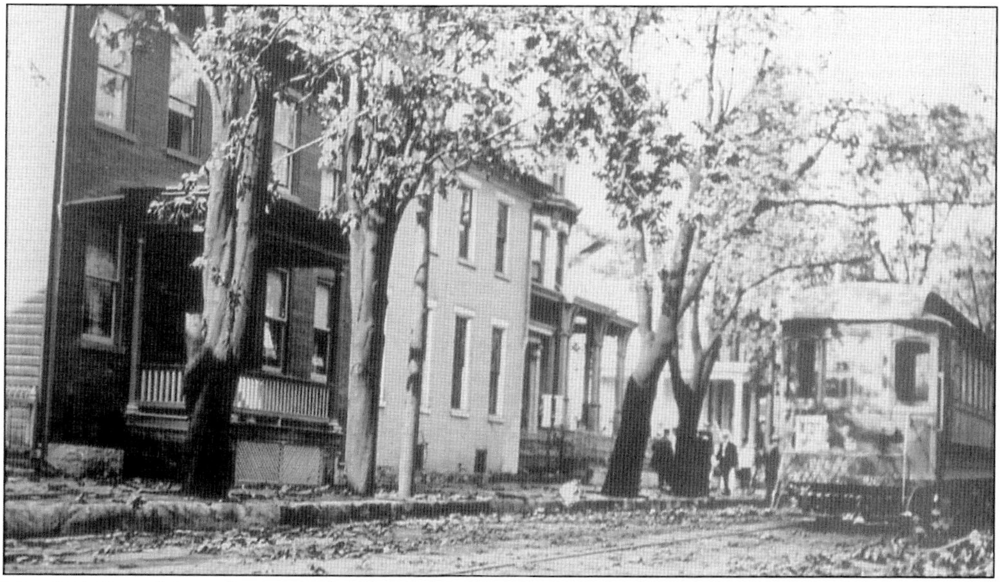

No. 314 East Main Street. This home, pictured to the far left of the trolley stop, was built for and owned by a single woman, Elizabeth Heisey, in the 1860s and inherited matrilineally for over 80 years by Mary Heisey Gingrich, Alice Cowell, Emma Gingrich, and Sallie Risser. The Buck family purchased the residence in 1949 and lived there until 1988, when the current residents, Helen Traglia and Thomas Hockley, purchased the home. (Courtesy of Dick and Betty Streicher.)

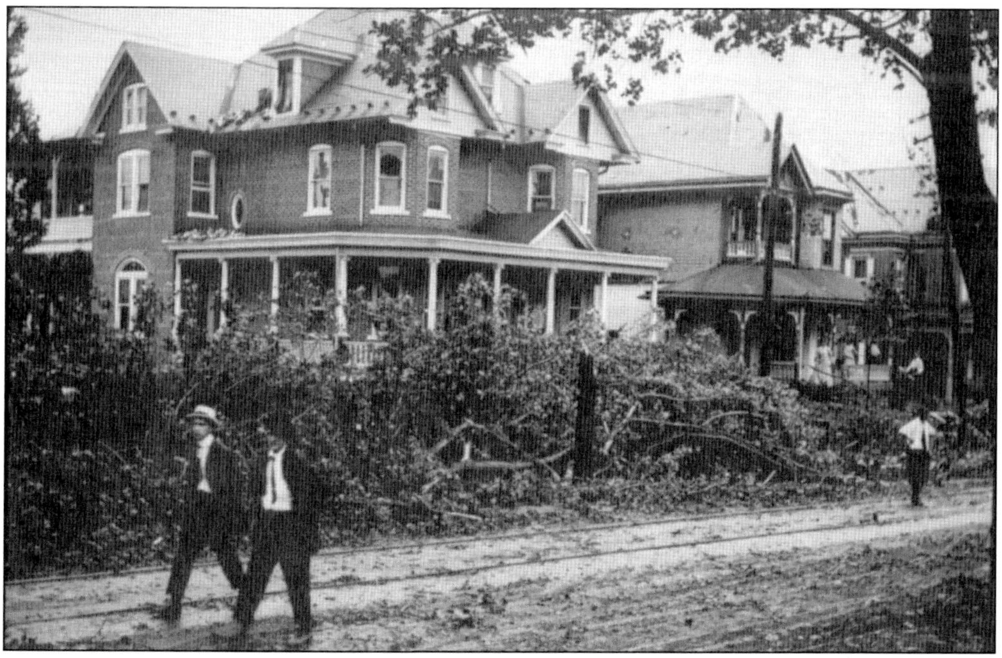

Nos. 313 and 315 East Main Street. This picture shows the north side of the 300 block of East Main Street in August 1915, shortly after a cyclone blew through Annville. (See page 13 for an overview of the cyclone's path.)

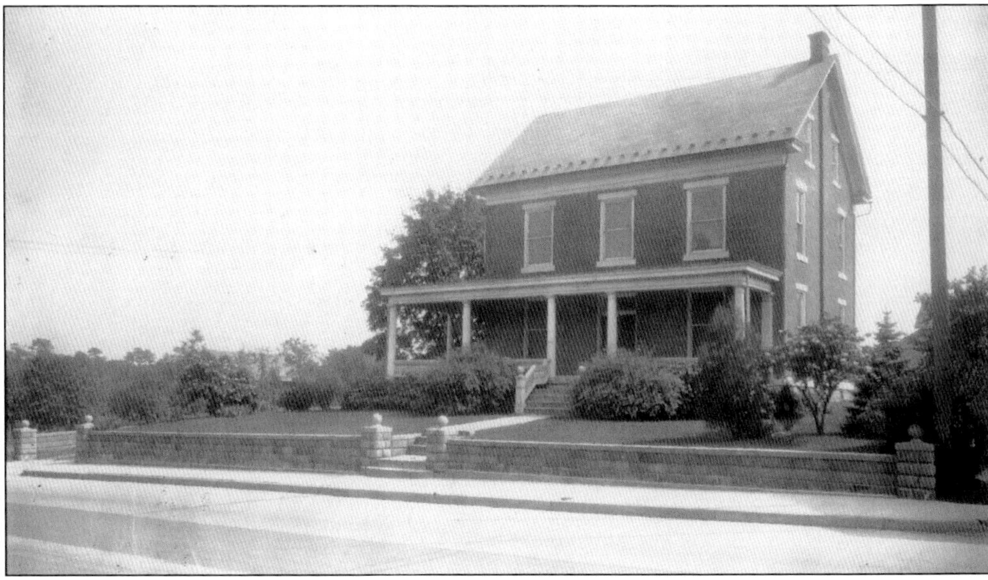

No. 330 East Main Street. This home was built around 1900 by Tobias Bomberger, who established Annville's first electric company in 1902. In 1933, Bomberger was struck and killed by a vehicle while crossing East Main Street. The house was sold to Bryl and Louise Nye in 1934, who grew prize orchids in a greenhouse at the back of the property. In the 1940s, the wraparound porch deteriorated and was dismantled. Bryl died after falling from a ladder on the property in 1975; the following year, the house was sold to the Gacono family, owners of Prudential Gacono Real Estate (50 West Main Street). In 1984, the property transferred to David and Ruth Troxell, who sold the home to Michael and Laura Charelian in 2007. (Courtesy of Laura and Michael Charelian.)

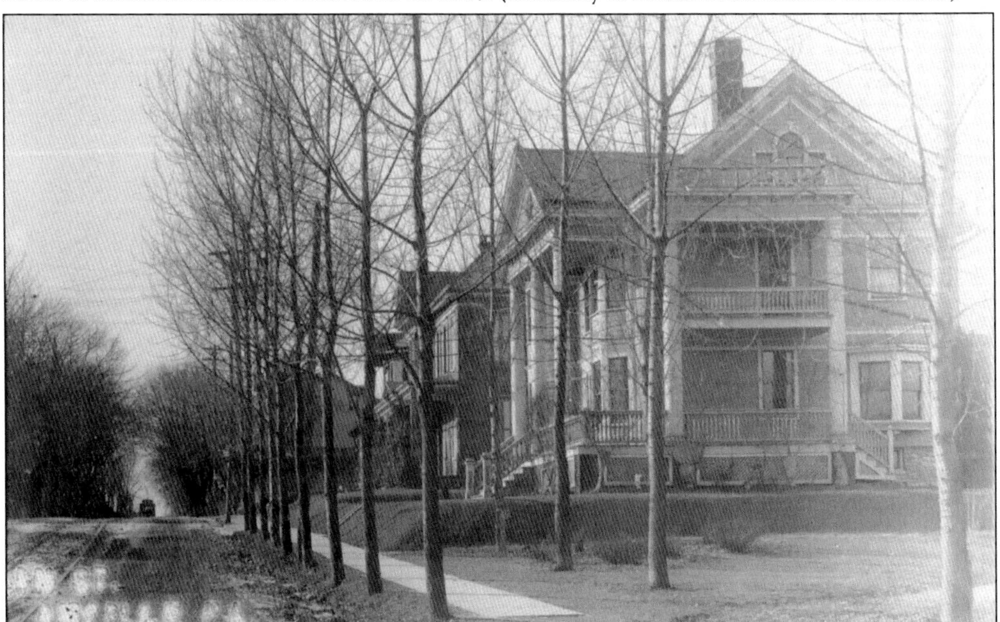

No. 337 East Main Street. In the 1890s, the Hartz family built this home in a Neoclassical style, which was somewhat unusual for the area. Note the tall trees that lined East Main Street in the early 1900s. (Courtesy of Blanche Schaeffer.)

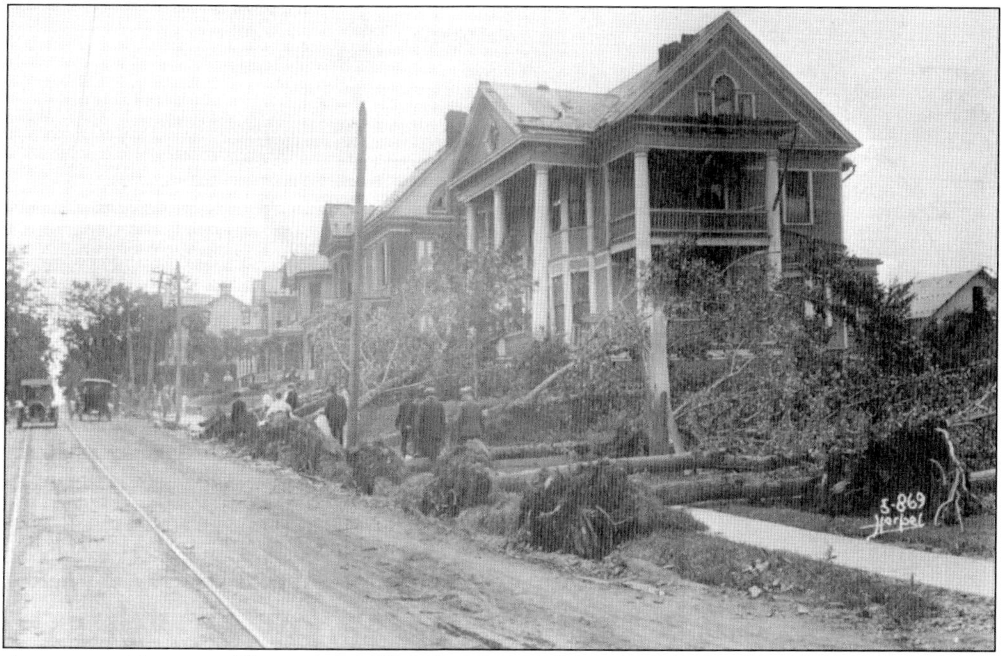

AFTER THE CYCLONE. The cyclone of 1915 uprooted the trees in front of the Hartz residence and twisted the easternmost front column of the building off of its base. The house later served as the longtime residence of the Paul J. Burke family.

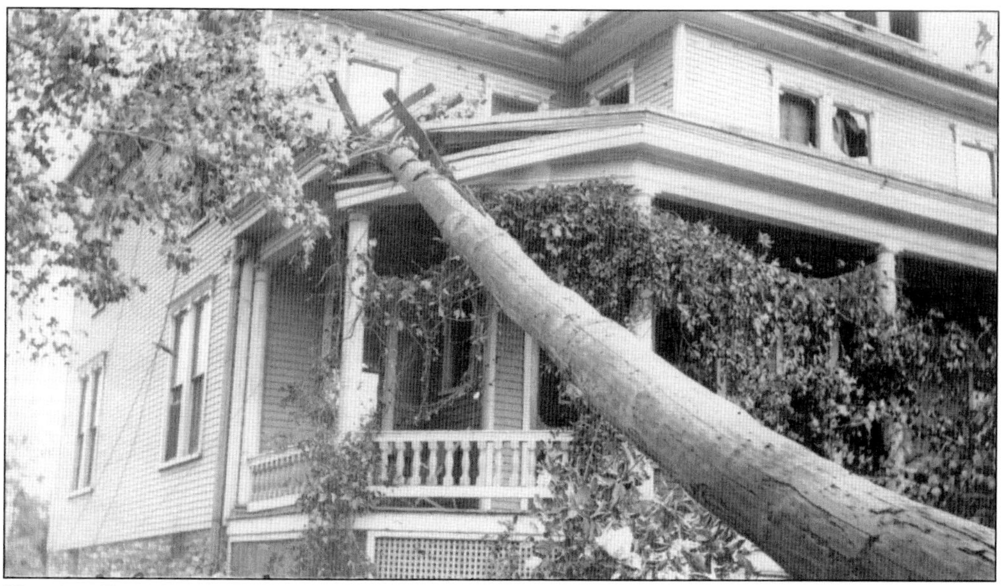

NO. 403 EAST MAIN STREET. A telephone pole knocked down by the 1915 cyclone damaged the porch of John E. Lehman, a professor of mathematics and astronomy at Lebanon Valley College from 1887 to 1928.

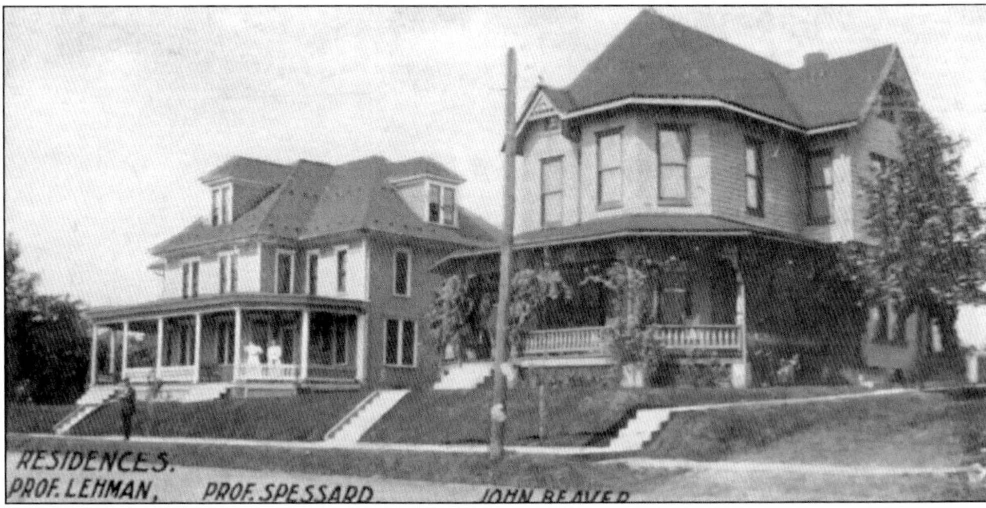

Nos. 403, 405, 411, and 413 East Main Street. Harry E. Spessard, a professor of English and Latin at LVC from 1898 to 1912, lived at 405 East Main Street next to Professor Lehman, earning the area the title "Professor's Row" at the time. When Alma Light lived at 405 East Main Street from 1930 to 1959, the house came to be known as the "Lighthouse." The residence at 413 East Main Street, built for the Beaver family in 1896, is distinctive in part due to its exterior shingle-work.

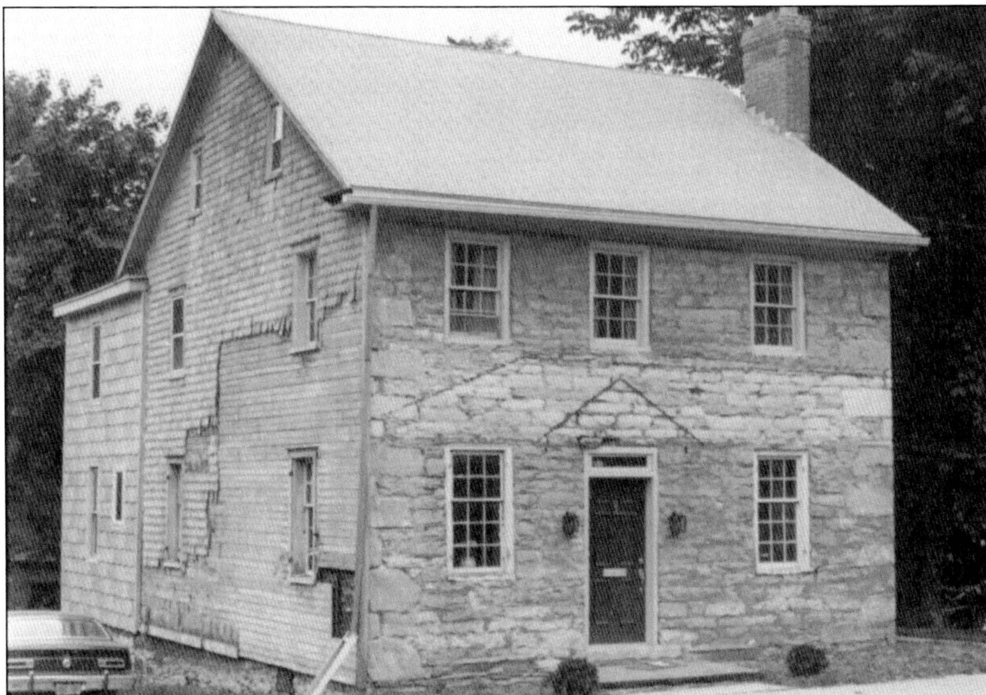

No. 414 East Main Street. According to lifelong Annville resident and local historian Anna Kreider, George Washington stopped at a tavern located here on his way west. This picture of the building was taken before its current owners, Bob and Carol Werni, renovated the early 18th-century limestone farmhouse in the early 1980s. "The Barn," located to the rear of the property, housed Annville Frozen Food Service in the 1970s and 1980s and now provides office space for a firm that specializes in advanced mathematics. (Courtesy of Bob and Carol Werni.)

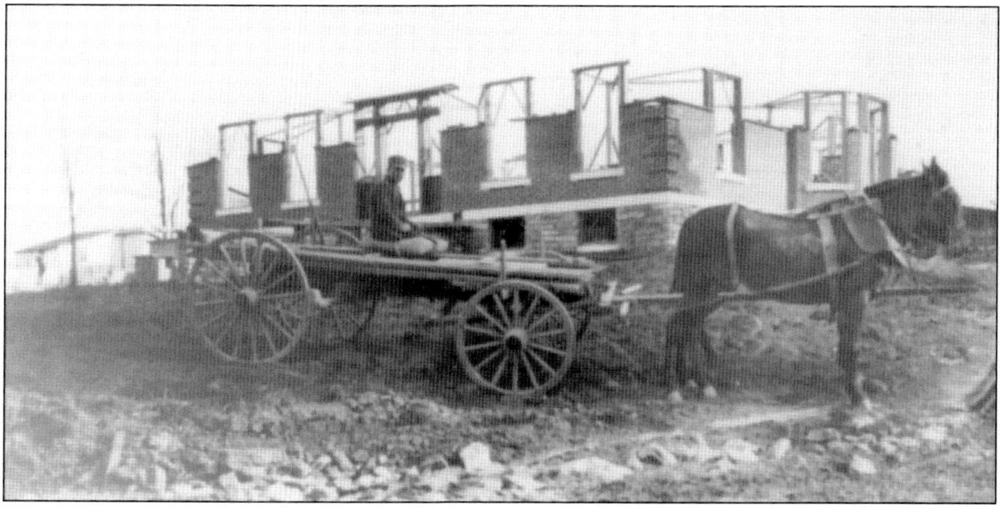

No. 444 East Main Street. In November 1905, four teams of horses hauled 369 loads of dirt and limestone to this location for the grading of the property. The men who drove the teams earned 12¢ an hour. Pages of detailed notes and pictures from the construction of the house as coordinated by its original owners, Bishop Job and Mary Mills, remain there today. When Edith Mills, the daughter-in-law of Bishop Mills (who was also a local musician of note), died in 1978, the house was purchased by a young artist named Bruce Johnson and his family. Here, at "Gallery 444," the Johnsons sold Bruce's highly coveted watercolors and line drawings. As a result of remarkable success, Bruce was featured on the cover of the April 1994 edition of *Money* magazine. In 2005, the historic home of "the Bishop of LVC" was sold to the incoming chaplain of the college, Paul Fullmer, and his family, who live there presently. (Courtesy of Paul and Becky Fullmer.)

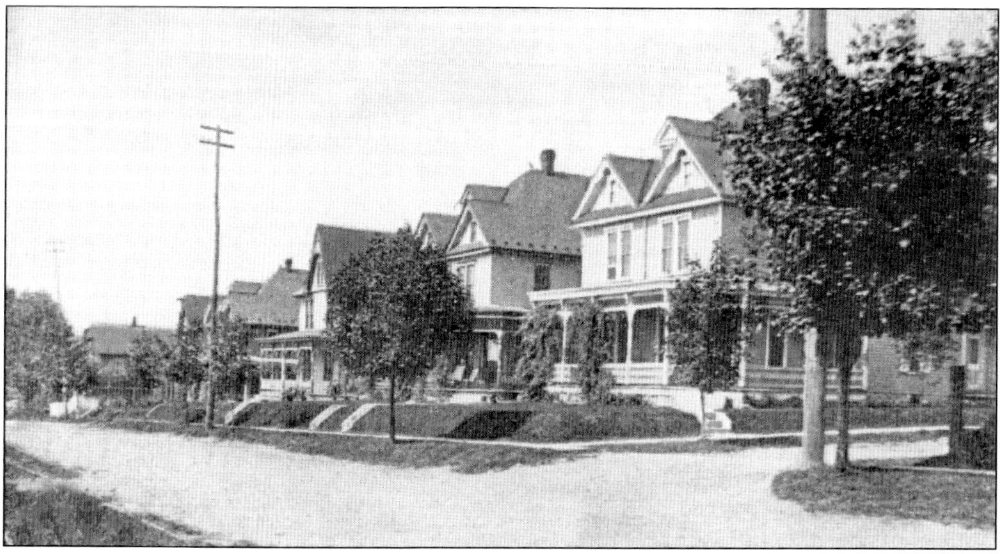

Nos. 459–461, 467–469, and 471–473 East Main Street. These large residences, built in the late 19th century, constituted "Professors Row" at the turn of the 20th century. The home at 467–469 was built by Dane Eberly, professor of Latin language and literature at LVC from 1876 to 1884. Professor Eberly's entire estate was willed to the college upon his death in 1910, establishing a professorship in languages and an interest-free student loan fund.

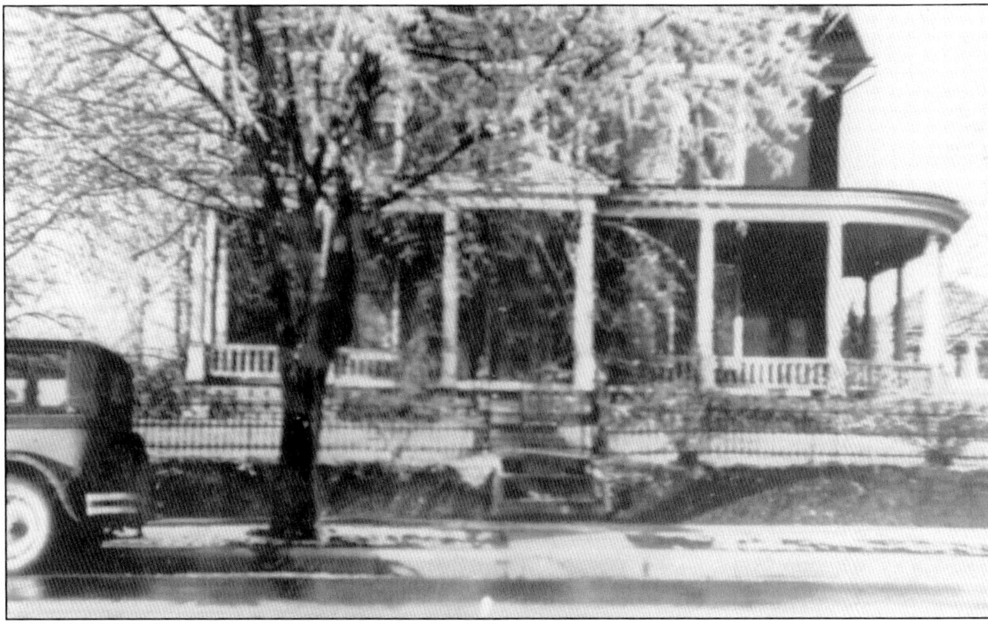

NO. 515 EAST MAIN STREET. This stately home was built around 1898 by Aaron S. Kreider, the youngest son of David Kreider Sr. (See pages 97–98.) A.S. Kreider was a prominent grain merchant and owner of a large shoe factory in Annville. (See page 116.) Though difficult to discern, this rare early picture of the house inspired David and Jill Palanzo to rebuild the large wraparound porch in 2007. The wrought-iron fence and circular driveway are original to the house. (Courtesy of David and Jill Palanzo.)

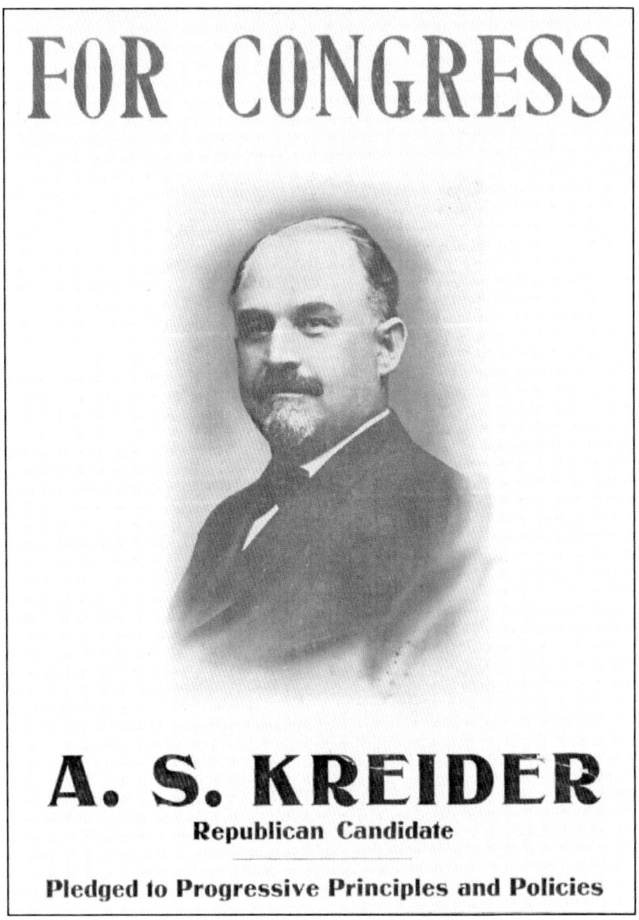

CAMPAIGN POSTER. Following a successful run for the US Congress in 1912, A.S. Kreider served as Pennsylvania's 18th District representative from 1913 to 1923. In 1921, the house at 515 East Main Street was sold to Alvin Kettering, whose daughters would establish the Jigger Shop in Mount Gretna prior to World War II.

Nine

Nos. 500–300 East Maple Street

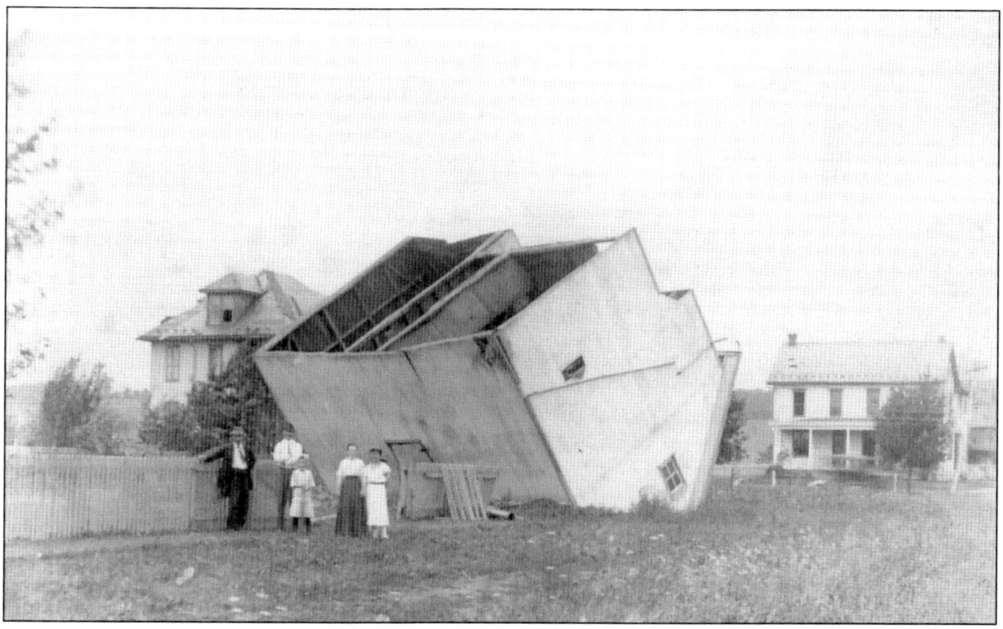

Saylor and Maple Streets. The 1915 cyclone blew A.S. Kreider's barn from the back of his property at 515 East Main Street all the way to the corner of Saylor and Maple Streets. Residences at 459–461 and 452 Maple Street are seen in the background.

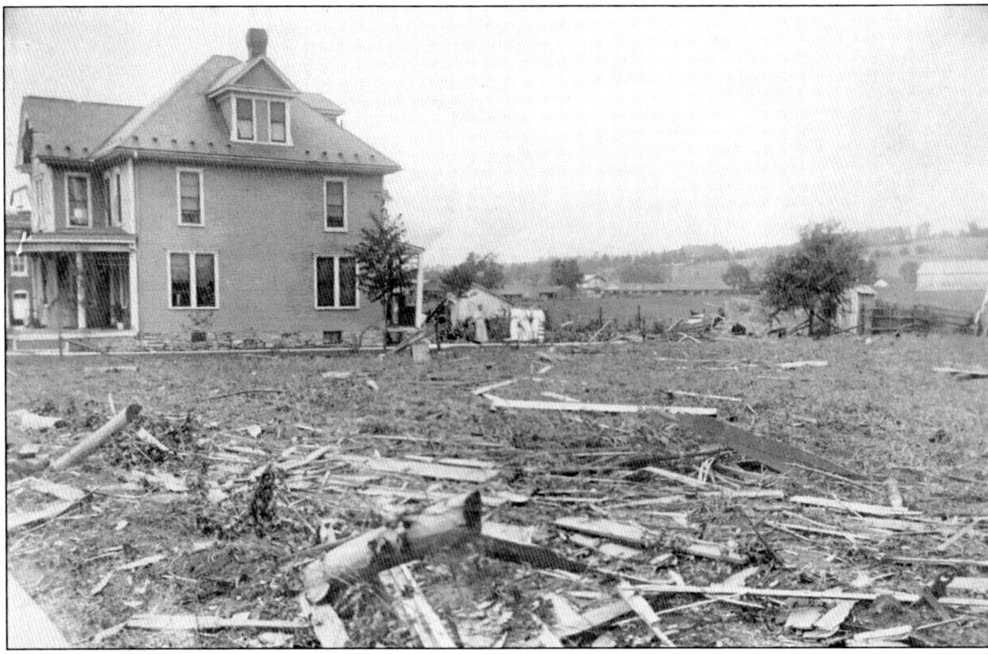

No. 515 East Maple Street. At the time that the cyclone of August 1915 hit East Maple Street, the house at 515 was the only residence on the north side of the block. (See page 13 for an overview of the cyclone's path.) (Courtesy of Robert and Suanne Long.)

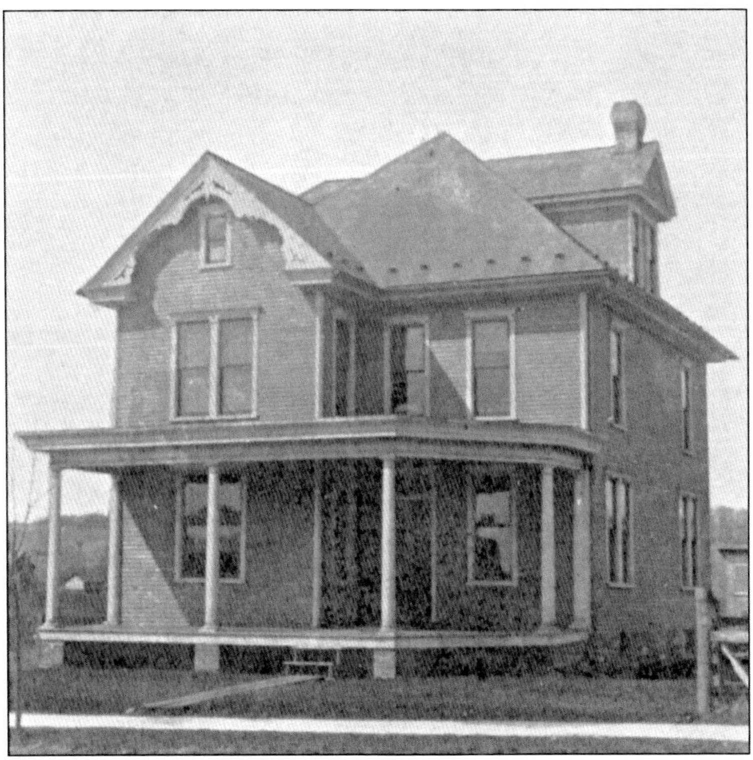

No. 515 East Maple Street. This picture shows the solitary home on the north side of this block, as it looked from the front in 1910. (Courtesy of Lebanon Valley College.)

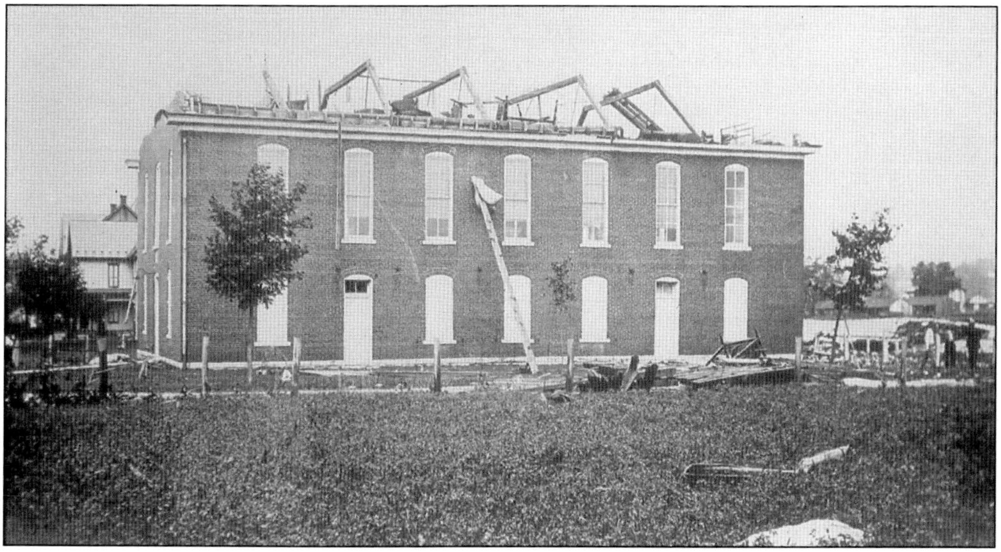

No. 495 East Maple Street. Kitty-corner from 504 East Maple Street stands the Annville Church of the Brethren. It was just eight years after the church was dedicated on April 21, 1907, that the August 1915 cyclone blew the gable ends and roof from the building. Repairs were made, and the church was able to serve the congregation again until a fire seriously damaged it on February 22, 1947. Material from the first church was saved and used for the new building, which was completed in November 1949. (Courtesy of Dick and Betty Streicher.)

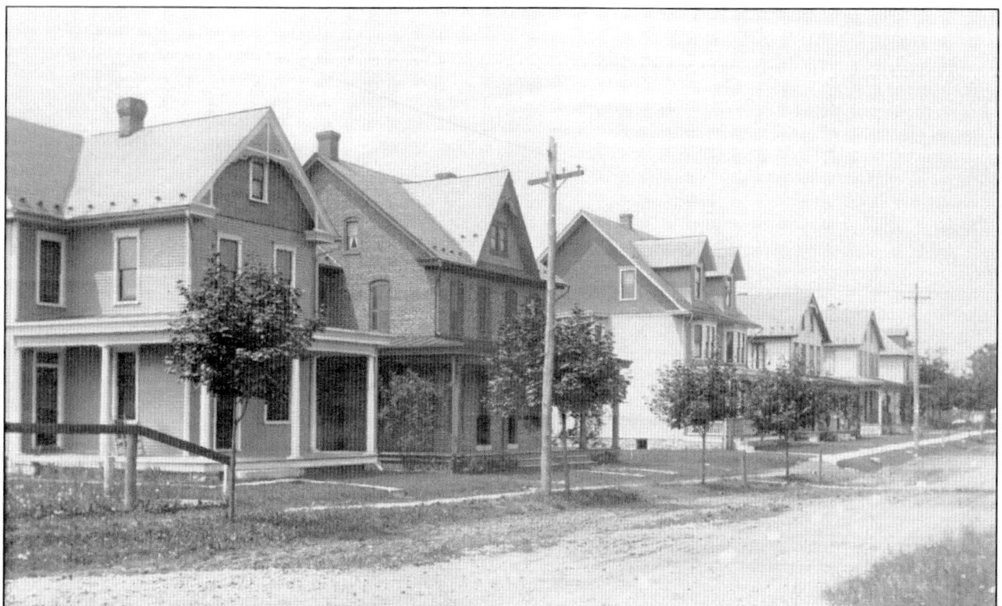

East Maple Street's 400 Block. The maple trees of Maple Street are young in this early picture of the south side of the 400 block taken around 1910. (Courtesy of Robert and Suanne Long.)

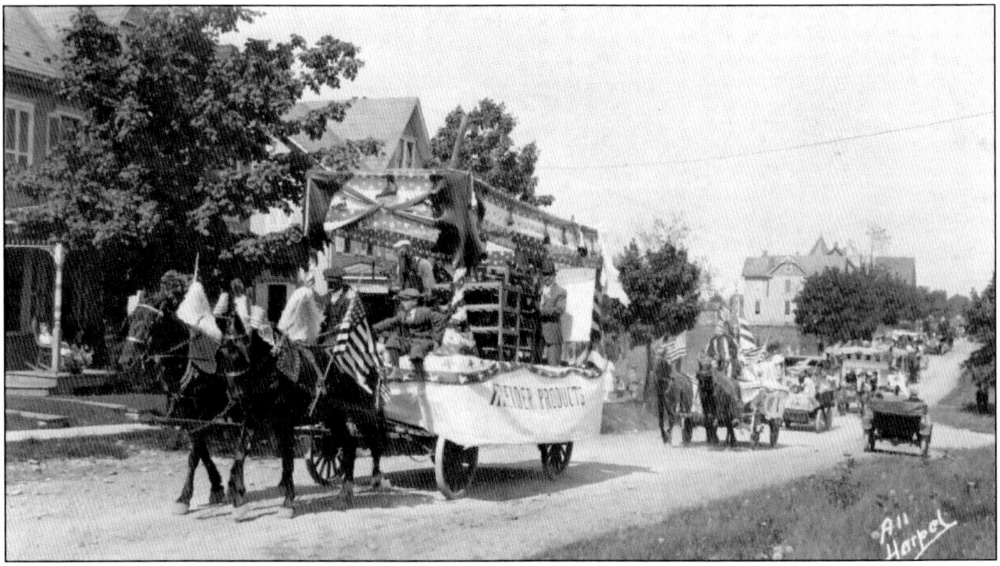

NOS. 447, 457, AND 459 EAST MAPLE STREET. This picture of a 1910s parade reveals that the north side of the 400 block of East Maple was not yet developed. (Courtesy of Dick and Betty Streicher.)

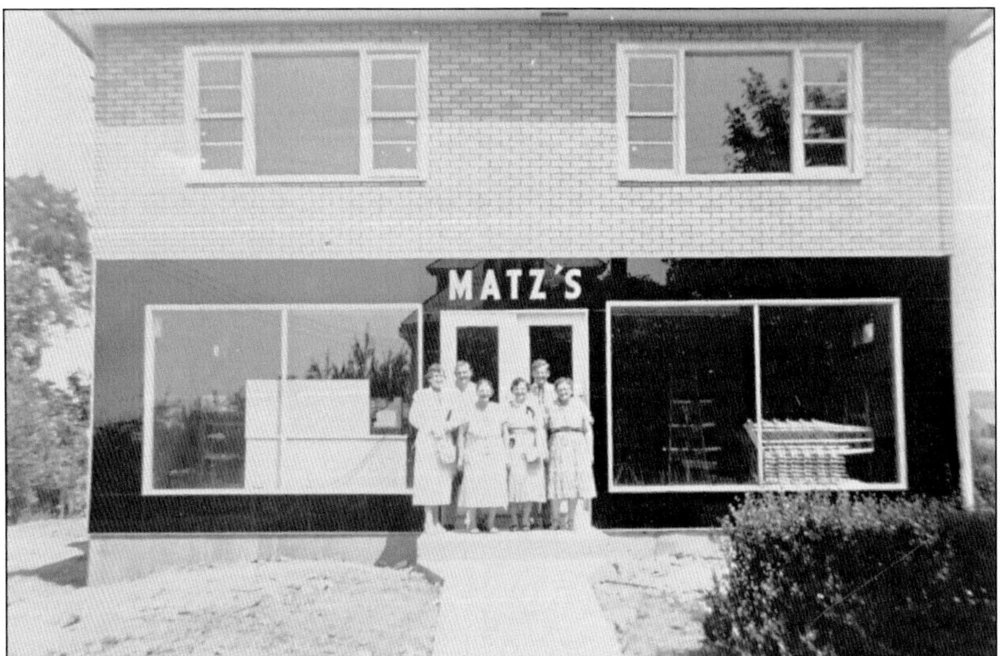

NO. 445 EAST MAPLE STREET. This picture was taken on August 1, 1953, shortly after Harold Matz opened a store on the block. Matz was a relative of the Keller family, who had operated a store at 337 East Maple Street since the 1900s. (See page 110.) The space continues to serve business purposes. (Courtesy of William Matz.)

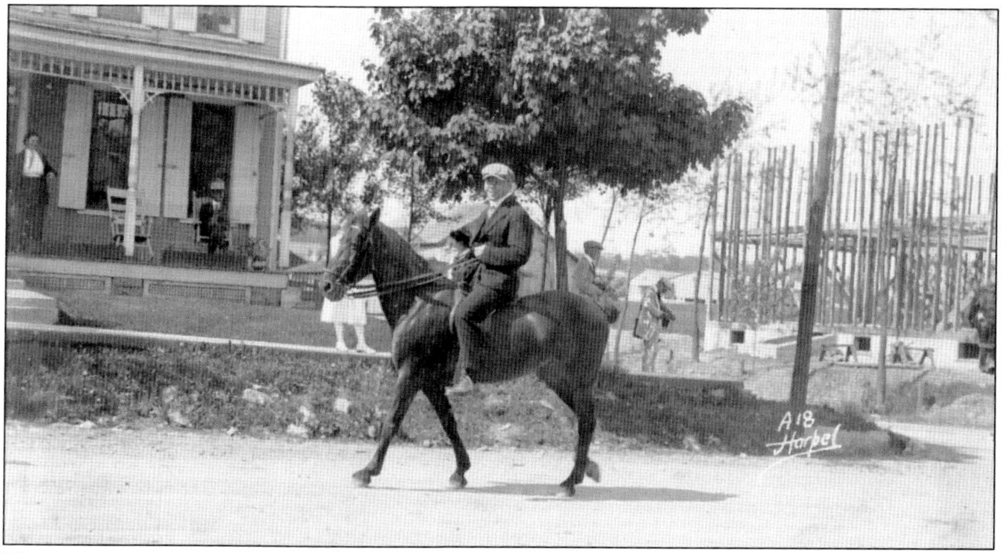

Nos. 345 and 403 East Maple Street. A single horseman on parade passes by a home that is under construction at the direction of Christian Gollam (1859–1943) and his wife, Rosalin Gollam (1862–1925). (Courtesy of Dick and Betty Streicher.)

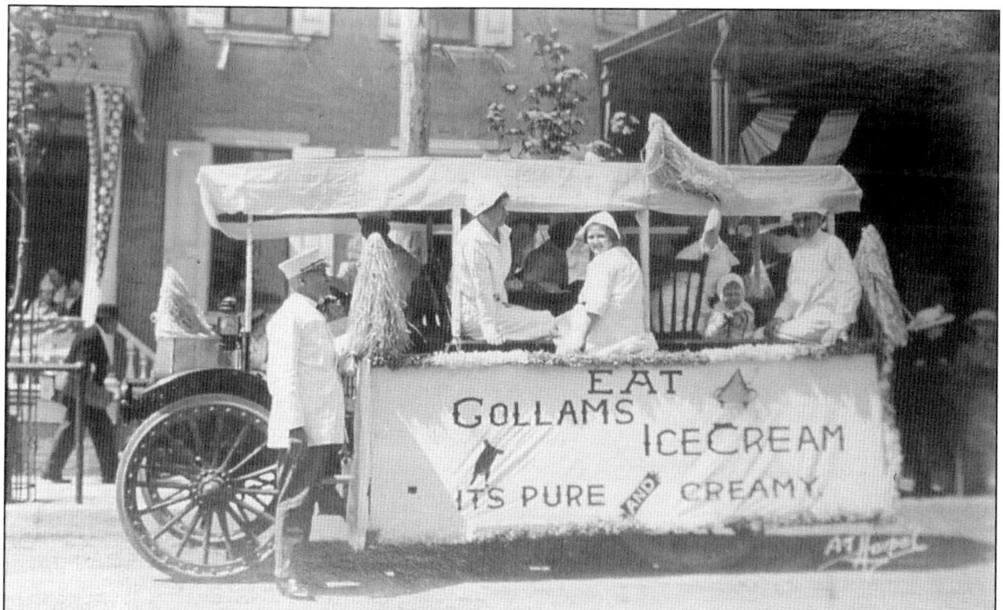

Gollam's Ice Cream. From the 1900s to the 1940s, the Gollam family earned their livelihood by selling ice cream. (See page 83 for a picture of one of their first restaurants in downtown Annville.) (Courtesy of Dick and Betty Streicher.)

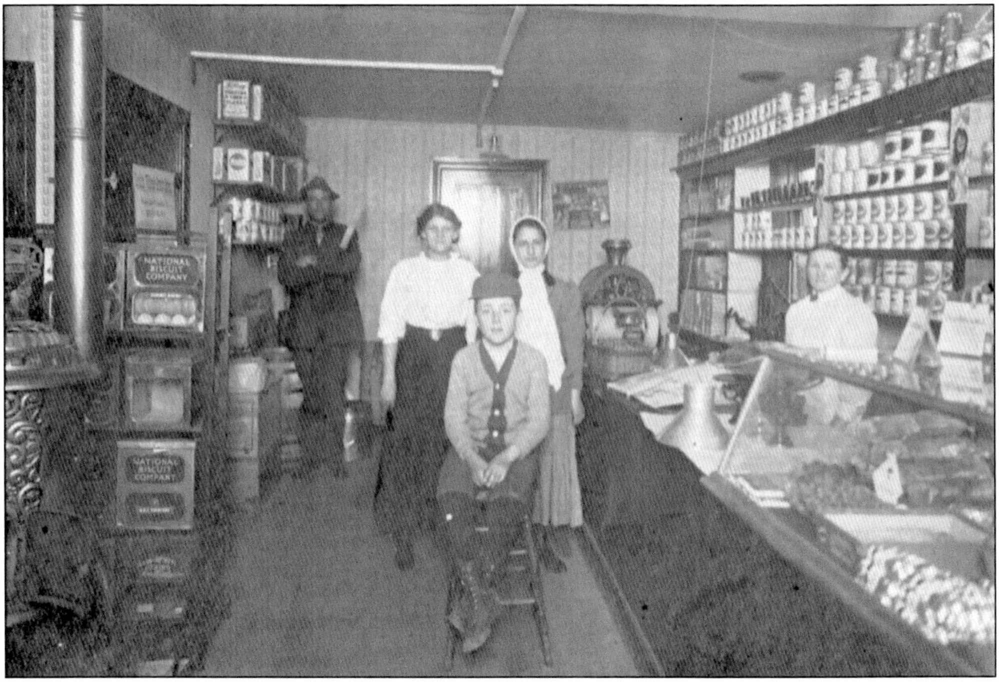

NO. 337 EAST MAPLE STREET. Jacob Keller (1862–1932) and his wife, Mary Miller Keller (1858–1936, behind the counter), built a home and storefront for Keller's Store at this location. From left to right, their daughters, Anna Keller Matz (1896–1971) and Lydia Keller (1891–1966), stand in the center of the picture. The store operated here until the 1930s when it was moved to 445 East Maple Street. (Courtesy of William Matz.)

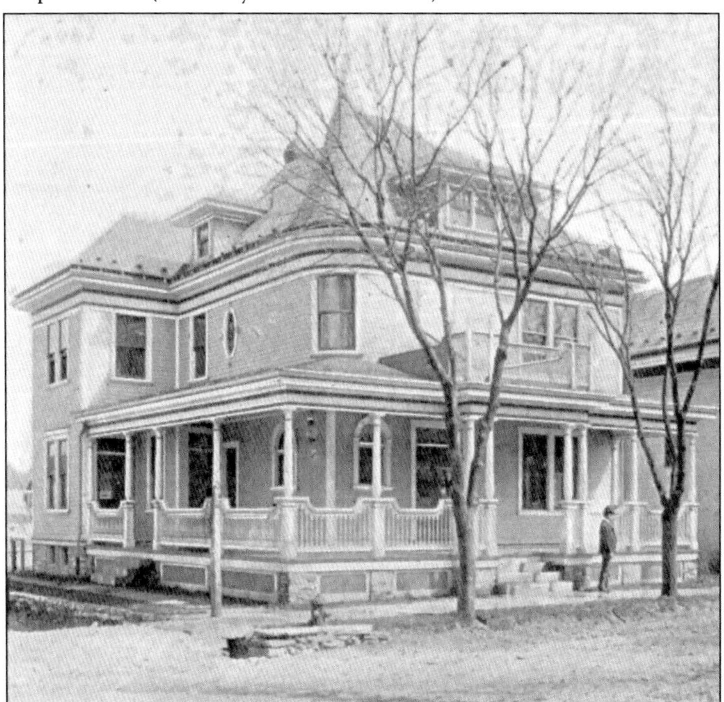

THE PARSONAGE. Originally built for Hervin U. Roop, president of Lebanon Valley College from 1897 to 1906, this home was later purchased by Annville United Methodist Church for use as a manse. The college purchased the house from the church in 2009 and is considering renovating it for use as a hospitality house. (Courtesy of Lebanon Valley College.)

Ten

Off to College

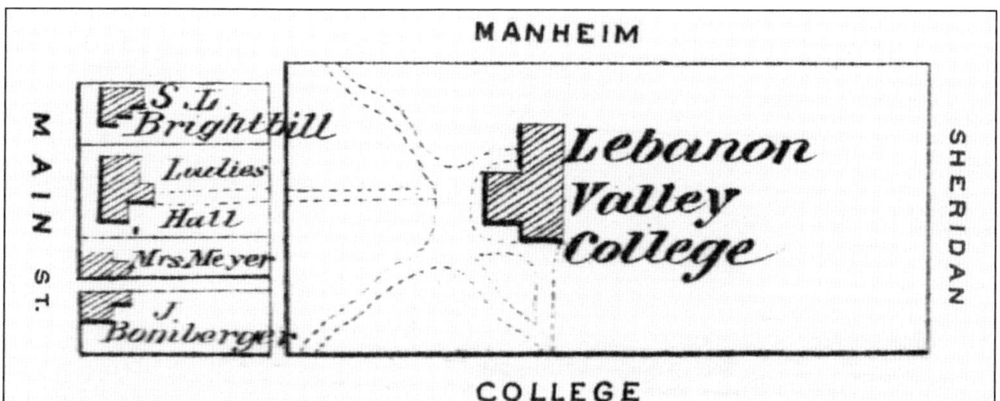

Lebanon Valley College Property, 1875 Map. This portion of the *County Atlas of Lebanon, Pennsylvania* details the building footings and surnames of residents on the land owned by Lebanon Valley College (LVC) and adjacent properties as they existed in 1875. Note, in particular, that only two sides of the northern Administration Building face North College Avenue at this time.

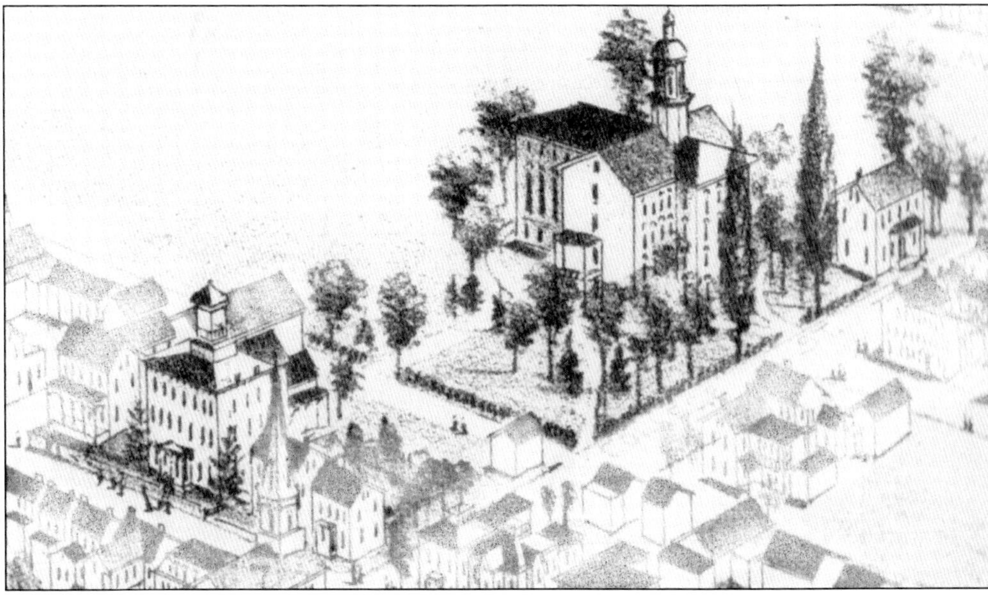

LVC PROPERTY, 1888 VIEW. T.M. Fowler's panoramic view of Annville portrays the buildings owned by Lebanon Valley College and adjacent properties, as they appeared from the southeast in 1888.

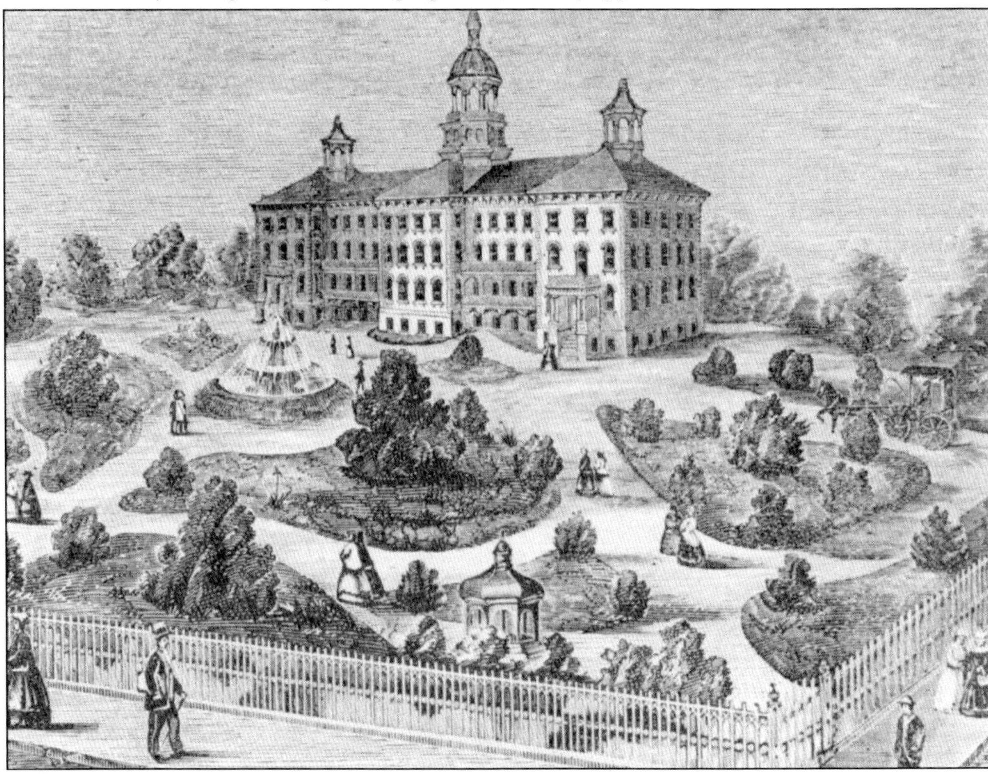

A GRAND VISION. Despite its elegance, this sketch of the college Administration Building from the 1867–1868 catalogue never came to fruition. Rather than five, only two walls faced North College Avenue when the building was completed in 1867. Compare the footings from this image with the sketch in the 1875 atlas on the previous page. (Courtesy of Lebanon Valley College.)

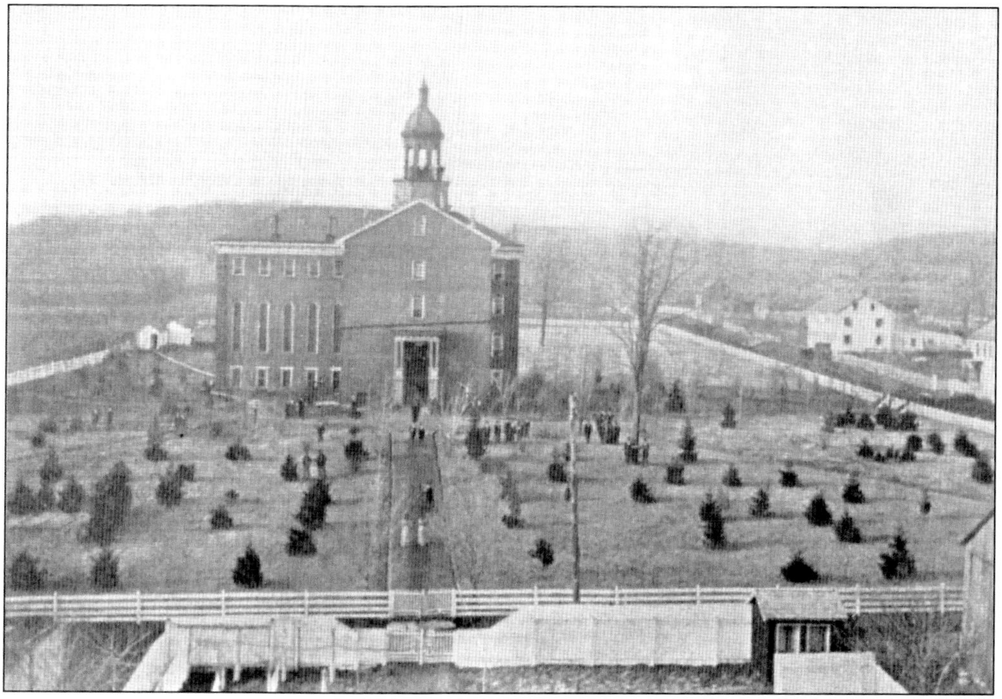

THE ADMINISTRATION BUILDING. This early picture, taken sometime around the 1870s or early 1880s, features the western wing to the left, which housed the chapel on the first two levels and the boys' dormitory on the third. (Courtesy of Lebanon Valley College.)

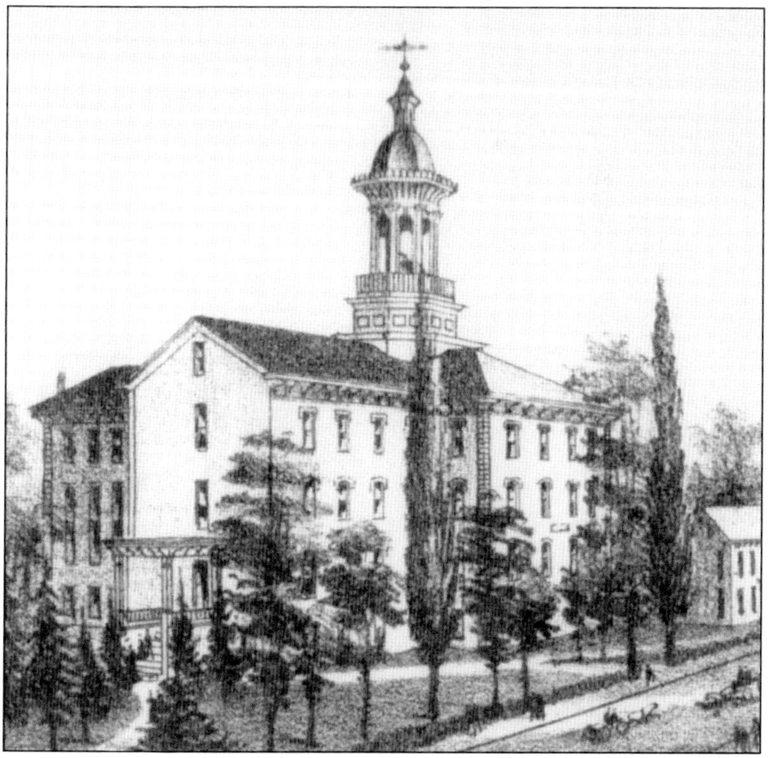

A CLOSER LOOK. Some detail of the two walls facing North College Avenue, as well as the wing extending to the west, can be seen in this sketch from the 1888 view of Annville. The frame building to the northeast side of the structure, dedicated to the sciences, music, and the library, was moved to 336 East Sheridan Avenue in the 1890s to make way for Engle Hall. (See page 116.)

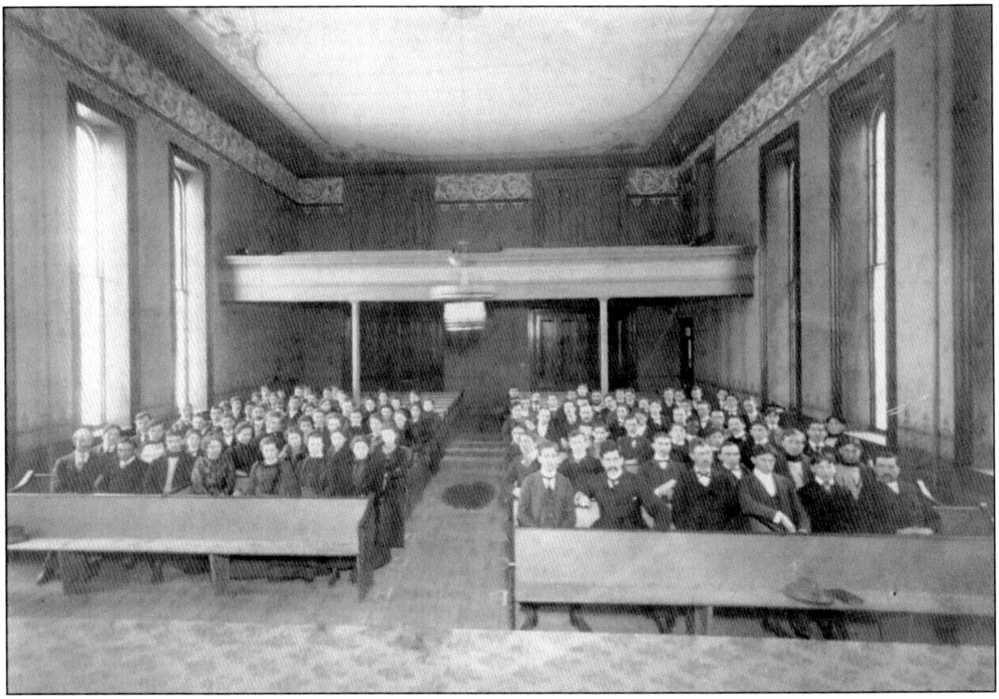

CHAPEL SERVICE. This picture shows the students of Lebanon Valley College on March 19, 1900, as they gathered for mandatory worship services, which were held in the chapel of the western wing of the Administration Building. (Courtesy of Lebanon Valley College.)

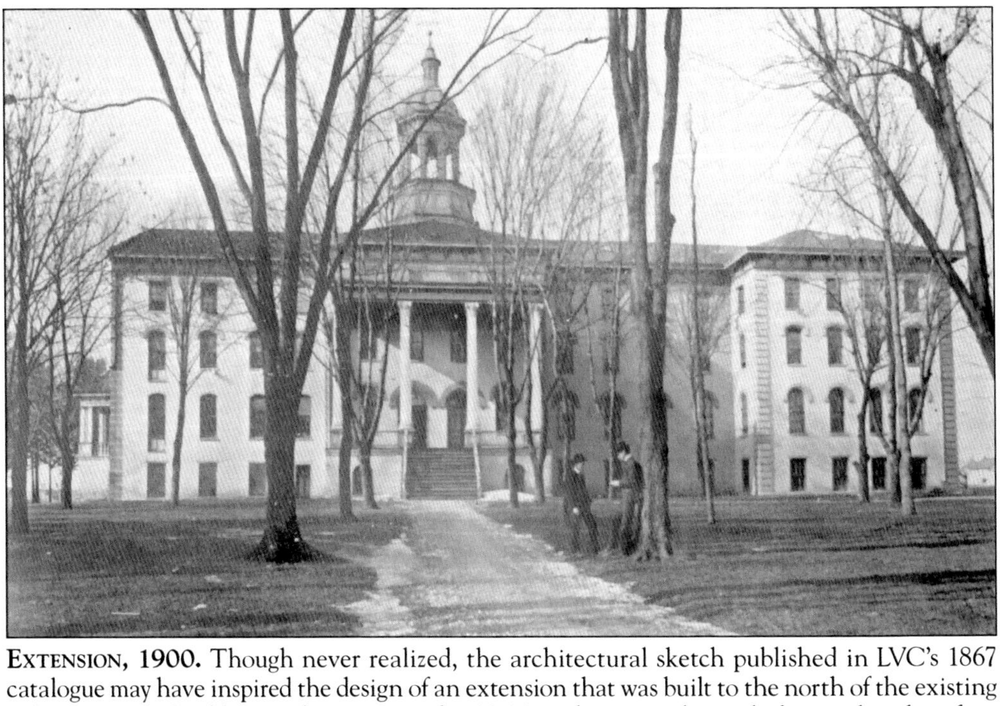

EXTENSION, 1900. Though never realized, the architectural sketch published in LVC's 1867 catalogue may have inspired the design of an extension that was built to the north of the existing Administration Building in the summer of 1900. Note, however, that only four, rather than five, walls face east toward North College Avenue. (Courtesy of Lebanon Valley College.)

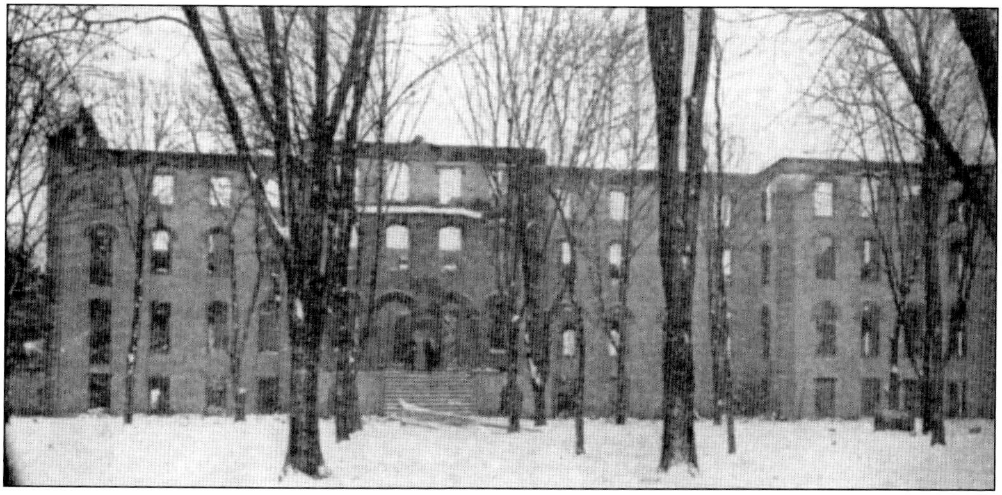

THE 1904 FIRE. Just four years after the completion of this significant addition, on Christmas Eve in 1904, the Administration Building was hollowed by a devastating fire. The source of the blaze was never determined. By the end of the year 1905, a new Administration Building had risen in its place, designed by Annville native Abner A. Ritcher. Many of the stones from this burned-out building would supply other construction projects in Annville. (See page 15.) (Courtesy of Dick and Betty Streicher.)

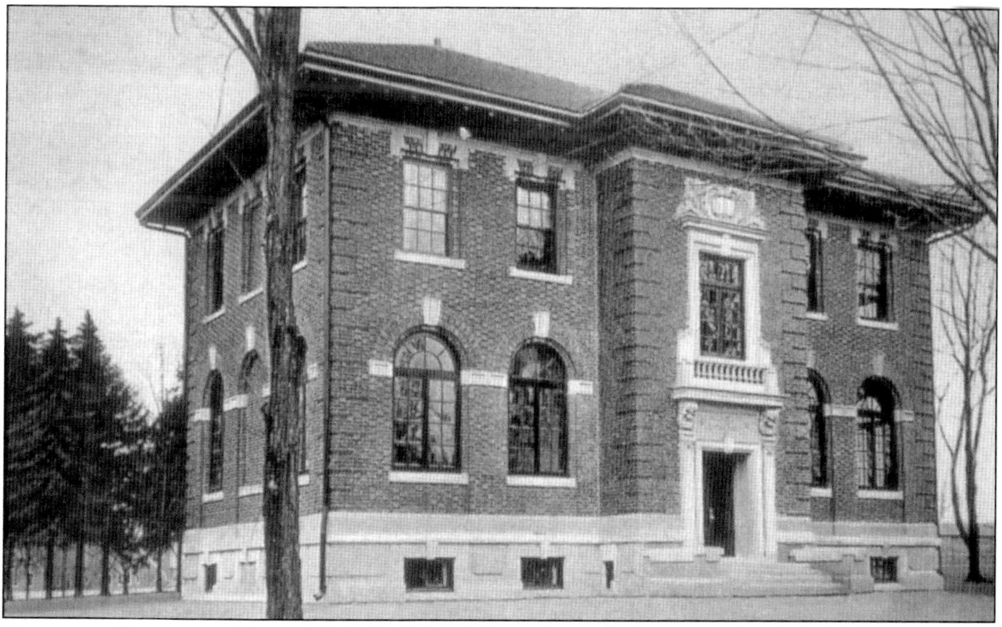

CARNEGIE BUILDING. Glancing to the left of the Administration Building, one notices a stately edifice in Italian Renaissance style with stone trimmings. Andrew Carnegie contributed money for this building, designed by Abner A. Ritcher. Construction of this college library building was completed in 1904. The structure would later serve as the headquarters for Student Services before becoming the college's Office of Admission. (Courtesy of Dick and Betty Streicher.)

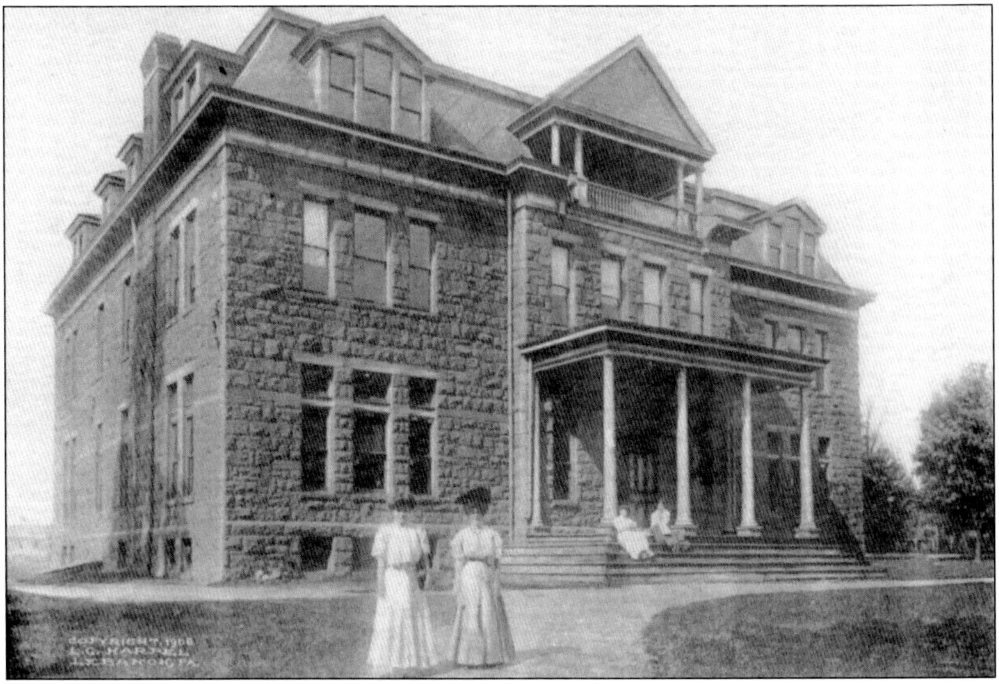

Music Conservatory. This conservatory once stood in the place where Blair Music Hall now stands. Completed in 1899, Engle Hall was the first in a series of edifices constructed as part of a building campaign that lasted until 1906. (Courtesy of Blanche Schaeffer.)

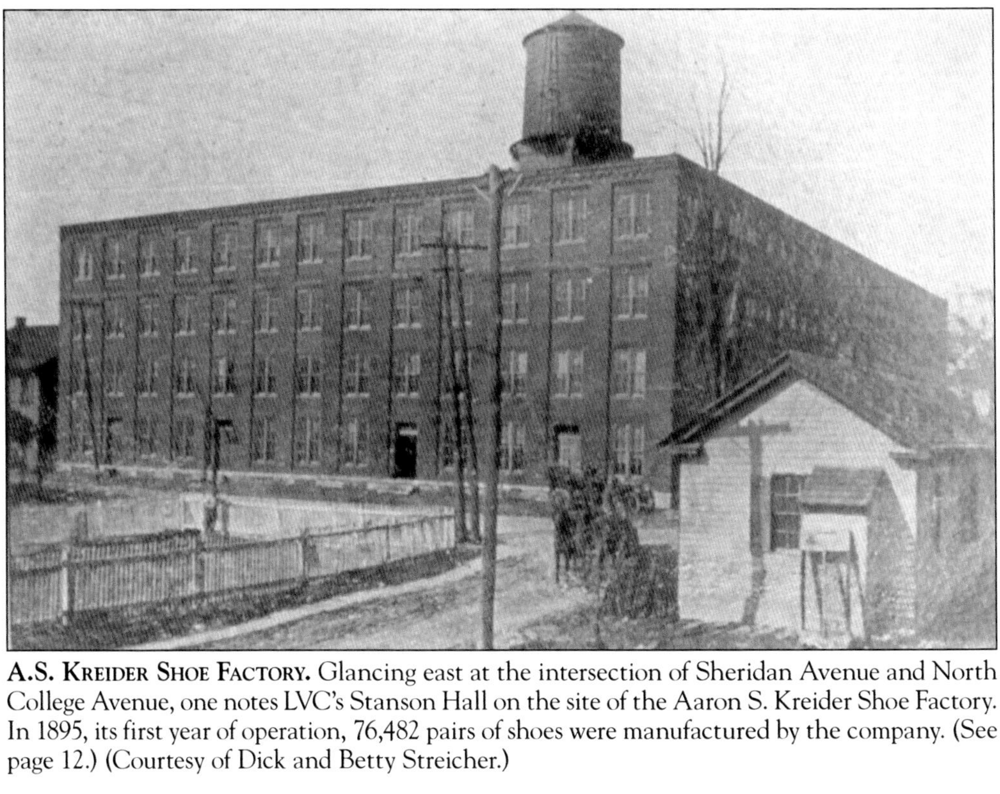

A.S. Kreider Shoe Factory. Glancing east at the intersection of Sheridan Avenue and North College Avenue, one notes LVC's Stanson Hall on the site of the Aaron S. Kreider Shoe Factory. In 1895, its first year of operation, 76,482 pairs of shoes were manufactured by the company. (See page 12.) (Courtesy of Dick and Betty Streicher.)

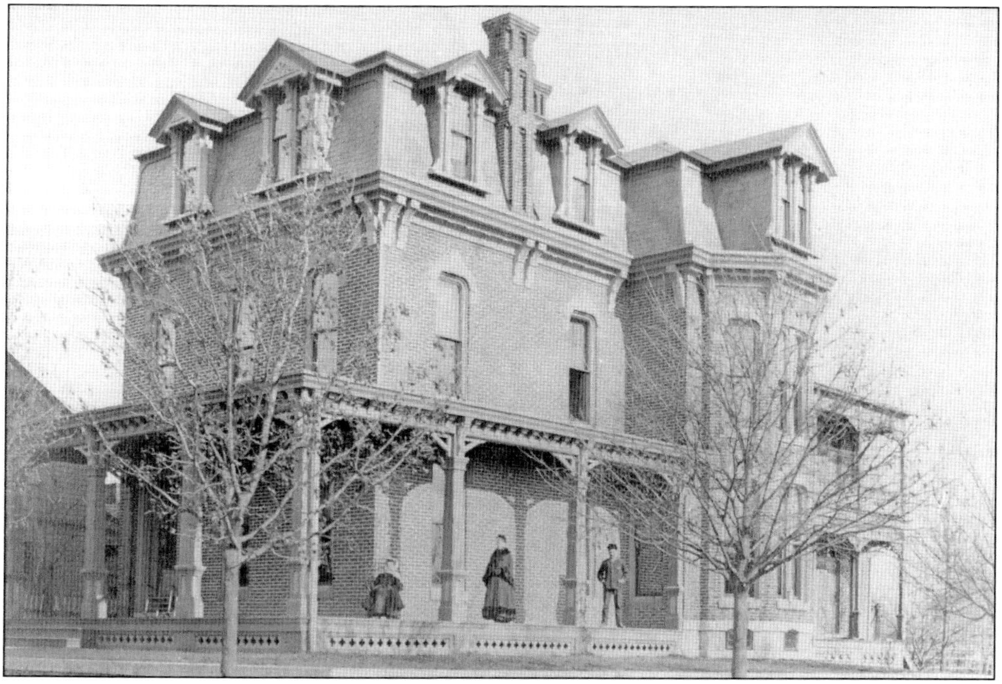

NO. 206 NORTH COLLEGE AVENUE. This house, once located on the northeast corner of Sheridan and North College Avenues, was built as the residence of the Joseph Kreider family in the 1890s. (See page 98.) Subsequently, the house became home to the Coover family and the David L. Saylor Jr. family. After being purchased by Lebanon Valley College in 1963, the building was referred to as Saylor Hall. It housed the mailroom, music practice rooms, several administrative offices, and, for a time, the art department. In 1973, the mansion became a women's dormitory before being razed in the 1980s. All that remains today is the limestone retaining wall that surrounded the yard. (Courtesy of Lebanon Valley College.)

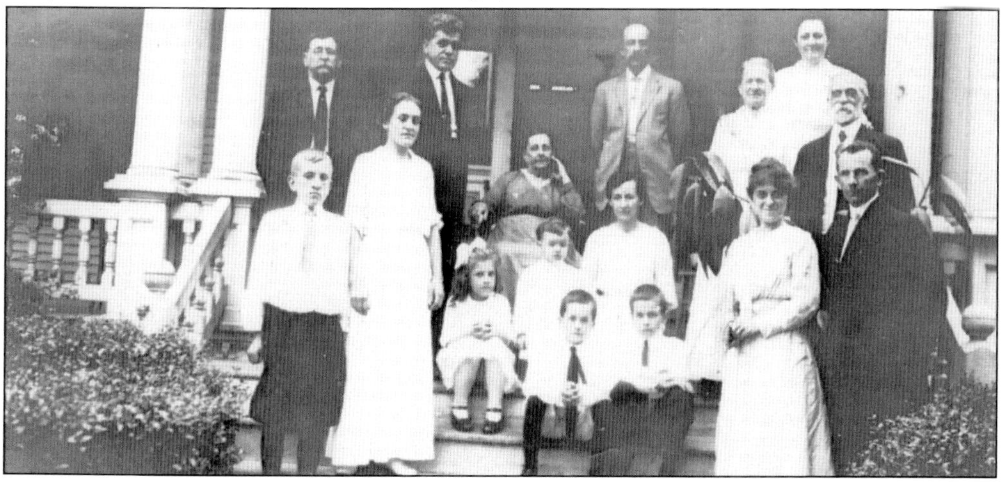

NO. 222 NORTH COLLEGE AVENUE. Directly north of the intersection of Sheridan and North College Avenues is a residence that is currently known as North College. Prof. Alvin E. Shroyer (top row, second from left), a member of LVC's class of 1900, and his family moved into the house in 1909 when he returned to the college to teach Greek and religion. Professor Shroyer died from pneumonia in 1920 at 45 years of age. (Courtesy of Anne Shroyer Shemeta.)

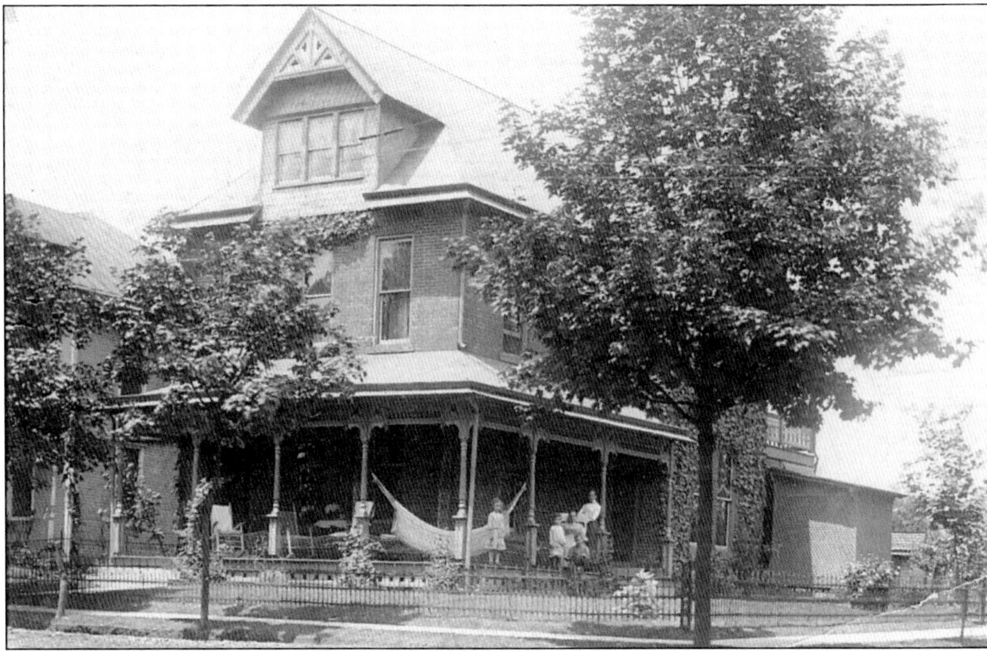

No. 83 East Sheridan Avenue. Although built in the 1890s for David Kreider Jr. (see page 98), it was Kreider's grandson David Shroyer (1904–1983) and his wife, Frances (1906–1992), who would occupy the residence for the greatest length of time, raising four children here. In the early 1990s, the family sold the home to Lebanon Valley College for use as a health center. (Courtesy of Anne Shroyer Shemeta.)

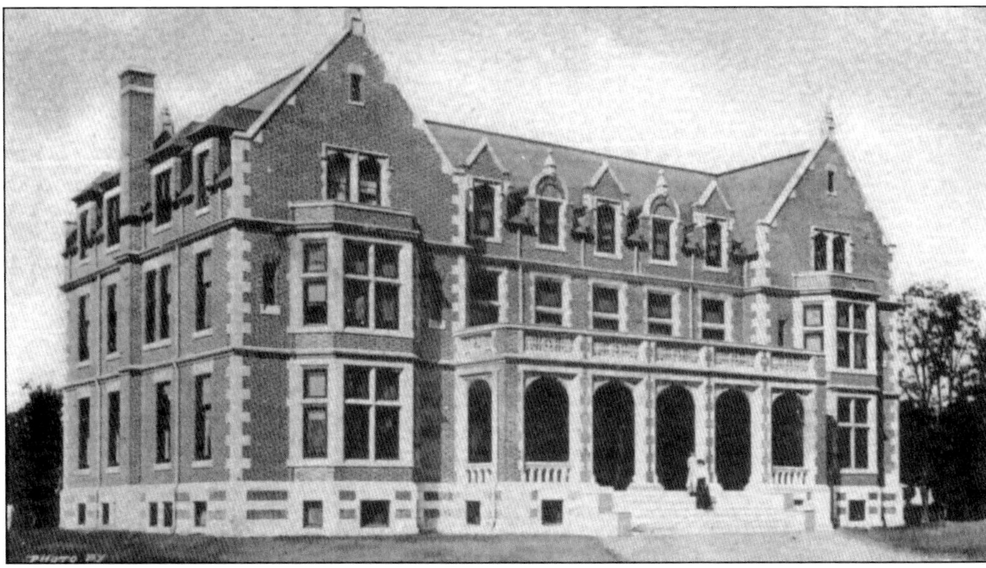

North Hall, Site of Miller Chapel. This new residence for women, built to complement housing for ladies offered at South Hall (see page 90), was constructed as part of the building initiatives that added seven new buildings to the campus in 1905–1906. The Elizabethan-style building would house female students until men were moved into the facility in 1957, changing the name to Keister Hall. The current chapel replaced the hall in 1966 as part of the college's centennial celebration. (Courtesy of Dick and Betty Streicher.)

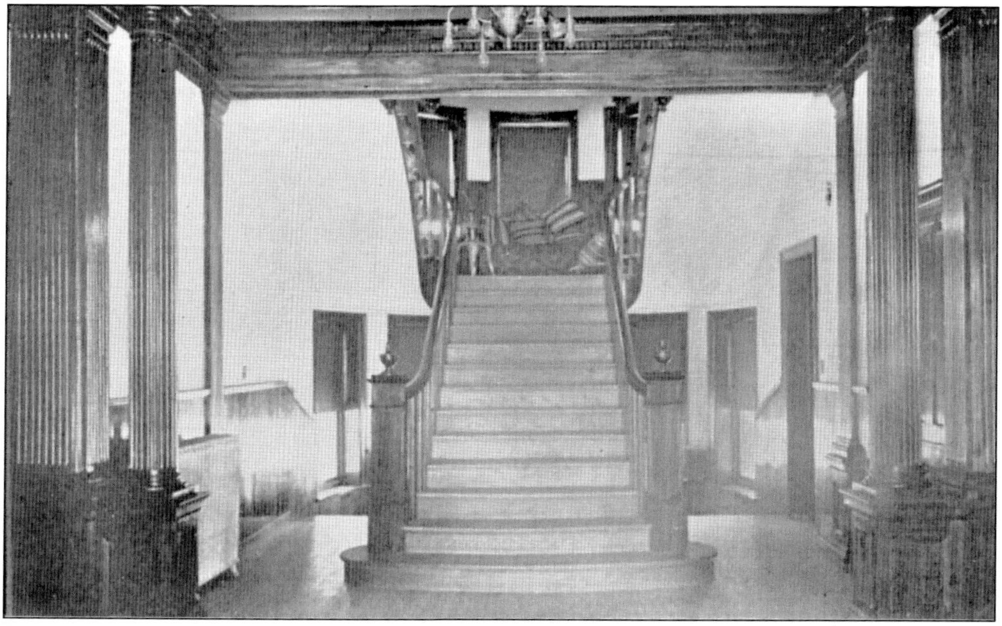

INTERIOR OF NORTH HALL. Surrounded by the elaborate woodwork that characterized the facilities built for the college in the early 1900s, a young male student would wait here in order to meet with a lady resident of the hall. (Courtesy of Lebanon Valley College.)

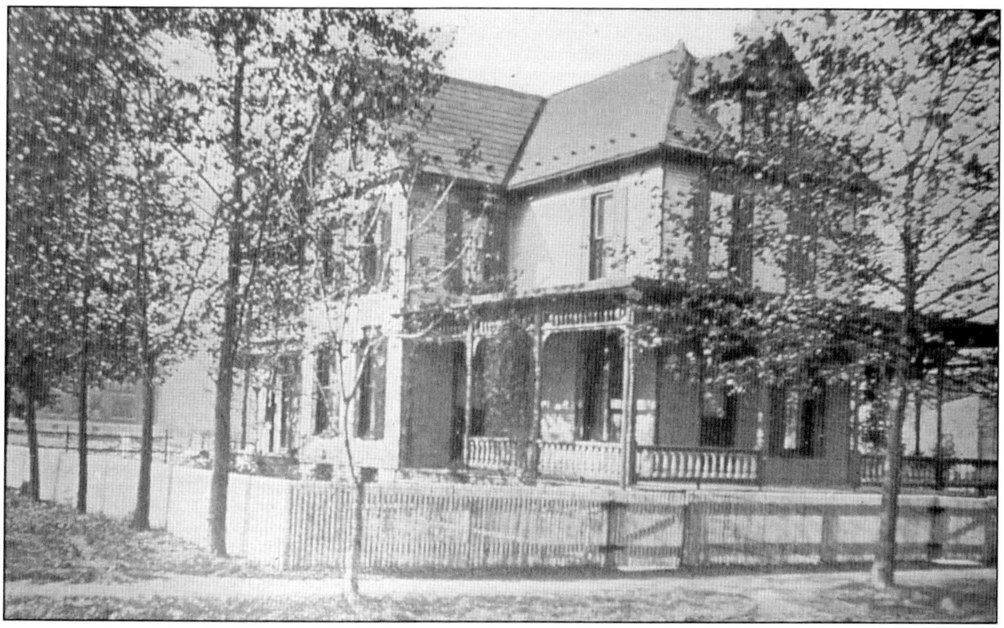

NO. 26 EAST SHERIDAN AVENUE. This home, one of two similar homes that once occupied the space immediately north of the current Lynch Memorial Hall, served as the primary residence of President Lynch from 1932 until it was razed in 1949 to make room for the construction of Lynch Memorial Hall. (Courtesy of Dick and Betty Streicher.)

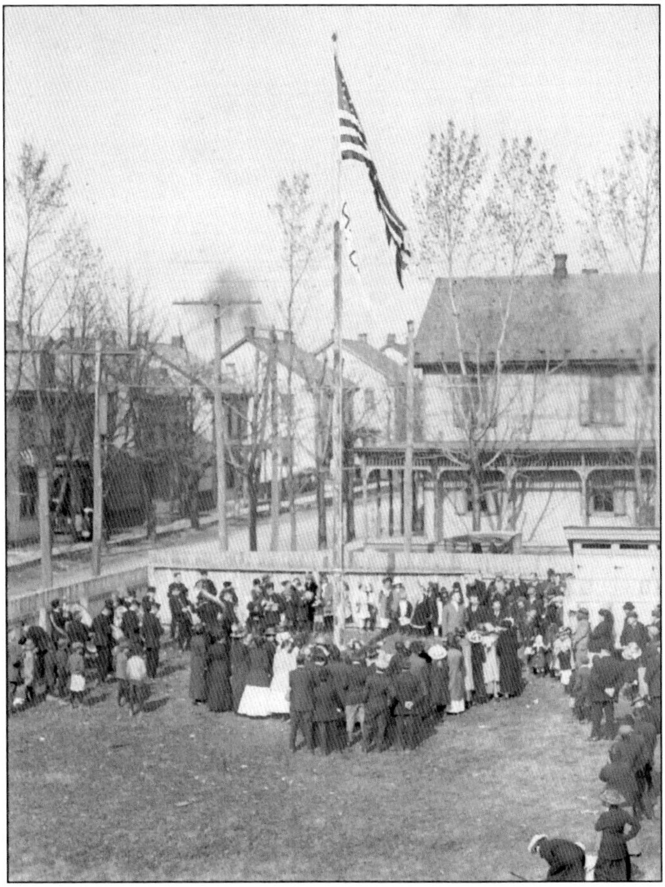

Flags and Handkerchiefs. Looking past the president's house to the west in the 1900s, one would see the home of Della Herr Thomas (16 East Sheridan) and property belonging to a flag factory on both sides of North White Oak Street. In this picture, looking east along East Sheridan Avenue, employees of the factory gather to celebrate the completion of their first flag. Handkerchiefs were also manufactured at the facility. (Courtesy of Dick and Betty Streicher.)

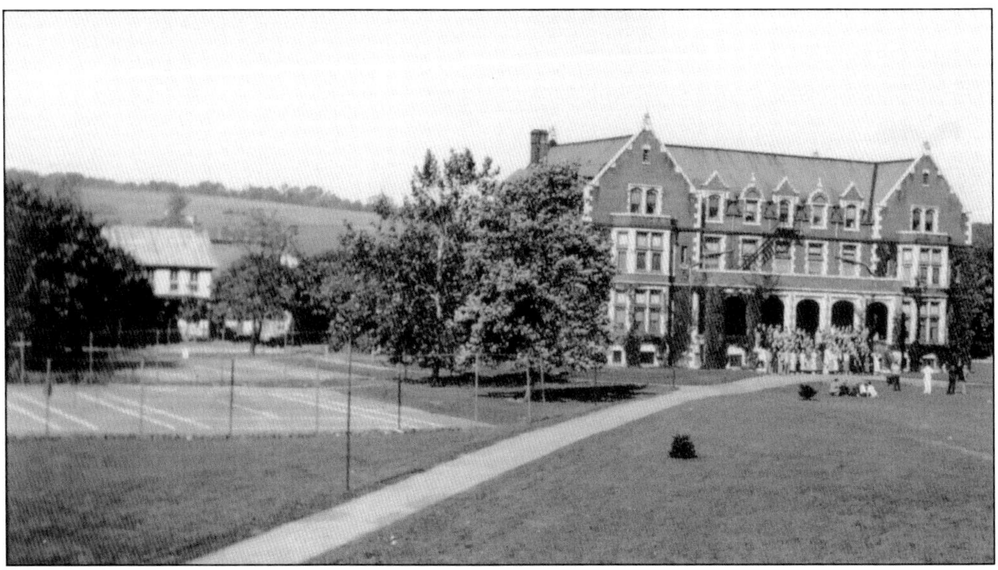

Tennis Courts. Walking south along the west side of Miller Chapel, one passes by open space that once served as LVC's tennis courts. The Lynch Memorial Building was eventually built on part of this land. (Courtesy of Lebanon Valley College.)

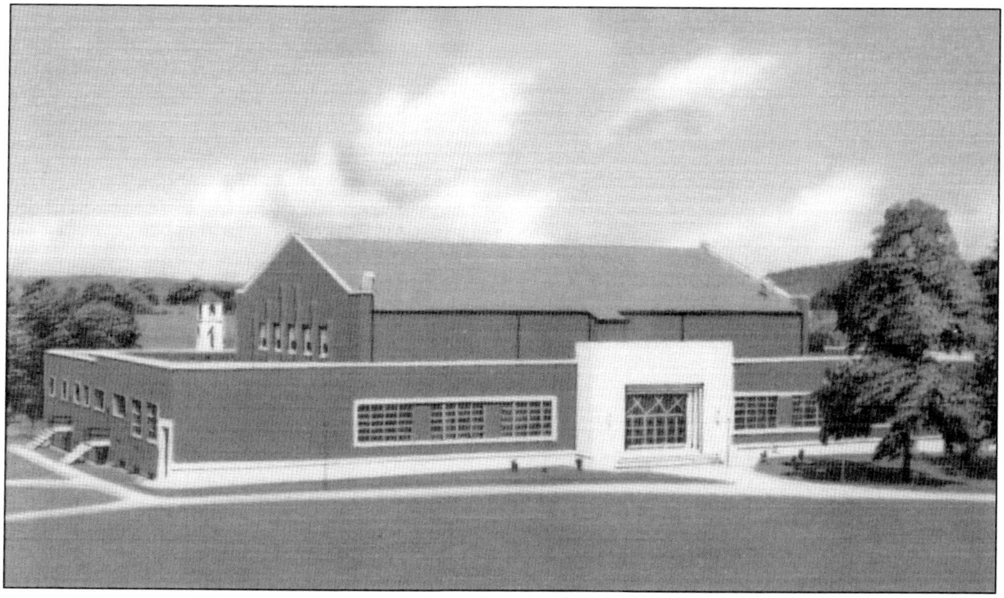

LYNCH MEMORIAL BUILDING. As though from the seedlings of the tennis courts, Lynch Memorial Hall was built in 1950 to provide new physical education facilities, a timely replacement for the well-worn basketball courts in the lower level of the Administration Building. Not long after the construction of the Arnold Sports Center in the 1990s, the Lynch Memorial Building would undergo a creative transformation. The building now houses a large open atrium and coffee bar, as well as several academic departments. (Courtesy of Blanche Schaeffer.)

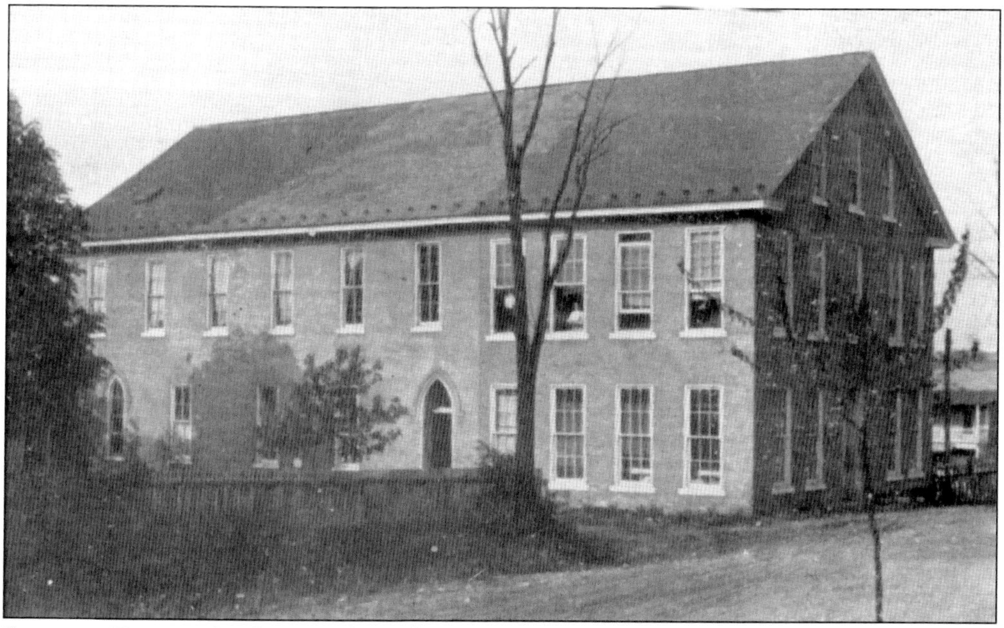

STOCKING FACTORY. Looking southwest between Lynch Memorial and the Neidig-Garber Science Center to the other side of North White Oak Street, one sees a large building constructed in the late 1890s, the A.R. Kreider and Brother Hosiery Mill. The college originally purchased the building in 1955 to house the chemistry and biology departments. In the 1990s, it was divided into apartments for students at Lebanon Valley College. (Courtesy of Dick and Betty Streicher.)

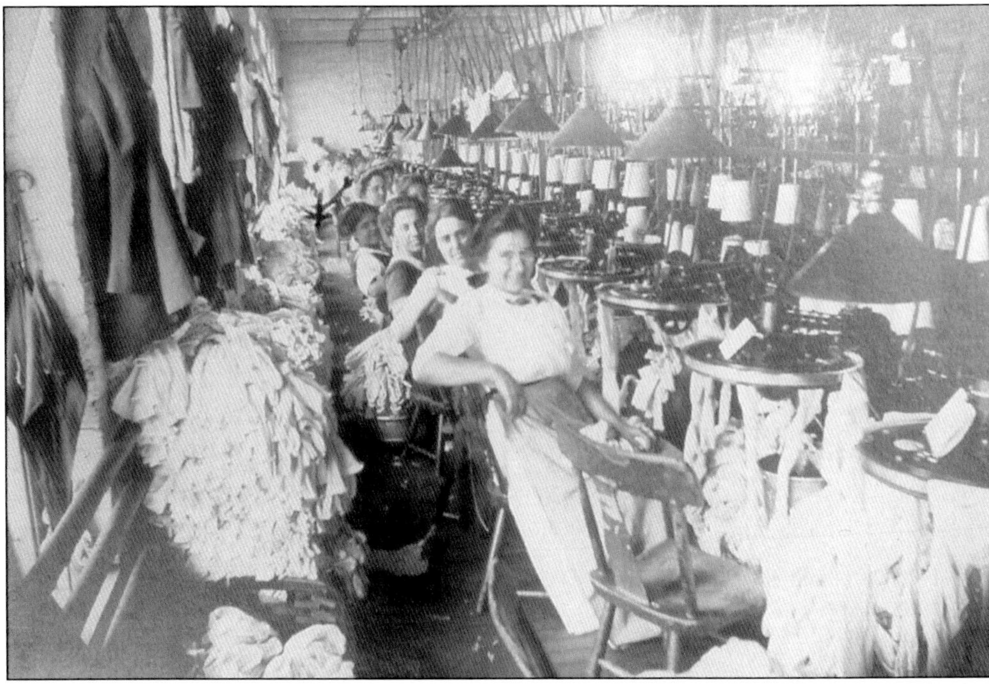

Knitting Hosiery. A. Raymond and Edwin Kreider, children of Andrew and Emma Kreider (see page 94), had originally established the hosiery mill in January 1900 with just a few employees. (Courtesy of Dick and Betty Streicher.)

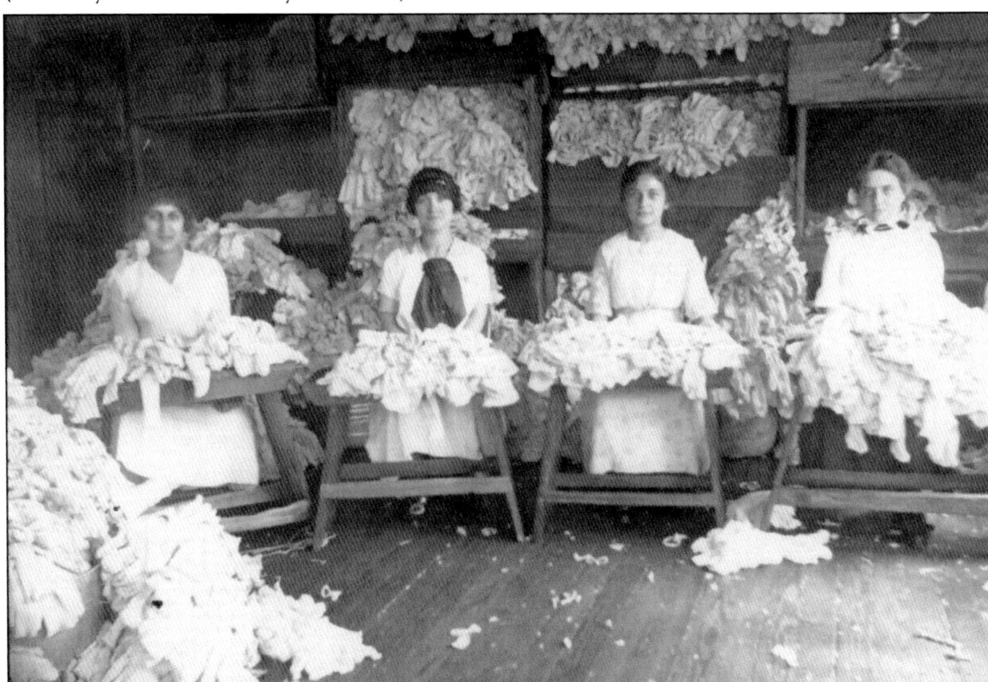

Hosiery Inspection. By 1919, the business employed more than 400 people, producing approximately 2,400 pairs of socks per day. (Courtesy of Dick and Betty Streicher.)

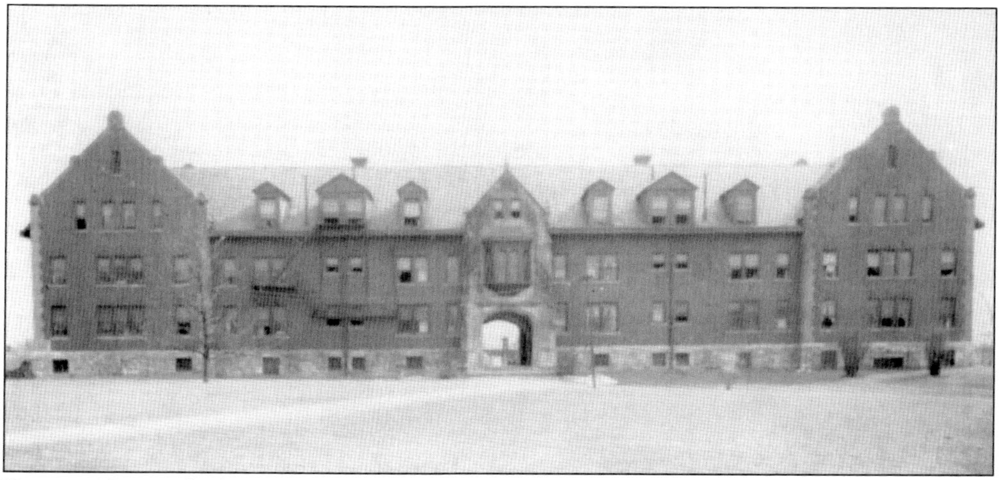

Kreider Hall. The large residence hall in Oxford-Cambridge style pictured here once stood on the ground where LVC's Neidig-Garber Science Center was built beginning in the late 1970s. Following the destruction of the men's dormitory on the third floor of the Administration Building by the fire in 1904, Kreider Hall was constructed for men as part of the building initiatives that added seven new buildings to the campus in 1905–1906. Despite the efforts of residential proctors, extreme dilapidation had transpired by the 1930s, prompting Dean Clark Carmean and his wife, Edna, to move in with the men. It was not long before the dormitory was much improved and the Carmeans could move to a private residence. (Courtesy of Blanche Schaeffer.)

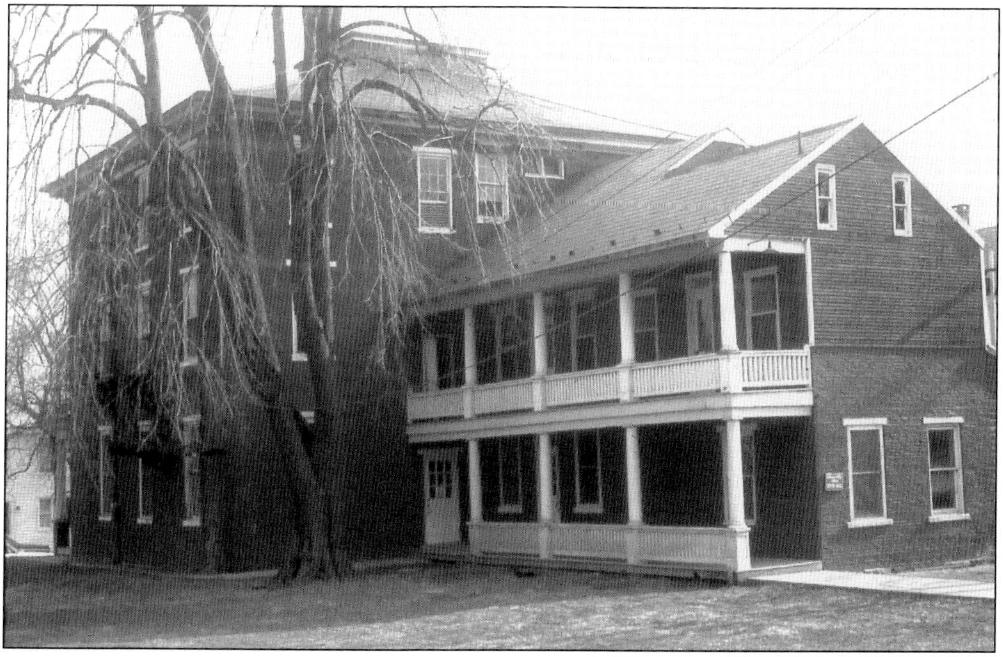

Back through South Hall. Passing along the site of Gossard Memorial Library—now Bishop Library—a turn to the south between two complementary rounded walls, one belonging to the library and the other of the Carnegie Building, leads one down a small set of steps to O. Pass Bollinger Plaza. This picture represents the building that a pedestrian would have seen if passing through this plaza between 1857 and the 1970s. In the early and mid–20th century, the public school system utilized the back lower level of this building for its second-grade classrooms. (See page 90.)

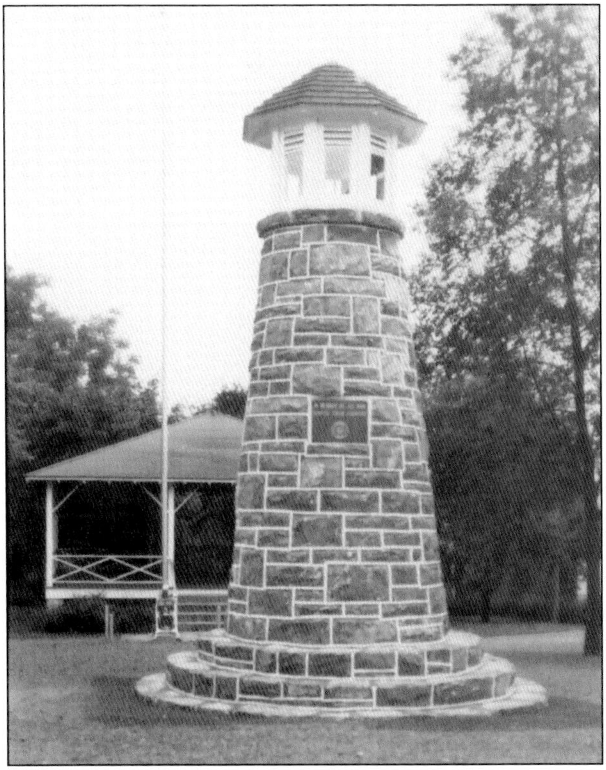

No. 35 South Manheim Street. Returning to East Main Street, pedestrians may turn right to access Manheim Street via a crosswalk, located just 100 yards to the west. One block to the south, at the intersection of Manheim and Queen Streets, stands the Connor-Streicher American Legion. The legion utilized a former Annville school in its initial construction. The 20-foot-tall, functional limestone lighthouse just west of the building was erected around the time of the founding of the Legion in 1922 "in memory of all who served their country."

The Playground. In the early 1900s, these lots held the large community playground and snack bar pictured here.

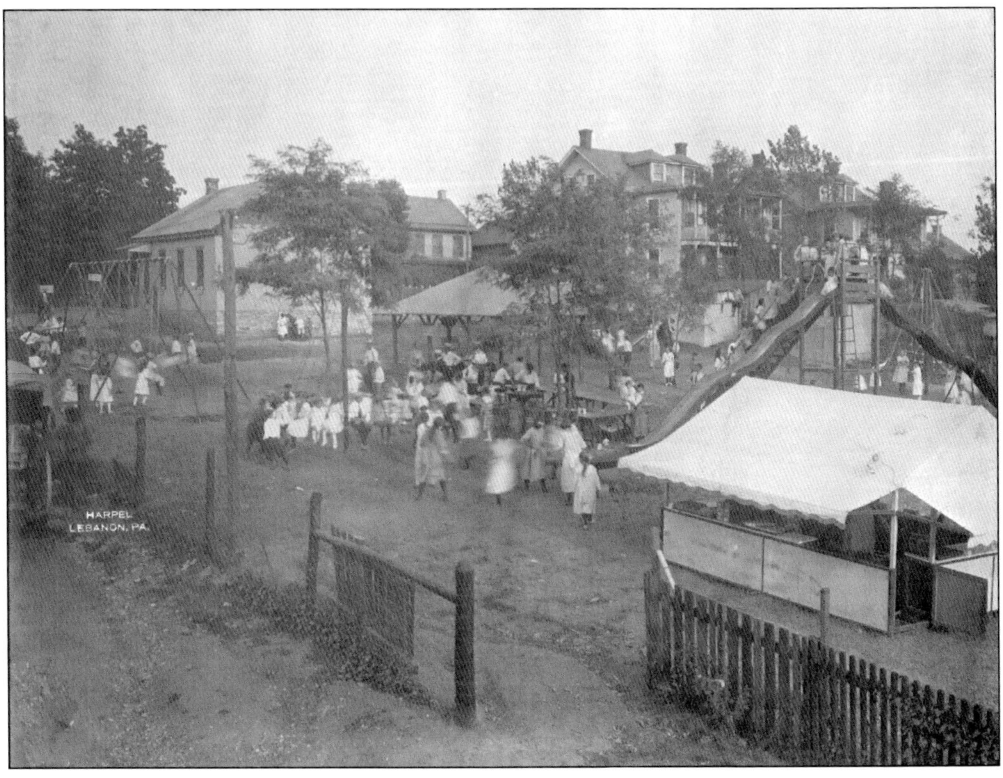

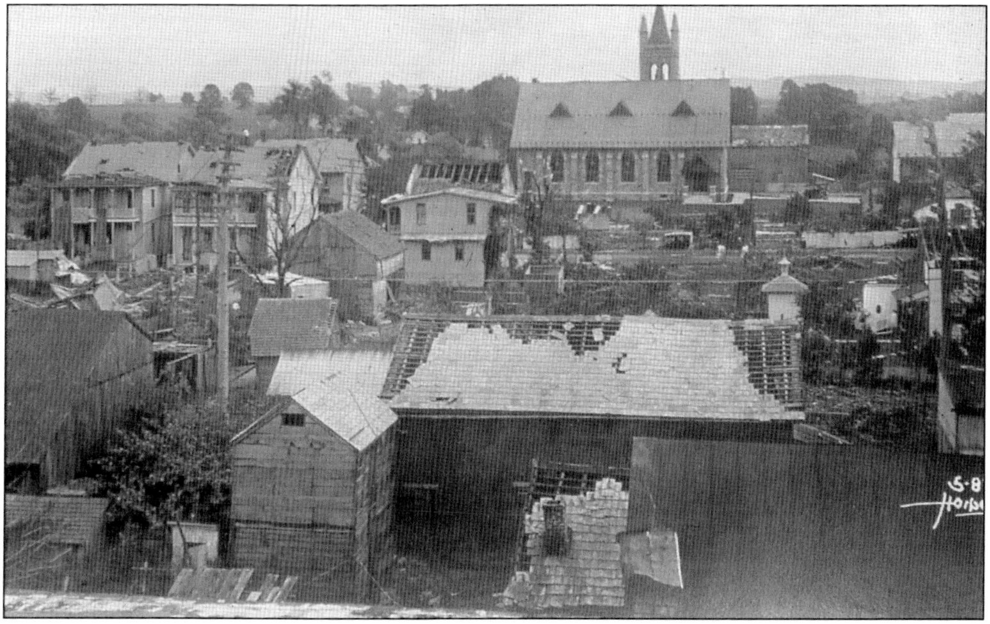

Homes after 1915 Cyclone. This 1915 view of the back of homes along the first block of East Queen Street from South Manheim Street reveals the damage done by the cyclone. (Courtesy of Dick and Betty Streicher.)

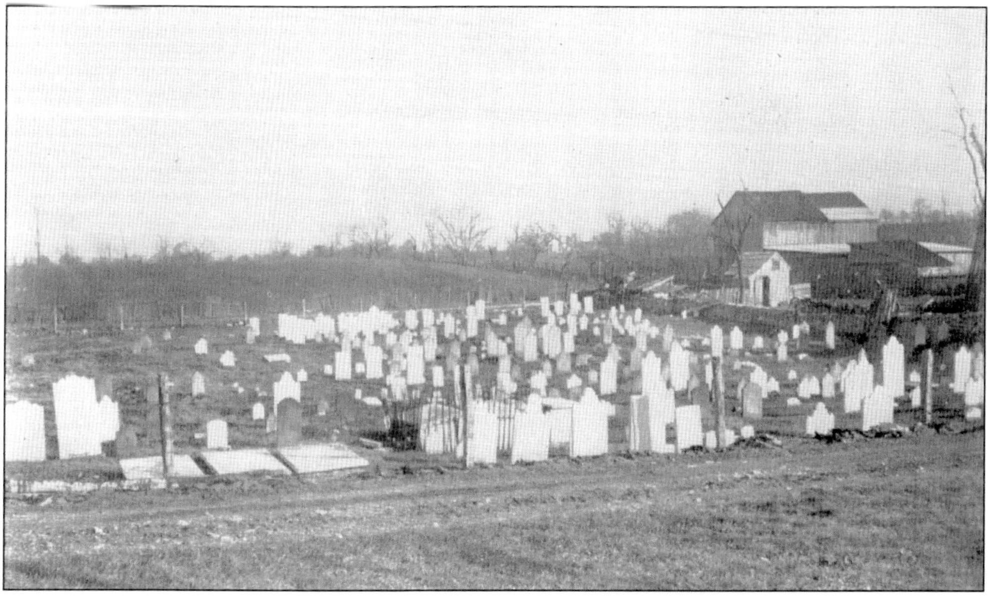

No. 200 South White Oak Street. A large marker in the middle of the park to the east of Christ Church United Church of Christ notes that the space used to be a cemetery. The bodies of 494 of Annville's earliest residents, including piano manufacturer John Shertzer and many members of the Raiguel family of pioneers, were buried here from 1804 to 1891. Though most of their stories are lost forever, we can honor the contributions of those who came before us as we walk through Annville in celebration of what the town has been, has become, and may be. Requiescant in pace.

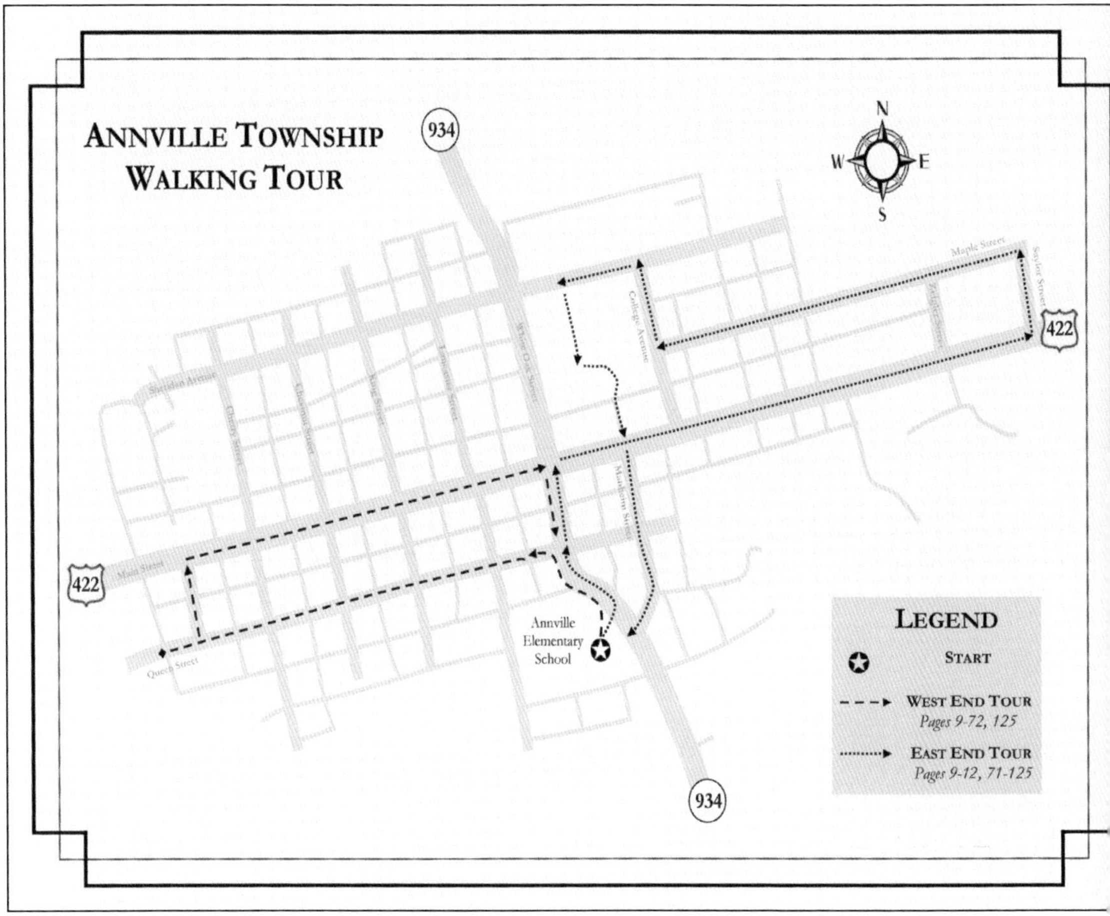

WALKING TOUR MAP. Two walking tours of Annville are described on this map, one to the west and one to the east. Both tours have their start at the 200 block of South White Oak Street. Leaving cars behind in the parking lots of Annville Elementary School or Christ Church (after requesting permission to do so), walkers may gather on adjacent lawns. A walk through either end of town will result in a historic tour that lasts approximately 90 minutes.

BIBLIOGRAPHY

Beers, Frederick W. *County Atlas of Lebanon, Pennsylvania*. Philadelphia: F.A. Davis, 1875.

Bierman, E. Benjamin. *A Visit to Annville Sixty Years Ago*. Lebanon, PA: Lebanon County Historical Society, 1899.

Billings, Philip A. *Porches: An Introduction to Citizens of Annville, Pennsylvania*. 2 vols. Lebanon, PA: Donald Blyler Offset, 1983–1985.

Croll, Philip Columbus. *Ancient and Historic Landmarks in the Lebanon Valley*. Philadelphia: Lutheran Publication Society, 1895.

Egle, William H. *History of the Counties of Dauphin and Lebanon in the Commonwealth of Pennsylvania*. Philadelphia: Everts and Peck, 1883.

Flory, Doris M. *Union Hose Company, Annville: January 12, 1912–January 12, 1987*. Lebanon, PA: Donald L. Blyler Offset, 1987.

Ford, Arthur L. *Cinderella and the Seven Dwarfs: Lebanon Valley College's 1952–1953 Basketball Team's Improbable Run to the NCAA Sweet Sixteen*. Annville: Lebanon Valley College, 2007.

Kreider, Anna. *Annville Landmarks Including Memory Portraits and Annville Industries, 1733–1912*. Unpublished manuscript, 1962.

Nalley, Lori Unger. *The Herr Family of Annville, Pennsylvania: 220 Years and Counting*. Morgantown, PA: Masthof Press, 2008.

Richter, Fredric, Kenn Kreiser, and Richard and Betty Streicher. *A Pictorial History of Annville*. Lebanon, PA: Donald Blyler Offset, 1983.

Shenk, Hiram H. *The Annville Academy*. Lebanon, PA: Lebanon County Historical Society, 1904.

Stein, Thomas S. *Annville's Oldest Burial-Place and Its Memories*. Lebanon, PA: Lebanon County Historical Society, 1915.

Stein, Thomas S. *Granny Forney's Cake and Beer Shop*. Lebanon, PA: Lebanon County Historical Society, 1927.

Stein, Thomas S. *The Marshalls of Berks and Lebanon Counties, Pa.: A Historico-Biographical Sketch Portraying the Careers of a Family of Physicians*. Annville: Hiester, 1915.

Wallace, Paul A.W. *Lebanon Valley College: A Centennial History*. Annville: Lebanon Valley College, 1966.

Warner, Joseph H. *Annville: Township and Town*. Lebanon: Lebanon County Historical Society, 1910.